Managing High-Intensity
Internet Projects

ISBN 0-13-062110-2

Selected Titles from the
YOURDON PRESS COMPUTING SERIES
Ed Yourdon, *Advisor*

JUST ENOUGH SERIES / YOURDON PRESS
DUE, Mentoring Object Technology Projects
MOSLEY/POSEY, Software Test Automation
YOURDON, Managing High-Intensity Internet Projects

YOURDON PRESS COMPUTING SERIES
ANDREWS AND STALICK Business Reengineering: The Survival Guide
BOULDIN Agents of Change: Managing the Introduction of Automated Tools
COAD AND MAYFIELD with Kern Java Design: Building Better Apps and Applets, Second Edition
COAD AND NICOLA Object-Oriented Programming
COAD AND YOURDON Object-Oriented Analysis, Second Edition
COAD AND YOURDON Object-Oriented Design
COAD WITH NORTH AND MAYFIELD Object Models, Strategies, Patterns, and Applications,
     Second Edition
CONNELL AND SHAFER Object-Oriented Rapid Prototyping
CONSTANTINE The Peopleware Papers: Notes on the Human Side of Software
CONSTANTINE AND YOURDON Structure Design
DEGRACE AND STAHL Wicked Problems, Righteous Solutions
DEMARCO Controlling Software Projects
DEMARCO Structured Analysis and System Specification
FOURNIER A Methodology for Client/Server and Web Application Development
GARMUS AND HERRON Measuring the Software Process: A Practical Guide to Functional
     Measurements
HAYES AND ULRICH The Year 2000 Software Crisis: The Continuing Challenge
JONES Assessment and Control of Software Risks
KING Project Management Made Simple
PAGE-JONES Practical Guide to Structured Systems Design, Second Edition
PUTNAM AND MEYERS Measures for Excellence: Reliable Software on Time within Budget
RUBLE Practical Analysis and Design for Client/Server and GUI Systems
SHLAER AND MELLOR Object Lifecycles: Modeling the World in States
SHLAER AND MELLOR Object-Oriented Systems Analysis: Modeling the World in Data
STARR How to Build Shlaer-Mellor Object Models
THOMSETT Third Wave Project Management
ULRICH AND HAYES The Year 2000 Software Crisis: Challenge of the Century
YOURDON Death March: The Complete Software Developer's Guide to Surviving "Mission
     Impossible" Projects
YOURDON Decline and Fall of the American Programmer
YOURDON Modern Structured Analysis
YOURDON Object-Oriented Systems Design
YOURDON Rise and Resurrection of the American Programmer
YOURDON AND ARGILA Case Studies in Object-Oriented Analysis and Design

Managing High-Intensity Internet Projects

Edward Yourdon

PRENTICE HALL PTR
UPPER SADDLE RIVER, NJ 07458
WWW.PHPTR.COM

Editorial/production supervision: *Kathleen M. Caren*
Acqusition Editor: *Paul Petralia*
Editorial Assistant: *Justin Somma*
Marketing Manager: *Debby van Dijk*
Manufacturing Manager: *Alexis R. Heydt*
Cover Design: *Nina Scuderi*
Cover Design Director: *Jerry Votta*
Series Design: *Gail Cocker-Bogusz*

© 2002 Prentice Hall PTR
Prentice-Hall, Inc.
Upper Saddle River, NJ 07458

The publisher offers discounts on this book when ordered in bulk quantities.
For more information, contact
Corporate Sales Department,
Prentice Hall PTR
One Lake Street
Upper Saddle River, NJ 07458
Phone: 800-382-3419; FAX: 201-236-714
E-mail (Internet): corpsales@prenhall.com

Printed in the United States of America

10 9 8 7 6 5 4 3 2 1

ISBN 0-13-062110-2

Prentice-Hall International (UK) Limited, *London*
Prentice-Hall of Australia Pty. Limited, *Sydney*
Prentice-Hall Canada Inc., *Toronto*
Prentice-Hall Hispanoamericana, S.A., *Mexico*
Prentice-Hall of India Private Limited, *New Delhi*
Prentice-Hall of Japan, Inc., *Tokyo*
Prentice-Hall (Singapore) Pte. Ltd., *Singapore*
Editora Prentice-Hall do Brasil, Ltda., *Rio de Janeiro*

*To my extended family—mother, fathers, wife,
daughter, sons and sisters—who remind me on a
daily basis what life's priorities are all about.*

Contents

Introduction

> Risk! Risk anything! Care no more for the opinion of others, for those voices. Do the hardest thing on earth for you. Act for yourself. Face the truth. ∎
>
> Katherine Mansfield, in *The Journal of Katherine Mansfield*, 1927.

The first question that people ask me about managing high-intensity Internet projects is: *"What's different?"* The very nature of the question implies that IT professionals and managers assume that *something* must be different about managing such projects … but at the same time, they suspect that many of the fundamentals of project management must still exist. Thus, there is often a sigh of relief when I tell an audience of IT managers that *nothing* is different about managing high-intensity Internet projects, and an air of excitement and dread when I tell them that *everything* is different.

The objective of this book is to focus on what's different, though I'll also take the opportunity to remind you occasionally about the fundamental principles of project management so that you dare not forget in the midst of your excitement over exotic new Internet-based technologies. As a reader, I'll assume that you're familiar with the basics of organizing, scheduling, estimating, recruiting, and supervising the myriad details associated with an IT development project. Thus, I won't try to explain what a Gantt chart is used for, or why someone would believe that a work breakdown structure is a critical tool for managing projects, nor will I give you a blow-by-blow description of the typical life-cycle activities of analysis, design, coding, and testing. But I'll also assume that you're unaware of, or unprepared for, some of the unique pressures and difficulties associated with the kind of high-intensity Internet projects that are being launched in thousands of companies around the world today. Specifically, here's what's different about such projects:[1]

- *Users and managers are becoming more demanding.* Many of today's Internet-based projects are defined as "mission-critical," so there is far more visibility and pressure than was often the case with traditional IT projects.

- *Many Internet-based projects require business process re-engineering (BPR) to succeed.* This is just like the early days of the client/server era in the early 1990s, during which we learned that 80% of BPR initiatives were failures.

- *Peopleware issues are often exacerbated.* There is a shortage of advanced, specialized skills, combined with decreasing company loyalty, and the inclusion of project team members with no formal IT background.

- *The pace of business demands faster implementation of Internet-based projects.* As a result of "death march" project schedules, many development teams abandon all attempts at organized processes or methods and resort to extemporaneous hacking, which lead to disastrous results.

- *Internet-based projects are often exposed to much greater risks than before, because they can be accessed by anyone, anywhere in the world.* Familiar issues such as performance, reliability, security, and privacy take on greater importance than may have been the case with traditional projects.

- *New technologies are emerging faster.* New hardware technologies range from 3G (third-generation) wireless technologies (which were on the horizon while this book was being written) to new development environments (e.g., Microsoft's .NET initiative) to new programming languages and collaboration tools.

Each of these points is discussed in more detail below, and each point forms the basis of a subsequent chapter.

---

1. See also "Success in e-projects," Edward Yourdon, *Computerworld*, Aug. 21, 2000.

1.1   Users and managers are becoming more demanding

During the last few years, many pundits, university professors, consultants, and business magazines have exhorted management to "reinvent" their companies to take advantage of Internet-based supply chains, global e-commerce possibilities, and internal efficiencies. In many cases, there was a great deal of hype associated with these exhortations—but it's important to realize that many business managers took them seriously. In some cases, they believed that their very existence was threatened; for instance, a traditional bookseller might well have felt threatened by Amazon, and a traditional newspaper publisher might well have felt threatened by the existence of Internet-based news. And wherever the Internet offered the opportunity to access new markets, new customers, new products, or new services, there was enormous pressure to be first to market and thus exploit the opportunities before additional competitors arrived on the scene.

As this book was being written in mid-2001, the hype associated with the Internet had begun to fade and was being replaced in some companies with jaded cynicism. Perhaps it's because the Internet has now become a more familiar technology; in both the business world and society. As of early 2001, for example, surveys indicated that approximately 50% of U.S. households had access to the Internet, and the figure was approximately the same in many other industrialized nations around the world. Perhaps the hype has faded because of the collapse of the "dot-com" industry in the 2000-2001 period; no longer do we necessarily expect a startup company to have a greater market capitalization than General Motors just because its name is XYZ.com. In any case, many companies had scaled back or postponed their e-business plans by the early part of 2001,[2] and there may be a brief respite of a few years before we see a return to the frenetic pace of the late 1990s.

But the hype has not disappeared completely, and the demands of the business community for Internet-based systems have not disappeared, either. Yes, there are a few simple Internet-based projects, and a few situations where business managers casually say to the IT department, "Whenever you folks have some spare time, would you mind creating a little Web site for us?" Indeed, as Cohen, Grochow, and Raiffa point out (see Figure 1.1), the majority of Internet/Web-based applications in the late 1990s were nothing more than simple, static Web pages.

It's more common today to see organizations regarding the Internet as a "disruptive technology" that creates a global, 24-by-7 business environment

---

2. See "CFOs on e-business: Not So Fast," Thomas Hoffman, *Computerworld*, Mar. 1, 2001.

for their products and services, instead of the Monday-to-Friday, nine-to-five business environment in which they interacted primarily with pre-existing customers in their local marketplace. Using the Internet for both internal operational purposes and also for external customer-facing activities is no longer optional for any but the smallest of businesses, and for all but the smallest business, the Internet forces business managers to reconsider such fundamental questions as:

- What business are we in?
- What is our core competence?
- What basic assumptions and constraints about the marketplace, and about our products and services, are still relevant in today's Internet-based economy?

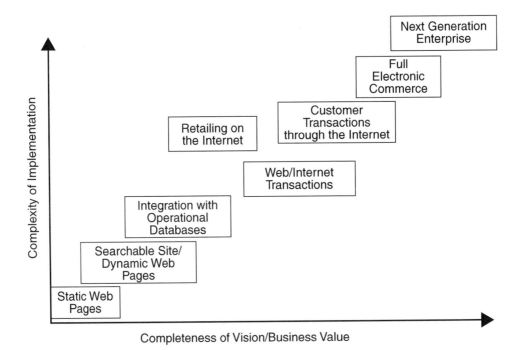

FIGURE 1.1 Different types of Internet-based systems.[3]

Many companies are just now beginning to realize that the Internet is providing their customers with far more power than ever before; not only can customers compare prices and service offerings from many competitors

---

3. From "Business Value and the World Wide Web," Judith N. Cohen, Jerrold M. Grochow, and Mark J. Raiffa, *Cutter IT Journal*, Dec. 1996.

more easily than before, they can also interact with *other customers* to share experiences and even aggregate their individual orders to obtain better prices. Until the Marketing/PR Department of XYZ Corp. discovers that there is an active Web site called "WeHateXYZ.com"—visited daily by thousands of irate XYZ customers who want to share their experiences with one another—they don't really understand the familiar phrase: "The Internet changes the traditional relationship between suppliers and customers."[4]

So, what does all of this have to do with the issue of *managing* Internet-based projects? Aside from the general observation that these projects tend to be more intense and high-pressured than the traditional projects we may have worked on previously, it also implies that there will be more emphasis on the politics associated with such a project. As we'll discuss in Chapter 2, this means that the project manager has to be more concerned than ever with questions such as:

- Who has the political power to declare the project a success or failure?
- Who are the key stakeholders in the project, in addition to the official owner of the project?
- What are the key criteria by which success or failure will be determined?

The official and visible aspects of project success may involve an aggressive deadline, a tight budget, and the ability to accomplish the work with a limited staff; but the invisible criteria for success are likely to involve the re-engineering, or reinvention, of business processes. Hence, there is likely to be a great deal of emphasis on *negotiations* concerning deadlines, schedules, budgets, and project staffing. These are familiar topics for most project managers, but the negotiations often turn out to be more intense and demanding for Internet-based projects. More importantly, though, there is likely to be more emphasis than ever on BPR; we'll discuss this in more detail below.

1.2   Many Internet-based projects require BPR to succeed

As noted earlier, the IT industry went through another technology upheaval in the early 1990s, when client/server technology first appeared on the scene and companies had the chance to replace mainframe-based, "dumb termi-

---

4. For an eloquent and detailed discussion of this point, see *The Cluetrain Manifesto,* Christopher Locke, Rick Levine, Doc Searls, and David Weinberger, Perseus Books, 2000. If you're too busy or lazy to buy the book, visit the authors' Web site at www.cluetrain.org.

nal" systems with decentralized GUI-based applications. While there was a great deal of fascination with the hardware and software technologies associated with client/server systems, it quickly became apparent that *real* business improvements would only be accomplished if the *business processes* were re-engineered when the new technologies were deployed. This led to the popularization of a new buzzword—"BPR," for business process re-engineering—and it also introduced some less popular buzzwords like "downsizing" and "right-sizing" as companies attempted to use the new technologies to eliminate clerks, administrative personnel, and layers of middle management.

Curiously, many of the lessons and experiences associated with this era have already faded from memory; indeed, when I use the term "BPR" in seminars and presentations today, I find that many of the current generation of Internet-savvy developers and managers have no idea what I'm talking about. As a result, they're also unfamiliar with the work of such management gurus as Michael Hammer, who helped evangelize the BPR movement in the early 1990s with his seminal book, *Reengineering the Corporation.*[5] And perhaps more important, they're unaware of the sobering assessment made by Hammer toward the end of the 1990s: *80% of the BPR initiatives had failed to achieve their objectives.* The reason for the failure, in most cases, had little or nothing to do with the glamorous client/server technology; in most cases, it had to do with politics, culture, and the difficulties of organizational change.

In the extreme case, both the client/server projects of the last decade and the Internet-based projects of the current decade were sometimes launched with no business model for identifying benefits, revenues, customers, or any rationale for success—other than the *Field of Dreams* theory that "If we build it, they will come." This is the common explanation for the failure of so many dot-com enterprises, and it also explains the failure of many internal e-business projects that companies have launched.

But not all BPR projects of the client/server era were spectacular failures, and not all of the ill-considered Internet projects will be as visibly catastrophic as the collapse of Pets.com or wine.com. Many of the less visible BPR failures of the 1990s turned out to be, in Hammer's words, "re-paving old cowpaths"—that is, using new technology to carry out the same old

---

5. See *Reengineering the Corporation: A Manifesto for Business Revolution*, Michael Hammer and James Champy, Harper Business, 1993. For subsequent perspectives from the same authors, see Michael Hammer's *The Reengineering Revolution*, Harper Business, 1995; James Champy's *Reengineering Management: The Mandate for New Leadership*, Harper Business, 1995; and Michael Hammer's *Beyond Reengineering: How the Process-Centered Organization is Changing Our Work and Our Lives*, Harper Business, 1996.

(inefficient) business processes slightly faster and cheaper with new hardware and software. Alas, the same thing is happening today with the latest technology: the Internet. For example, one government agency decided that the Internet would be a wonderful technology for replacing its paper-based, hard-copy employee directory, which was updated on an annual basis by the Human Resource Department, and was thus obsolete for most of the year. The new system had a slick, colorful Web interface and could be accessed by employees anywhere in the government agency; unfortunately, the Human Resource Department insisted that only it could update employee-related information … which it continued to do on an annual basis. Thus, the new system saved a lot of paper and provided a user-friendly means of displaying information, but the information was still fundamentally obsolete because the organization refused to change its business processes.

Managers of high-intensity Internet projects must realize that part of their role is to be the BPR champion or facilitator, to ensure that the underlying business processes *are* re-engineered when the new technology is deployed. But there is a big risk here: Most project managers lack the authority or political power to impose BPR on the business departments that are clamoring for new Internet technology. There is no magic solution to this problem, and no guarantee for success. We will discuss the BPR issues associated with Internet projects in considerable detail in Chapter 3.

1.3   Peopleware issues are often exacerbated

For most of the past decade, if not longer, IT organizations have been faced with a shortage of technical skills. In some cases, this has led to deferral and postponement of projects; in other cases, it has led to understaffed projects, with three developers trying to accomplish what normally would have been assigned to a team of five. But during the hey-day of the dot-com era, it also led to inflated salaries, outrageous employee benefits (e.g., a new car as a signing bonus), and unrealistic expectations on the part of freshly minted college graduates who expected stock options and compensation packages on a par with Bill Gates.

The collapse of the dot-com industry in the early part of this decade has reduced both the expectations of employees and the shortage of personnel, but not completely. Employers no longer have to pay outrageous salaries to find someone with basic HTML or JavaScript skills, but it's still difficult to find experienced veterans with specialized skills in the areas of networking, security, wireless technology, and the latest tools from IBM, Microsoft, and Sun. Thus, the hysterical hiring frenzy of the late 1990s and early 2000s may have disappeared, but IT organizations are likely to continue facing the same kinds of skill shortages that they had in the mid-1990s, late 1980s, and before. And to whatever extent that an Internet development project involves the very latest bleeding-edge technologies, companies are likely to continue facing severe shortages that could cause projects to be postponed or understaffed.

The dot-com frenzy of the late 1990s also led to an increase in mercenary behavior, with talented developers jumping from one job to another without any concern for company loyalty. On the other hand, this is a phenomenon that can also be traced back to the client/server era, in which IT departments made cold-blooded decisions to replace highly paid COBOL programmers with younger, cheaper Visual Basic programmers. The Dilbert-style cynicism that pervaded many IT organizations during this period has continued to this day, so that both employers and employees have forsaken any pretext of loyalty and long-term commitment; the result is that managers of high-intensity Internet project cannot necessarily assume that their team will remain intact for more than a few months.

As this book was being written in spring 2001, the dot-com collapse and associated economic slowdown had made many IT professionals more cautious than before and less willing to accept job offers consisting of low salaries and stock options of dubious value. At the same time, it made some of them more cautious about abandoning stable jobs in boring brick-and-mortar companies to work on glamorous Internet projects in new startup companies; as a result, project managers may have found a little more personnel stability than in recent years. On the other hand, the same economic slowdown led to cuts in training budgets and various other belt-tightening decisions that may have exacerbated a somewhat tenuous peopleware situation in some IT organizations. This can be a particularly serious problem in companies that expect their IT developers to work long overtime hours on high-pressure Internet projects; it can be extremely demoralizing to learn that the Accounting Department won't approve a $5 expenditure for a dinner-in-the-office slice of pizza and can of soda at the end of a 14-hour workday.

It's important for the manager to be aware of these problems, especially because many of today's Internet projects also involve team members who have no formal IT background. It's enough of a shock to hear the members of one's project team say, "Testing? What's that? Doesn't this stuff just *work* when we build it?", but it can be a deeper shock to realize that the artists, musicians, programmers, and subject matter specialists have an entirely different set of assumptions, expectations, and attitudes about their role in the workplace. Just as with BPR, there is no instant solution to the peopleware problems associated with high-intensity Internet projects. We'll discuss these issues in more detail in Chapter 11.

1.4   The pace of business demands faster implementation

For someone entering the IT industry today, it's amazing to think that once upon a time, application development projects had 7-year schedules. Well, maybe not *every* project lasted that long, but it was extremely common throughout the 1970s, and even the 1980s, to see projects that took 3–5 years from initiation to full-scale deployment. One of the interesting consequences of the client/server revolution of the early 1990s was that the 7-year projects got turned into 7-month projects, on almost an overnight basis. Again, not *every* client/server project had this characteristic, but it was extremely common to see a mandate from senior management that no IT development project would be allowed to take longer than an annual budget cycle, from beginning to end.

For those who had been accustomed to the leisurely pace of a 7-year project, this was quite an adjustment. Not only did we see the introduction of programming tools and development environments that supported faster development cycles (e.g., the replacement of batch-oriented COBOL development with interactive tools like Delphi, PowerBuilder, and Visual Basic), but we began to see IT organizations replacing the old-fashioned, time-consuming waterfall development process with various forms of rapid application development (RAD) processes. But a client/server project lasting 6 months, 9 months, or 12 months still had some time available for traditional activities like documenting requirements, developing design models, and conducting code reviews.

Now, for better or worse, we're living in "Internet time," and our Internet development projects have accelerated what was already a rather fast-paced schedule of activities. The old-fashioned projects that once took 7 years and got compressed down to 7 months in the client/server era are now being squeezed into 7 weeks. This is not an exaggeration. One of the large software development firms that I'm associated with regularly takes on client assignments to build Internet-based systems that are described by the client as "mission-critical," and for which the development schedule is 4 weeks long.

In some cases, the accelerated schedule is mandated by competitive pressures or "market window" opportunities; in other cases, it's mandated by emotional demands from senior managers who seem to believe that outrageous development schedules can be achieved by executive fiat. And to some extent, all of this reflects the steadily accelerating pace of everything in society today: We're all living in Internet time, and our IT development projects are just a reflection of that fact.

But the consequences for the IT project manager are serious: The imposition of an "impossible" deadline and a breakneck schedule tempt the developers into abandoning all forms of documentation, planning, thinking, analyzing, and formal software development processes and methods. This was bad enough in the early 1990s, when most of the developers at least knew what kinds of processes and methods they were abandoning. But today's Internet systems are often being developed by recent university graduates whose entire exposure to software engineering consists of an introductory course in Java programming. This may seem like an unnecessarily harsh criticism if the university graduate has a degree in software engineering or computer science; but even in this case, we're talking about people who have only worked on solo projects (i.e., their own programming assignments) lasting somewhere between a few hours and a semester.

Refer back to Figure 1.1 and it's easy to see why the early Internet systems did not require a great deal of formal methodological detail: We were building simple Web applications that merely displayed HTML-based pages of information. But many organizations are now beginning to tackle Internet projects that are large enough and complex enough that at least some of the old-fashioned ideas of planning, analyzing, and implementing software development processes are not only relevant, but downright necessary.[6]

For the relatively small, fast Internet development projects that still represent the majority of today's projects, the emerging trend is to use so-called "agile" or "light" software development methodologies to strike a compromise between the bureaucratic paralysis associated with the more formal, rigorous methodologies of the past and the utter anarchy that characterized so many of the Internet development projects of the late 1990s and early

---

6. A small illustration of this point: In the midst of writing this chapter, a new book arrived in the mail—it's a 410-page tome from Steven Splaine and Stefan P. Jaskiel entitled *The Web Testing Handbook*, STQE Publishing, 2001. A few years ago, testing would have been delegated to those innocent users naïve enough to install a beta version of a Web system; and even today, most of what takes place under the heading of "Web testing" is informal, hurried, and completely ad hoc in nature. Most Internet developers would probably express skepticism that there is even enough to say about Web testing to fill 410 pages!

2000s. Striking such a balance is one of the toughest jobs for the Internet project manager; we'll devote an entire chapter to this topic later in the book.

1.5   Internet-based projects are often exposed to much greater risks than before

Just getting out of bed in the morning is a risky proposition; everything we do in life has associated risks. And certainly, this has been true of all IT development projects since the beginning of the computer era; there are numerous surveys, articles, and books that document the relatively low percentage of such projects that have been finished on time, within budget, and with users who feel that their requirements have been properly understood and implemented.[7] For Internet systems, as with most other types of computer systems, there are the potential problems of performance (poor response time), reliability (frequent crashes or incorrect results), security (vulnerability to hacking or illegal entry), privacy (disclosure of confidential information to unauthorized persons), and so forth.

But there are at least two reasons why Internet-based systems often have more severe risks than older, traditional systems. The first reason is obvious: By its nature, an Internet-based system is exposed to the entire global population. A teenage hacker in Moscow or Minneapolis or Mozambique may decide to invest his or her considerable skills to hack an organization's Internet system to: (a) shut it down completely, (b) steal money or valuable information, (c) prevent anyone else from accessing the system through "denial-of-service" attacks, (d) post embarrassing messages or pornographic pictures on the system, or (e) all of the above. And second, even without attempting such destructive behavior, it may turn out that several thousand (or million) such teenage hackers decide to visit a system at the same time, thus overloading it to the point where nobody can use it at all. While this might have been theoretically possible with the client/server and online systems of the 1990s and 1980s, it was rarely a practical issue simply because the developers and operators of such systems had more direct control over the community of actual and potential users.

A related point is worth mentioning: Many of today's systems have relatively short lifetimes from an operational perspective. Consider, for example, the Web site and related Internet applications associated with the

---

7. See, for example, *Patterns of Software Systems Failure and Success*, Capers Jones, International Thomson Computer Press, 1996.

Olympics, which lasts for approximately two weeks, once every four years; for a more extreme example, consider the Internet system developed to support the Hollywood Oscar awards, for which the ceremonies last approximately four hours. If such a system fails, or is overloaded, or is successfully attacked by vandals or hackers, there may not be enough time to recover from the problem before the associated event is finished. Obviously, not all Internet systems fall into this category, but it reminds us that one of the important ramifications of Internet time is that we no longer have a leisurely period during which to analyze and repair operational failures, and then restore the system in a calm, orderly fashion.[8]

All of this puts more emphasis than ever on careful planning and testing; we may have been able to get away without them in the early Internet projects, but not any longer. Perhaps more important, today's Internet projects are different from the more traditional projects that many of us have managed in the past because they require a greater emphasis on risk management as a significant part of project planning and project management. We'll discuss this topic in more detail in Chapter 10.

1.6   New technologies are emerging faster

Finally, Internet projects are likely to be different than other projects that have taken place within an IT organization simply because they represent the leading edge of technology within the organization. At the same time, the subject matter or business domain associated with the project may either be old or new, which gives us the four distinct possibilities illustrated in Figure 1.2.

In the lower left quadrant of Figure 1.2, we see a combination of old technology and old business/subject matter practices—for example, the implementation of an old-fashioned batch mainframe payroll system in COBOL. Presumably, such projects are still taking place in various parts of the world, and presumably they continue to provide value, though sometimes they are simply re-implementations of an even older technology that has collapsed from old age.

---

8. Indeed, this same kind of pressure exists for day-to-day operational systems, simply because of their global exposure and the enormous user community that they serve. When AOL, eBay, Amazon, or any of the stock brokerage day-trading systems crash and remain out of service for more than a few hours, it becomes a major news event.

Of more interest are the situations represented in the top left quadrant and bottom right quadrant, that is, the combination of new and old. As discussed earlier, the use of new technology (such as the Internet) to automate old business practices is simply the re-paving of cowpaths, and we are almost certain to see some pressures when moving a project into the top right quadrant so that new technology can be employed to help an organization conduct its business in an entirely new way.

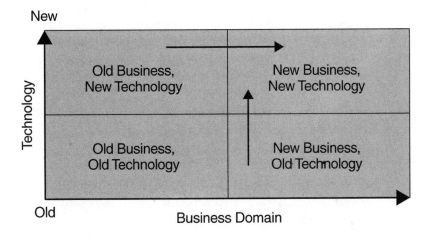

FIGURE 1.2 The combination of technologies and business domains.

Similarly, it's possible to imagine a radically new and different set of business processes being carried out with old-fashioned technology; sometimes a simple spreadsheet or flat-file database may be sufficient technology to support an innovative business process. But chances are that we'll feel pressure here, too: If the new business is effective with old technology, there's a reasonable chance that it will be even more effective with new technology.

In any case, today's Internet project managers are likely to find themselves coping with new hardware, new architectures, new programming languages, new development environments, new databases, and new standards. Of course, this has been true for each of the waves of technology that have swept through the IT industry during the past 50 years, beginning with the vacuum-tube ENIAC computer. A manager going through his or her first such transition may find the experience daunting, but someone who has been in the field for 10 years or more is likely to recognize that today's new technologies are, in Yogi Berra's terms, "Déjà vu all over again." Of course, the new technologies—whether they are today's Internet-related technologies or the next-generation technologies of the middle or later part of this decade—can represent a serious problem if the IT staff doesn't have adequate expertise in the technologies.

This usually leads to a rather chaotic period of a few years, in which the organization outsources some of its high-tech requirements, recruits new employees to acquire the needed skills, trains some of its existing staff to upgrade their skills, and tries to do the best it can with whatever superficial skills it happens to have. Similarly, there is often a rather chaotic period during which new versions of tools, languages, and development environments are introduced by the technology vendors—a period in which the technology doesn't work reliably, or isn't supported adequately by the vendors. Whether it's IBM, Microsoft, Sun, or any one of a dozen other high-profile vendors, such criticisms and accusations were common during the early stages of the Internet era. And as long as these vendors continue to introduce dramatically new technologies, it's likely to continue being a problem.

We'll discuss the role of tools and technologies in the development of Internet-based systems later in this book, in Chapter 12, but my experience has been that new technologies are not the fundamental causes of project failures. In rare cases, the entire project—and the associated business justification for the project—may depend on advanced technology that doesn't work at all, or doesn't get delivered when the vendor promised. But more often, the technical problems are little more than the "straw that breaks the camel's back," providing a handy scapegoat to cover up the more fundamental problems of poor planning, poor management, or poor development processes.

While the specific tools, products, and technologies associated with the Internet may be new and different for many IT managers, the *general* issues associated with new technologies have been discussed for many years. As Geoffrey Moore explained in his popular book, *Crossing the Chasm*[9] in the early 1990s, new technologies are adopted by five distinct segments of the marketplace, beginning with "innovators" and ending with "laggards" (refer to Figure 1.3). What Moore did not explicitly note in his book, and what many IT managers have failed to recognize, is that the period of time between the innovators and the laggards, *for the adoption of IT technologies*, is usually between 14 and 20 years. Thus, the adoption of Java and many of today's familiar Web-based technologies reached the "early adopter" stage

9. See *Crossing the Chasm: Marketing and Selling High-Technology Products to Mainstream Customers*, Geoffrey A. Moore, Harper Business, 1991. See also his follow-up book, *Inside the Tornado*, Harper Business, 1995.

by early 2000, but it's likely to be closer to 2010 before the laggards make a commitment.[10]

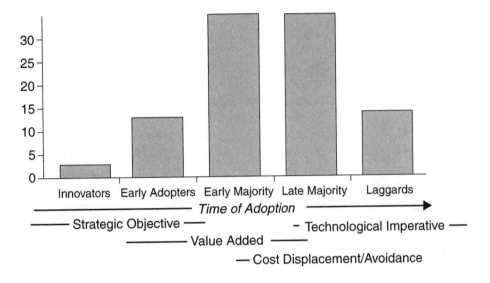

FIGURE 1.3 The adoption of new technologies.

In any case, the issue of technology adoption is one that Internet project managers must be aware of, for the projects they are managing represent the organization's effort to introduce and deploy the latest IT technologies. Thus, it's important for project managers to understand whether their organizations have traditionally been innovators, laggards, or somewhere in between with respect to new computer technologies; for example, were they among the first to introduce Windows 2000, Linux, object-oriented programming, client/server technology, CASE (Computer-Aided Software Engineering) technology, relational databases, structured programming, and a long list of other technologies? Or were they content to let someone else be the pioneer, and settle instead for the second-prize title of early adopter? Or were they part of the mainstream community, or perhaps even a laggard? Chances are that whatever organizational behavior was exhibited with previous technologies will be repeated again with the Internet, unless the com-

10. The figure of 14–20 years for the adoption period of computer technologies was identified by Sam Redwine in his paper (co-authored with W. E. Riddle) "Software Technology Maturation," *Proceedings of the 8th International Conference on Software Engineering*, London, Aug. 28-30, 1985, pp. 189-200. If it's any consolation, technology adoption takes far longer in other disciplines; it has been argued, for example, that it took the military 75 years to go from the technology of muskets to the technology of rifles.

pany has a new leader who is determined to make the company either more adventurous or more conservative than it has been in the past.

In many cases, it's also important to understand whether one's customers, vendors, suppliers, and partners are innovators, early adopters, mainstream participants, or laggards. Indeed, one of the main reasons for the failure of so many dot-com companies was not that *they* were unsuccessful in deploying sophisticated Internet technology, but rather that the marketplace on which they depended was more conservative than had been estimated. Of course, it's possible to build an Internet-based system whose technologies are used solely by internal employees, but for a larger and larger percentage of the Internet systems being built today, the very *raison d'etre* of the system is to facilitate more effective communications with individuals and organizations *outside* the corporate boundary. And if those external entities are not yet using the latest wireless/Web/Internet technologies, it may not matter whether you were successful at implementing such technologies internally.

1.7   Conclusion

So, what's different about managing high-intensity Internet projects? Well, you still have customers and users who have to be satisfied. You still have schedules and deadlines that someone expects you to meet. You still have a budget that you're not supposed to exceed. You still have a team of developers whose work is abstract and intangible, but whose progress and deliverables still have to be managed, assessed, and controlled. You still have to plan and organize, and you still have to cope with politics. Plus, you still have to deal with unexpected surprises in every facet of the project, from technological glitches to perverse users to headstrong developers. In those senses, nothing has changed. A project is still a project, even if it is a high-intensity Internet project.

On the other hand, much of the familiar terrain of project management has changed so drastically that it's a whole new ballgame. A project operating on a 4-week schedule is *qualitatively* different than a project operating on a 4-month schedule; as a colleague of mine observed, if it takes you a week to realize that your programmers haven't produced any working code, you've lost 25% of the entire project schedule. Similarly, an Internet-based project whose launch is broadcast on the national TV news (as was the case for another colleague of mine) is operating in an entirely different world than an old-fashioned project that had the luxury of being rolled out in a carefully controlled fashion to one branch office after another. The differences, as we've seen in this introductory chapter, can be both profound and daunting.

ঽঽ ঽঽ ঽঽ ঽঽ ঽঽ

But that doesn't mean that we should give up. Indeed, one of the intriguing lessons from the dot-com era (which implies that it's now part of past history, much like the Age of the Dinosaurs) is that very few, if any, projects failed because of mistakes in traditional project management. They may have run out of money, and they may have discovered that there weren't enough customers willing to pay enough money to generate a profit. But most of the systems *did* get built, and they did have real customers who got real products and services from Internet systems. So, with a little bit of luck, and a lot of hard work—and with the guidelines, warnings, and insights that I'll provide in the subsequent chapters of this book—it's possible to succeed.

So, while you may be sobered by some of the problems mentioned in this chapter, you shouldn't give up. Indeed, by the time you finish this book, you should be ready for almost anything … except, perhaps, whatever comes *after* the Internet!

ঽঽ ঽঽ ঽঽ ঽঽ ঽঽ

Project Politics and Negotiations

Many project managers assume that the first things they need to do when they've been given the responsibility for a new project are plan and organize. Obviously, those are essential functions, but they're not usually the *first* things that you need to do with a high-intensity Internet project. Indeed, the initial activities are more political in nature, involving such questions as: "Who are the key players in this game?" and "How will I know whether we've won or lost this game when the project is over?" Obviously, this has nothing to do with PERT charts and Gantt charts, and it doesn't even have anything to do with scheduling and estimating, or asking the end-users for a list of their requirements. But if you ignore these initial political considerations, you greatly increase the risk of failure.

This may seem like an extreme statement, particularly if you've spent the last several years managing traditional IT development projects with rational schedules and user expectations. In such projects, the political landscape is familiar, the players are known, and the rules of engagement are respected by all parties. But Internet projects are intrinsically risky—not just because of the insane deadlines and frantic schedules, but for all of the other reasons discussed in Chapter 1. During the late 1990s, there was an air of euphoria about the Internet and the Web, and such projects might not have appeared risky at the time; but as we've come to see in the past few years, the real risk during that period may have been unrealistic expectations. And now, during the early part of the new decade, we seem to be facing an emotional backlash: IT project managers may find themselves facing unexpected hostility and skepticism from a user community that assumes *all* Internet projects will suffer the same fate as the bankrupt dot-com ventures.

Many IT managers squirm with discomfort whenever the conversation turns to politics. "I'm not a politician, and I don't like to get involved with corporate politics," they complain. "I'm a professional, and all I want to do is help my team build the best possible system." This is a noble sentiment, but the reality is that a good portion of any manager's job is spent dealing with politics; as former President Lyndon Johnson once said, "I only think about politics 18 hours a day." Some political tasks—for instance, motivating and supervising the individual members of a project team—are so familiar that a veteran manager handles them from instinct and long years of experience. But when the project management terrain changes, as is often the case with a high-intensity Internet project, then it becomes necessary to focus consciously on the key political issues.

2.1   Identifying the key players

The first thing a project manager needs to do is identify the key players in the Internet project that he or she is managing. Because of the risks associated with such projects, your chances of success are zero if you don't know who your friends and enemies are. Not only that, it's also important for everyone on the project team to be aware of this information, because in today's Internet age, it's impossible for project managers to hide their team in a back room somewhere while they fight all of the political battles.[1]

---

1. To illustrate this point, it's worth noting that when an IT project fails in a sufficiently spectacular fashion that customers and suppliers begin suing each other, the first things the lawyers ask for (during the "discovery" phase of the lawsuit) are the email archives of everyone involved. It often turns out that a senior manager has sent an email message to the project team that says, "We WILL deliver this project on time, no matter how impossible it may seem. I do not want to hear any disagreement about this point." And it's also common to find email messages from a lowly programmer or testing professional that say, "Boss, we're doomed—we might as well re-name this project 'Project Titanic.' We've discovered 314 fatal bugs in the latest build of the system, and there is absolutely NO WAY that the project will be finished on time."

Who are the key players on a typical Internet project? They usually include some combination of the following:

- The *owner*—This is the person who pays for the system, and who is ultimately responsible for its success or failure. Indeed, the key thing about this individual is usually that he or she has the authority to determine whether or not the project *is* a success or failure. On the other hand, the owner is not necessarily the person who will use the system; in the extreme case, the owner doesn't have a computer on his or her desk, and doesn't know the difference between a Web browser and a football.

- The *investor*—This is the person who provides, or authorizes, the funds required to build the system. This may be a venture capitalist (VC) or investment banker if the Internet system is intended to be a separate legal entity, or it may be the CEO or Board of Directors if the system is being internally funded. In the more mundane situation, the investor is simply the business manager who has the authority to commit funds for the project. It's important to remember that the investor has the authority to reduce budgets and withdraw funds if he or she loses faith in the project.

- The *user*—This is the person who will actually use the system once it has been developed. Typically, of course, there are *many* users, and they may or may not belong to a single organizational category (e.g., sales representative or field-service technician). Indeed, they may not even be employees of the organization; they may be external customers, or they may be employees of the supplier/vendor/partner organizations with whom the Internet system will interact. Typically, these are the people whose day-to-day business processes will be most heavily affected by the new Internet system; as such, they may be either wildly enthusiastic about the system or deeply resentful and hostile about the upheaval it will create in their lives.

- The *stakeholder*—This is the person(s) whose interests, influence, power, ego, and/or fortunes are affected by the success or failure of the project, and who is in a position of power to affect the outcome of the project in either a direct or indirect fashion. Stakeholders may thus become allies or obstacles to project success, and they may operate behind the scenes by whispering encouraging or discouraging words in the ears of the owner, the investor, or the user(s). It's thus vitally important for the project manager to identify the stakeholders, analyze their perspectives and opinions about the project, and take whatever steps are necessary to gain their support.[2]

A final note: Because e-business and other Internet systems often change the way an organization conducts its day-to-day affairs, the traditional identification of owners, users, and stakeholders may be inaccurate. Make sure you know who *really* will be affected by the introduction of a new Internet system, and make sure you know who *really* cares whether the project succeeds or fails. Otherwise, you're likely to get blindsided from individuals you least suspect.

In the best of all worlds, the project manager wants the full commitment and support of the owner, the investor, the users, and the various stakeholders.[3] But different members of this group are likely to have different levels of commitment, some of which may be publicly stated, and some of which may not. To further complicate things, the level of commitment from your official and unofficial sponsors, champions, and stakeholders may change on a day-to-day basis, depending on the state of the economy, the stock market, and the most recent corporate quarterly earnings report.

For the manager who dislikes politics, the nuances of commitment and support may seem irrelevant. But it's worth remembering that one of the primary reasons why the massive Y2K remediation effort succeeded in so many organizations is that—for the first time *ever*!—the IT department actually had a *substantial* commitment from the CEO and the Board of Directors to take the necessary steps to repair the computer systems. The reason was simple: The CEO and the Board had been advised by the lawyers that the penalties for failure were staggering, and they were advised by the business managers that day-to-day operations would cease if the computer systems were not Y2K-compliant. Not only that, they were required by the Securities and Exchange Commission (SEC) to disclose the extent of their risks in their financial reports, so that everyone could see how vulnerable they were.

Y2K obviously has nothing to do with Internet systems, but the success that we had with that technical challenge raises the obvious question: Do you have the same level of support and commitment from your senior management for the Internet project that you're about to undertake? Have they given you their home telephone numbers and told you to call them any time, day or night, if you're running into trouble?

---

2. For an excellent discussion of this point, see "Project Clarity Through Stakeholder Analysis," Larry Smith, *Crosstalk: The Journal of Defense Software Engineering*. Dec. 2000.

3. There's actually a difference between commitment and support, as illustrated by the parable of the chicken and the pig who argued with each other about who played the most important role in providing breakfast for the farmer. "I'm very involved, and I fully support the effort," said the chicken, noting that it was her role to produce the eggs for the farmer's breakfast. But the pig replied, "Yes, but I'm *committed*: I provide the bacon for the farmer's breakfast."

2.2   Determining the basic nature of the project

In a previous book,[4] I suggested that high-risk projects could be categorized with a simple two-dimensional grid, as shown in Figure 2.1: The horizontal axis is easy to understand: Some projects have a greater chance of success than others. But the vertical axis is equally important, particularly when it comes to motivating the members of a project team to exert super-human effort to achieve an otherwise impossible deadline. To understand the nature of the vertical axis of Figure 2.1, all you have to do is ask one simple question: "Would you be willing to sign up for another project like this one?"

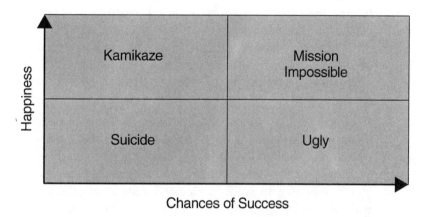

FIGURE 2.1 The four types of high-risk projects.

At the end of the 1990s, most Internet projects fell into the "mission impossible"[5] category: Everyone assumed that they would succeed (through a combination of talent, hard work, and luck), and everyone assumed that success would lead to an IPO, lucrative stock options, and various other combinations of fame and fortune. It's important to remember that, along with the project manager and the members of the team, all of the other key players (owner, investor, users, and stakeholders) also believed in the mission impossible nature of the projects.

---

4. *Death March: The Software Developer's Guide to Surviving "Mission-Impossible Projects,"* Prentice Hall, 1997.
5. In this context, "mission impossible" is meant to imply the glamorous Hollywood image portrayed by Tom Cruise in two movies by the same name—or, for members of an older generation, the television series from the 1960s and 1970s, in which Peter Graves and his team *always* succeeded with their mission, and returned in the following week's episode for yet another impossible mission.

Alas, there are not as many mission impossible Internet projects as there were a few years ago; the collapse of the dot-com industry destroyed that illusion in many companies. Today, it's more likely that an Internet project will be characterized as an "ugly" mission, which means that senior management is prepared to sacrifice the health and happiness of all the project team members (including the project manager) to succeed. And in most cases, the project *will* succeed—but there will be a lot of blood on the floor when it's over.

Within some government agencies today, there are "kamikaze"-style Internet projects springing up under the heading of "e-government"—they have little or no chance of success, but everyone feels that they are part of a noble venture, and is willing to make the personal sacrifices required. Until the Internet becomes so mature that the laggard segment of the marketplace begins building such systems, it's relatively unlikely that we'll see what Figure 2.1 characterizes as "suicide" missions—that is, projects with no chance of success, and whose team members are miserable victims who have no alternative but to accept the managerial edict of long overtime and high stress.

One of the unpleasant realities of high-risk Internet projects is that public assurances from stakeholders, investors, and the project owner may not reflect the reality of the situation. This was particularly evident during the final days of the dot-com frenzy, when project team members were constantly exhorted to work harder and faster, with the assurance that their team would be spun off into a public company whose shares would skyrocket. The reality was that the investors had announced that they were unwilling to provide any additional funding, which meant that the owners were in a desperate race to launch their Internet system before they ran out of cash.

In the post-dot-com environment, there are still many Internet system projects being pushed into the ugly or kamikaze quadrant of Figure 2.1 on the theory that they are mission-critical projects whose failure will somehow imperil the survival of the organization. That may be an accurate assessment for a dot-com startup enterprise, but many of the brick-and-mortar companies would manage to find a way to continue muddling along even if their mission-critical, Internet-enabled supply chain system was a month or two late. Thus, it's important for the project manager to maintain a sense of perspective and to try hard to distinguish between the political characterization of the project and the true reality.

2.3   Managing project definition: What does "success" mean?

For many of today's high-intensity Internet projects, the seeds of success or failure are sown on the first day of the project, long before any technical work is done. After all, success or failure is in the eye of the beholder. The key question the project manager must ask is: "Who is the 'beholder' who has the authority to declare success or failure, and what are the criteria that will form the basis of that declaration?"

As mentioned earlier in this chapter, the owner of a system is the person who has the authority to declare success or failure; but, the *identity* of the owner often changes drastically with Internet systems. As Professor Robert Austin observed in a recent survey,[6] 61% of all IT organizations reported that they had initiated traditional development projects in the past, but only 22% of all IT organizations were involved in initiating e-business projects. Similarly, 46% of senior managers had initiated traditional IT projects in the past, but only 30% were involved in initiating e-business projects. Business/operating units had initiated traditional IT projects in 46% of the companies responding to Professor Austin's survey, but only 20% had initiated e-business projects. 30% of marketing/sales groups had initiated traditional IT projects, but only 9% had initiated e-business projects. And 9% of finance groups had initiated traditional IT projects in the past, but only 2% had initiated e-business projects. Depending on whether an organization sees the Internet as a key enabler of improved cash flow, better sales, improved supply chain operations, or entirely new products and services, the champion of a new Internet project may be an entirely different person (or group) than was typically the case in the past.

It's also crucial for the project manager to understand the criteria by which project success or failure will be determined. Typical criteria include the following:[7]

- Finishing on time, or at least delivering a reasonable subset of the desired functionality of the system on or before the deadline
- Staying within budget

---

6. See "The Paradox of e-Business," Rob Austin, *Cutter Consortium Business Technology Trends and Impacts,* Nov. 2000.
7. For more discussion of the criteria for success in an Internet project, see "Spelling Success," Ed Yourdon, *Computerworld,* Feb. 19, 2001; "Long-Term Thinking," Ed Yourdon, *Computerworld,* Oct. 26, 2000; and "The Value of Triage," Ed Yourdon, *Computerworld,* Mar. 20, 2000.

- Delivering the required functionality, so that the system actually does what the users want it to do
- Providing a good enough level of quality, so that the system doesn't crash too often, provides an acceptable level of performance, and produces correct answers most of the time
- Getting the next round of VC funding, or launching the IPO

By contrast, a key indicator of a doomed project is that nobody can articulate what success really means, or the definition is so vague (e.g., "high-quality information will be delivered anywhere, anytime, to any relevant user who asks for it") that nobody can tell whether or not it has been achieved. Another key danger signal the project manager should watch for: strong disagreement among key stakeholders about the definition of success. Marketing may want the Internet system to increase sales, while Finance may wish to improve cash flow and reduce inventory. Meanwhile, the Customer Service Department may expect that an Internet-based system will enable customers to answer most of their technical inquiries through a Web browser, thus making it possible to reduce the number of employees in their department. And, senior management may have some vague notions that the Internet will allow them to "reinvent" their business, without explaining to the project manager what that really means.

The combination of these criteria and constraints may prove impossible to achieve, particularly if they are stated in a vague, ambiguous, and subjective manner. But even if the business objectives are crisply defined and clearly explained, the project manager may face the more traditional conflict among schedule, budget, and quality—hence the old saying, "You can have a fast system, or a good system, or a cheap system; pick any two out of the three." Thus, the pragmatic nature of success often depends on achieving a consensus as to which constraints (budget, schedule, quality) can be compromised or sacrificed. Since Internet projects tend to have extremely aggressive schedules and deadlines, this usually means that functionality, quality, or budget parameters have to be compromised or sacrificed—a message that the project owner may not wish to hear, but nevertheless must be stated.

The situation is compounded by a phenomenon known as "requirements creep," that is, the list of features/functions/requirements used to generate the budget and schedule for the project slowly grows as the project continues. Software metrics gurus like Capers Jones have observed that in traditional projects, the number of requirements increases at the rate of 1% per month; thus, a project lasting a year is likely to implement 12% more requirements than had been planned at the beginning of the project. And

unless the project manager incorporated 12% slack into the original estimate, chances are that the project will be 12% behind schedule, or 12% over
budget, or will require its developers to work 12% more overtime hours
than they had initially planned.

But if a 1% -per-month requirements creep is a traditional figure, from traditional projects; it's likely to be much higher for Internet projects, where the
end-users aren't quite sure what they want the system to do, and nobody is
quite sure what the technology is capable of providing. If the Internet project
is associated with fundamental changes to the users' business processes—a
topic we'll discuss in more detail in the next chapter—then there is also
likely to be a great deal of "requirements churn," where new requirements
aren't added, but existing requirements are likely to be modified on an
ongoing basis.

If the fundamental criteria for project success are "delivering required functionality to the user, on time and within budget," then the project manager's
natural instinct is to document the requirements as carefully as possible,
partly to form the basis for rational schedules and budgets, and also to form
a rational contract between the users and the development team. Alas, the
nature of most Internet projects is that they have few, if any, written requirements statements; part of the folklore of Internet projects is that there isn't
enough time to indulge in such obsolete, bureaucratic activities as documentation, and that the requirements will somehow emerge through a series of
iterative prototypes.

We'll discuss the process issues of documenting requirements,[8] as well as
iterative development techniques, in Chapter 6. But for now, the important
message for project managers is this: A great deal of political risk is created
at the beginning of Internet projects because nobody is quite sure what the
system is supposed to do at the critical point when budget/schedule commitments are being made. Not only that, the absence of a formal statement
of requirements makes it all the more difficult for the project manager to
identify the requirements creep and/or requirements churn that may be taking place.

If a formal requirements document does exist, then it can be used as the
basis for a rational renegotiation of schedules and budgets whenever the
user modifies or adds to the initial requirements; but this is usually predi-
cated on the notion that the ultimate success of the project will be determined *once*, at the end of the development and installation of the system,

---

8. For a discussion of this topic, see my article, "How to Help Users Write Good Requirements
   Statements," *Computerworld*, Nov. 2000.

based on the most recently revised budget and schedule. If the requirements are never fully documented at the beginning of the project, and if they emerge as the result of iterative prototypes of the system, then it doesn't make sense to define project success or failure in an all-or-nothing fashion. Thus, from a political perspective, it's important for the project manager to create an environment in which everyone can agree upon the criteria for interim success, culminating (hopefully) in a final success after the last prototype has been delivered.

To illustrate this point, consider the following sports metaphor: Under normal conditions, a baseball game isn't over until the last strike, of the last out, of the 9th inning. Thus, just because your team is losing at the end of the 8th inning doesn't mean that it has lost the entire game; and conversely, even if your team is ahead by 10 runs at the end of the 8th inning, that doesn't mean that it's guaranteed to win. But this traditional way of determining success or failure can be badly disrupted if a sudden thunderstorm forces the umpires to call a halt in play. If the thunderstorm occurs during the early innings, then the game is suspended, and play resumes the next day. But if the thunderstorm occurs during a late inning, and if the game can't be easily rescheduled, the umpires have the authority to declare a winner even if nine full innings have not been played. For the baseball manager whose team plays in a stormy climate, the message is clear: Play every inning as if it was the last one of the game.

There is one last political recommendation to make in this area: While undocumented or non-existent requirements make it difficult to develop an accurate budget, *ambiguous* specifications can be even more dangerous. As my colleague Tom DeMarco has observed,[9] an ambiguous specification is often a sign of unresolved conflict between diverse political camps—for example, different stakeholders—in the user community. DeMarco also notes that when IT professionals fail to identify a problem, they assume instead that it was *their fault that they couldn't understand the ambiguous specification.* Thus, it's important to note that we're not suggesting that you use the UML, structured analysis, or some other formal methodology to ensure that the requirements are well-defined; the point here is that the user community may be unwilling or unable to do so because of the political disagreements that eventually make them throw up their hands in frustration and say, "Well, we'll let the programmers sort that out when they get around to writing the code."

---

9. See *The Deadline: A Novel About Project Management*, Dorset House, 1997, page 216.

2.4   Estimating techniques

There is a fundamental truth that is just as true for Internet-related systems as it has been for every other kind of IT system developed in the past 40 years: *To accurately estimate the time, money, and resources needed for a development project, you need credible, accurate metrics from similar, previous projects.* But most IT organizations keep very few metrics about any of their previous projects, and they have little or no experience with Internet-related projects.

Thus, what is described as estimating in most organizations is either a sophisticated form of guessing, or a clumsy form of negotiating.[10] The situation is exacerbated by the phenomenon discussed earlier in this chapter: Most Internet-related projects begin without a clear description of the required functionality to be produced, either because the end-users are unsure of what they want or because the organizational culture believes that documenting such requirements is a bit of old-fashioned bureaucracy that can be dispensed with.

Many IT project managers disagree with this jaded assessment and assure me that they really *do* estimate how long they believe it will take to develop a certain amount of functionality with a certain group of developers. And perhaps the veteran project managers have internalized so much knowledge and wisdom about the development process that their estimating process is reasonably accurate and objective. But the majority of Internet-related projects that I saw during the late 1990s and early 2000s were managed by relatively inexperienced managers, which means that they had little or no prior estimating experience. To compound the problem, they often worked within a political climate that gave them a vested interest in believing their own optimistic predictions. Thus, when the owner or investor associated with the system asked the project manager, "Do you think we can get this new integrated Internet supply chain system developed in six months?", the project manager was likely to be thinking, "Hmmm, if I can pull this off, then I'll get a promotion and a bonus, and our company can go public, which will make my stock options worth ten zillion dollars!" Thus, it's no surprise that the project manager gave an enthusiastic "Yes!" to the question.[11]

So, what should you do when it's time to estimate time, budget, and resources for your Internet project, and then negotiate those estimates with the owner, user, and investors associated with the project? What's different

---

10. For another perspective on estimating-as-negotiation, see "Metrics and the Seven Elements of Negotiation," Michael Mah, *IT Metrics Strategies*, Apr. 2001.

about this process for Internet projects than it was for the non-Internet projects you used to manage in the past? The bottom line is simple: It's the same as it was before, but riskier. Whatever guidelines, tricks, techniques, or magical secrets you had for estimating client/server projects, or mainframe projects, or any other kind of IT projects can be used again in the new world, but you should realize, for all the reasons discussed above, that there's a greater chance that you'll be wrong. For most project managers, this means following the traditional practice of breaking the entire project into small, discrete, relatively independent work activities and then soliciting a range of estimates for the time and effort associated with each such activity.

As we'll discuss in more detail in a later chapter, chances are that you won't base those estimates on the classic waterfall activities of analysis, design, coding, and testing. Instead, you'll base the estimates on deliverable versions or releases of the system, each of which will contain a negotiated chunk of functionality expressed in features or functionality. Thus, the estimating process is likely to be associated with a number of conversations, or negotiations, of the following kind:

- System owner: "We need to have this new Internet-based customer service system up and running in 12 months! Do you think you can get it done by then, or would you like to update your resume and look for a new job?"

- Project manager: "Well, that sounds feasible, and I'm certainly willing to give it my best shot. But I have to be honest with you and tell you that since we haven't even talked to the users to find out what they want the system to do, it could take considerably longer than 12 months. It could even take two or three years."

- System owner: "Well, that's just not acceptable! For all I know, our company might not even exist two years from now! But now you've made me wonder just how confident I can be about your promise to finish the project in 12 months."

- Project manager: "Well, I didn't *promise* anything; I just said that it sounded feasible. If you want a 'hard' promise, why don't we consider

11. Some 20 years ago, my colleague Tom DeMarco wrote a provocative book entitled *Controlling Software Projects* (Prentice Hall, 1982) that made a radical suggestion: Create a separate estimating group whose work is judged and rewarded by the accuracy of its estimates, not the political acceptability of its estimates. While it might seem radical within the IT world, other engineering disciplines have used this approach for decades, if not centuries. Perhaps because the IT industry is too immature, or perhaps because it is dominated by a "macho" culture, DeMarco's suggestion has generally been ignored. I don't expect that to change during the era of Internet-related systems development.

something more focused and limited with a shorter timespan of, say, 2–3 months?"

- System owner: "Sounds good! What did you have in mind?"

- Project manager: "Well, how about an initial version of the customer service system that displays a list of frequently asked questions (FAQs) on their Web browser?"

- System owner: "That's it? That's all you're going to do? And that takes two months?[12] Why can't you do more? How about displaying the status of the orders that our customers have placed, so they can tell whether their orders will arrive on time?"

- Project manager: "Because that will require us to interface the new Internet system with the database of our legacy order entry system, and I think that's going to open a huge can of worms that we won't be able to cope with during the first two months."

- System owner: "Well, can't you at least do something fancy, like provide a search capability, so the customers can search through a 'knowledge base' of technical articles about our products?"

- Project manager: "Hmmm, I think we could incorporate that functionality in a second release of the system, perhaps a month after the first one. But it requires putting all of our technical articles online in some Web-browsable form, indexing all of the articles with the relevant keywords and search phrases, and then deciding which search engine we want to incorporate into our system. That's too much for us to do in the first version of the system."

- System owner: "Well, I still don't understand why the first version will take two whole months!"

- Project manager: "Well, how about giving me a day or two, so that my team can interview the relevant users to get a list of the *essential* features that we would have to have in the first release of the system? Then I'll ask my team members to do some careful estimating of how long it will take to implement each of those features, and I'll get back to you with a more refined estimate of how long it will really take to build the first version."

- System owner: "Why do you need a day or two? Can't you get that done this morning? Let's schedule a meeting for 2:00 this afternoon, after I get back from lunch…"

---

12. Note what has happened here: The project manager expressed an estimate in terms of a range of 2–3 months, and the system owner instinctively focused on the low end of the range, and turned that into a commitment.

Obviously, I've oversimplified things a bit here; among other things, the project manager may not want to explain to a non-technical system owner that at least a month of overhead effort will be required to build the first version of the system—to select the tools and technologies that will be used for the system, design a basic architecture and infrastructure, organize the team, negotiate the interfaces between the new system and all of the existing legacy applications and environments, and so forth.

Nevertheless, the basic concept makes sense: Instead of committing your team to deliver large unknowns with a large risk factor, try to negotiate a series of small unknowns with a smaller risk factor. Asking someone to make a promise that they'll deliver a large amount of unknown functionality in 6–12 months is crazy, but what's even crazier is that people do it all the time. In a situation like this, the system owner automatically focuses his or her attention on the 6-month figure, while the developers focus on the 12-month deadline, with the added assumption that if they're only a few months late, it won't be a big deal. But in today's fast-moving, highly-competitive, pressure-packed business environment, the difference between 6 months and 15 months *is* a big deal, and it can cause extremely painful consequences for all concerned.

By contrast, focusing on a promise to be delivered in a short 2–3 month timeframe introduces a lot more realism into the negotiation. Many business organizations already base their business plans around the concept of a fiscal quarter, so it leads to more specific discussions like this:

- System owner: "So, you're telling me that we'll have the first version of our new Internet system up and running by the end of the next quarter?"
- Project manager: "Yeah, I'm pretty sure we can do that. But the only way we can pull it off is to get the funding and hire the five people I need for the project team in *this* quarter."
- System owner: "Well, I can't get any more funding requests in front of the Budget Committee this quarter. And we've got a hiring freeze through the end of the next quarter because Wall Street is unhappy with the profitability that we reported for the last quarter."
- Project manager: "We're talking about basic physics here. With no money and no people, I can't build you a new system. I can't create software out of thin air."

For developers, even three months is a long period of time, and it often tempts them to make promises and commitments that they have no chance of fulfilling. Circumstances vary from one organization to another, and from one developer to another, but I've often found that it makes much more sense to continue partitioning and decomposing work activities until each assignable task involves no more than a week of technical effort. That allows the manager to have conversations like this with the project team:

- Project manager: "Okay, team, we've got to get the first version of our Internet-based customer service system up and running in three months. Is everyone comfortable with that?"
- Team (in unison): "Sure, boss, no problem!"
- Project manager: "Okay, fine. Now what that means is that you, Susan, will have to track down all of the existing FAQ documents in the customer service data, and convert them into HTML by next week. Can you do that?"
- Susan: "By next week? Sure, boss, no problem!"
- Project manager: "Great! And Billy Bob, you'll have to get a skeleton version of the Web server up and running in a week, so that everyone else will have something they can plug into. Can you do that?"
- Billy Bob: "By *next* week? You mean by *Monday* of next week? Are you kidding? I'm supposed to spend the next two days doing maintenance work on the old Blatzco system, and then I'm taking two days off to go whitewater rafting in Idaho. Maybe two weeks or three weeks from now would be reasonable, but I certainly can't get anything running by next Monday!"

In addition to the obvious explanations and excuses, the immediacy of the deadline imposed by the project manager forces Billy Bob to confront the fact that *he doesn't really know* how long it will take to build an initial skeleton version of a Web server *because he's never done it before*. Thus, his instinctive reaction is to build a buffer into his estimate, which leads him to say, "Maybe two weeks or three weeks...."

This may seem like a minor point, but it's extremely important. Notice that Billy Bob's response to the project manager is *not* "Jeez, boss, I really don't know how long this task will take because I've never done anything like this before. It could take a week of work if everything goes well, but it could also take two weeks if I run into problems..." There is no explicit acknowledgment of uncertainty, of risk, or of the instinctive defensive strategy of incorporating a buffer into the estimate.

Now imagine that *everyone* on the project team is faced with a similar situation, that is, doing something unfamiliar, with tools and technologies that haven't been used before, to deliver some functionality that hasn't been particularly well-defined. *Everyone* on the project team is thus likely to build a personal buffer into their own estimate, based on their own assessment of the risk and uncertainty, and also based on the confidence they have in their own ability to deal with such situations. If all of this was acknowledged openly and consciously, it might be manageable, but the more common situation is that it's hidden, buried, and not even consciously recognized by the individual members of the team.

Indeed, even if the individual buffers were consciously acknowledged, the project manager might encounter some problems. For example, what if Billy Bob discovers that his task is easier than had been anticipated? Will he tell the project manager that he has finished ahead of schedule and ask for a new assignment? Perhaps ... but there is also a phenomenon called Parkinson's Law, which states that: "Work expands to fill the time available." In other words, if Billy Bob thinks that he has a full two weeks to build the skeleton version of his Web server (a period of time which incorporates the risk buffer), then he'll actually spend the full two weeks.

So what? Well, the problem with this strategy is that it uses up some valuable buffer resources that might have been needed elsewhere. For example, what happens if Susan encounters some unanticipated problems in the task she was assigned? Perhaps it turns out that the Customer Service Department's FAQ documents are stored *only* on the manager's PC, and the manager is on vacation for the next two weeks. Or perhaps the FAQ documents were originally created with a now-defunct word processing package, for which there is no automated facility for conversion to HTML. Thus, instead of finishing her task in one week, as originally planned, it takes Susan two weeks. Assuming that Susan did *not* build an extra week of buffer into the schedule that she gave to the project manager, where does that extra week come from?

A new approach to dealing with issues like this is known as the critical chain strategy, which involves the "pooling" of safety buffers across several tasks and work activities within a project.[13] The critical chain approach was not yet being widely used when this book was written during the spring of 2001, but it appeared to be gaining popularity. In the meantime, there are some basic operational guidelines that managers of Internet-based projects should keep in mind:

---

13. See *Critical Chain*, Eliyahu M. Goldratt, North River Press, 1997; and "Software Critical Chain Project Management: Do Silver Bullets Exist for Schedule Reduction?", Richard E. Zultner, *Cutter Consortium Business-IT Advisory Service* Executive Report, Vol. 3, No. 10, Oct. 2000.

- There is likely to be a great deal of pressure imposed upon the project manager by the system owner, end-users, or investors, which means that the schedule, budget, and resources assigned to the project are likely to be optimistic and aggressive in nature.

- Since the detailed requirements of most Internet systems are unknown, or at least undocumented, at the beginning of the project, it's highly risky to make firm promises or commitments to deliver a full-blown system six months, a year, or two years into the future. And whether you like it or not, the political reality is that no matter how many caveats and qualifiers you attach to a long-term estimate, the system owners and end-users will interpret the estimate as a promise. Therefore, confine your promises to things that can be delivered within a matter of weeks, or 2–3 months at the outside.

- Because of the uncertainties associated with the individual tasks and work activities associated with Internet projects, each developer is likely to incorporate a buffer or safety factor into his or her own personal estimates. It's important for the project manager to make this activity explicit, conscious, and visible to everyone on the project team. Risk and uncertainty are facts of life with Internet projects, and it's better not to pretend that they don't exist.

2.5   Tools for assisting the estimation process

If you're managing an Internet-related project involving more than roughly half a dozen people for more than half a dozen months, you should consider acquiring a commercial estimating tool. There are several available in the industry; here is a brief list:

- KnowledgePlan, from Software Productivity Research
- SLIM, from Quantitative Software Management
- ESTIMACS, from Computer Associates
- COCOMO-2, available from several commercial vendors (see CoStar from SoftStar Systems)
- OnYourMarkPro, from Omni-Vista [14]

In the dozens of training seminars that I've conducted in recent years, I've generally found that less than 10% of IT organizations have acquired such tools, or have even heard of them; and even the organizations that have

---

14. Caveat emptor: I'm on the Technical Advisory Board at this company.

acquired an estimating tool rarely seem to use it. Maybe they're too expensive, or maybe they're too hard to use; maybe people have tried them once or twice with unsuccessful results. My personal suspicion is that IT organizations are reluctant to introduce a tool that would force them to acknowledge the unrealistic nature of their politically derived estimates, schedules, and deadlines.

In any case, I don't expect to see a dramatic increase in the use of commercial estimating tools on Internet-related projects in the near future. If your organization has used such tools in the past, I obviously recommend that you continue using them; but if none of the other project managers in your organization have used KnowledgePlan, SLIM, or ESTIMACS for previous projects, chances are you won't get approval to acquire such a tool for your Internet projects.

There is, however, one area where I think you *should* strongly consider using a commercial estimating tool: to help estimate the tradeoffs among schedule, budget, staff, and quality.

2.6   Tradeoffs among schedule, budget, staff, and quality

If there is one thing in common about all Internet projects, it seems to be that users, owners, and stakeholders want the system delivered faster than even the most optimistic project managers feel they can promise. Thus, if the project manager says, "My gut instinct is that it will take us 12 months to build this new e-commerce system," the response will be, "Too bad, we need to have it up and running in 6 months."

It's also possible that the negotiation will involve tradeoffs associated with people, for example: "We can't give you 10 Java programmers for your project; the best we can do is 5 over-the-hill C++ programmers,[15] and you'll have to train them in Java." Or perhaps it will involve money: "I know that you've estimated a development budget of $500,000 for this system, but we've got to figure out how to do it for $100,000." And on rare occasions, the system owners/investors will make a negotiating offer to exchange one scheduling parameter with another: "We know that your estimate calls for a

---

15. This probably means that they originally learned how to program in C, and while they pretend that they're writing C++ programs, the reality is that they wouldn't recognize an object if they fell over one.

12-month schedule, but we *must* get the system delivered in 6 months, so we'll give you twice as many people as you asked for."

Veteran project managers have known for a long time that the relationship among schedule, people, budget, and quality is not a linear one; as far back as 1975, Fred Brooks wrote a book called *The Mythical Man-Month*,[16] whose title emphasized the point that the notion of a unit of measure called the "man-month" (or, to be politically correct, "person-month") was a myth. Indeed, it appears that most of the critical relationships are not only non-linear, but require a third-order polynomial equation to describe accurately.[17] Since most of us are not very good at manipulating third-order polynomial equations in our heads, it helps to have a computerized estimating tool that can perform the calculations and provide a rational, objective estimate of how many more people will be needed if the schedule is going to be cut in half, or how many more defects can be expected if the staff size is frozen but the schedule is accelerated by 50%. Negotiations of this kind are almost inevitable with Internet time projects: There never seems to be an ideal environment where the optimal project team is given the optimal budget and an optimal schedule to do the best possible job.[18] Thus, as suggested earlier, you should definitely consider acquiring a commercial estimating tool to assist in the otherwise emotional, subjective process of negotiating tradeoffs with the system owner and/or investors.

At least one of the estimating tools facilitates another kind of political negotiation between the project manager and the owner/investor/user community—a negotiation involving *risk*. Consider the chart shown in Figure 2.2, which was produced by Omni-Vista's OnYourMarkPro estimating tool. The tool allows the project manager to stipulate the project start date and the number of developers to be assigned to the project; it also allows the manager to identify all of the requirements associated with the project, together with an estimate of the number of person-days required to implement each of the individual requirements. Using a standard COCOMO-based estimating formula,[19] OnYourMarkPro then produces (as one of several different

---

16. An updated 20th-anniversary edition of the book was published in 1995. See *The Mythical Man-Month*, Fred Brooks, Addison-Wesley, 1995.

17. See *Measures for Excellence: Reliable Software on Time, Within Budget*, Larry Putnam and Ware Myers, Prentice Hall, 1992.

18. For another perspective on this issue, see "Internet-Speed Deadline Management: Negotiating the Three-Headed Dragon," Michael Mah, *IT Metrics Strategies*, May 2000.

19. For more details on COCOMO (an acronym for **Co**nstructive **Co**st **Mo**del), see *Software Cost Estimation with COCOMO II*, Barry Boehm et al., Prentice Hall, 2000. The COCOMO model allows the project manager to specify numerous weighting factors to adjust for greater or lesser programmer skill, greater or lesser system complexity, etc.

displays and output reports) a chart showing the probability of achieving various end dates (i.e., deadlines).

Imagine the scenario where the system owner pounds his or her fist on the table and exclaims loudly, "We absolutely *must* have this new Internet system delivered by December 12th! And no, I can't give you any additional developers. We have an absolute hiring freeze, and we can't make an exception just for you! And I don't care about the technical problems you're having with Sun and Microsoft and IBM. It's *your* job to work all of that out!"

Figure 2.2 makes it possible for the project manager to say, "We're loyal, dedicated, and fully committed to doing the best that we possibly can. But given the work that has to be done, and the size of our project team, and the various other factors that can affect our productivity, our estimating model tells us that we have only a 70% chance of meeting a December 12th deadline. If you're willing to take that risk, so are we, but it's a risk that we need to share."

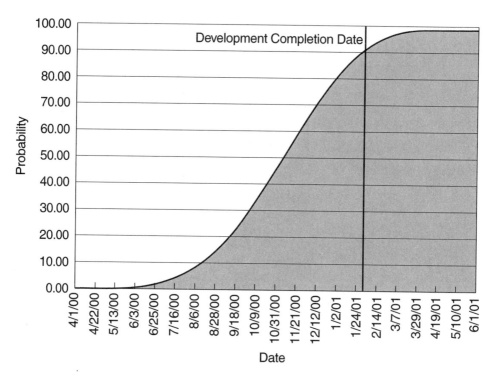

FIGURE 2.2 An output display from Omni-Vista's OnYourMarkPro.

In a typical political environment, the system owner is likely to respond with a call for patriotism, sacrifice, and dedication above and beyond the call of duty. But the underlying political message is this: "No, I don't want to share the risk. I want you, the project manager, to assume full responsibility for it. That's why I hired you! It's your job to manage the risk!" Unfortunately, there are some risks that are beyond the project manager's control, especially when they involve the software equivalent of laws of physics. No project manager in his or her right mind would promise to deliver a project within schedule, budget, or staffing constraints if it violated the law of gravity, or required traveling faster than the speed of light; and within a certain degree of accuracy, models like COCOMO help define what the speed of light is for software projects. It may be a politically unpalatable message, but it's still a message that needs to be heard.

The nature of the project manager's response in the hypothetical dialogue shown above is also politically important. Traditionally, a project manager faced with this situation would become belligerent and say, "No! Hell no! It can't be done! I refuse to accept such an outrageous schedule and deadline!" In some political environments, this is known as "pushing back," and is regarded as an acceptable negotiating ploy; the hope is that after a certain amount of yelling and shouting, a mutually acceptable compromise will be achieved.

Unfortunately, pushing back is not universally accepted, and in many organizations, the project manager who says "No" is accused of being disloyal, negative, and not a team player. Indeed, it often provokes the macho challenge/threat from the system owner, "Well, if you were a *real* manager, you'd figure out a way to make this work! I guess you're just not up to the challenge—maybe we'll have to find someone who *is* prepared to take on the tough assignments."

An estimating tool that produces a chart like Figure 2.2 allows the negotiating dialogue to move beyond the binary, all-or-nothing form of confrontation into a more mature, risk-sharing dialogue. Essentially, it allows the project manager to say, "Yes, I realize that it's my responsibility to do everything I can to make the project succeed. And I realize that the hiring freeze and budget constraints are *real* constraints that we can't change. And I will keep you fully apprised, Mr./Ms. System Owner, if the risk of meeting that December 12th deadline increases or decreases in the coming weeks. But it's unrealistic for you to pretend that it doesn't exist, and to assume that you can make it disappear by simply dropping it in my lap. It's here, and it's real, and it needs to be shared."

No matter how difficult or unpleasant such negotiations might be, it's *much* better to confront them at the beginning of the project, when there is a chance to establish a rational compromise. After all, even if the schedule, budget, and staffing resources can't be negotiated, the amount of deliverable functionality can be increased or decreased. But that's *not* possible if the reality illustrated by Figure 2.2 is ignored, and the negotiation is postponed until a week before the deadline. At that point, there is likely to be a great deal of partially finished work (e.g., design, coding, and even unit testing) that cannot be undone; merely jettisoning partially finished work won't recover all of the weeks of effort that have already been spent. Also, the software industry has known for more than 25 years that the desperate offer to add more people to a project a week before the deadline is not only useless but counter-productive; as Fred Brooks pointed out in *The Mythical Man-Month*, adding more people to a late software project just makes it later.

Thus, the operational recommendation here is very simple and straightforward: Negotiate early, negotiate often, and negotiate with as much objective estimating data as possible. Don't assume that the tradeoffs among schedule, staff, budget, and quality are linear; they are more likely to be exponential in nature.

2.7 What to do when rational negotiations are impossible

In a previous book,[20] I discussed the phenomenon of "death march" projects in which the project manager discovers that: (a) the schedule, deadline, budget, and/or staff resources are completely inadequate, and (b) sincere efforts to negotiate a more rational schedule/deadline/budget are impossible. In situations like this, the project manager has several options:

- Quit (the project or the company).
- Appeal to a higher authority. For example, send an email message to the CEO of the company to explain why the mission-critical Internet project is *not* going to be finished on time.
- Decide which rules you're going to break to achieve the irrational set of schedule/resource demands that have been imposed upon you. This may involve moving the team to a "skunk-works" environment so that they can work without interruptions, or it may involve ignoring the official software development process to eliminate time-wasting

---

20. *Death March: The Software Developer's Guide to Surviving "Mission Impossible" Projects*, Prentice Hall, 1997.

activities (e.g., forcing the users to document requirements that they don't understand).

- Redefine the project as a kamikaze, suicide, etc., and make sure entire project team knows it.

The key point is that the project manager must sincerely believe that the schedule, budget, and other project parameters are achievable, and must be able to explain his or her rationale to the members of the project team; otherwise, the project manager is guilty of conning, or lying to, the developers on the project team, which, in my opinion, is worse than whatever half-truths or non-truths are bandied back and forth between the project manager and the owner/investor/users during their negotiations.

2.8   Conclusion

There is a tendency for IT project managers to assume that *they* are in control of the events around them, and that their job is to plan, organize, monitor, and control those events. But as we have suggested in this chapter, the project manager is usually not even in control of the most fundamental aspect of the project: the determination of whether it has succeeded or failed. Someone else is paying the bill, someone else will be using whatever system is built, and someone else will ultimately decide whether all the hard work of a dozen Java programmers and Webmasters has succeeded or failed. Thus, the first things the project manager must do are identify the key players who will make the decisions and identify the criteria upon which the decisions will be made.

Arguably, the rest of the day-to-day activities of an Internet development project *are* under the project manager's control—once the critical parameters of schedule, budget, and staffing levels have been negotiated. But the most crucial aspects of an Internet project have relatively little to do with the Java code, Web pages, TCP/IP protocols, databases, or any other technical content. The most important determinants of success or failure (within the schedule/budget constraints) are the *business processes* that will be improved, redefined, and/or re-engineered as a result of the Internet. And the re-engineering of business processes turns out to be something in which the project manager is deeply involved, but over which he or she has little control. Thus, it's a critical activity, and we'll devote a great deal of discussion to it in the next chapter.

❧ ❧ ❧ ❧ ❧

Business Process Re-engineering

3

Observe always that everything is the result of a change, and get used to thinking that there is nothing Nature loves so well as to change existing forms and to make new ones like them.

Marcus Aurelius, *Meditations*. iv. 36.

3.1   Introduction

One can easily imagine a not-too-distant day when *every* computer system is connected to the vast global web that we call the Internet; at that point, it will no longer be relevant to distinguish Internet-related systems from non-Internet-related systems. But for at least the next several years, it's more likely that an Internet-related system will represent a significant change for an organization—not just a change in the programming language, networking architecture, or other technological details, but also a change in the way the organization does business.

Indeed, the most common justification for building an Internet system in the first place is that it enables a significant change in the organization's *business processes*. As noted in Chapter 1, this is not the first time we've seen this phenomenon: With each new wave of technology, computers have acted as a catalyst for such change. The introduction of the early mainframe computer systems allowed organizations to automate and improve what had previously been accomplished with paper and quill pen; subsequent generations

43

of online computing, desktop PCs, and client/server computing provided similar opportunities. Indeed, the introduction of client/server computing in the early 1990s caused such excitement that it introduced a new phrase into the business/computing vocabulary: *business process re-engineering*, or BPR.

With today's new Internet-based systems, a new wave of BPR has begun; indeed, it has not only revolutionized *internal* business processes, but has sometimes changed the very nature of a business itself. We'll discuss the external nature of such changes in the next chapter; in this chapter, we'll look at the internal nature of Internet-inspired BPR.

First, let's distinguish between BPR and the kind of incremental change that is often caused by the introduction of a new computer system. Here's a useful definition to keep in mind:

> *Business re-engineering is the fundamental rethinking and radical redesign of an entire business system—the business processes, jobs, organizational structures, management systems, values, and beliefs—to achieve dramatic improvements in critical measures of performance.*

Note the emphasis on fundamental and radical in this definition. A business user might approach you and say, "I'd like you to build me a Web-enabled version of my order entry system because I think it will improve our productivity by 3.14159%," and there might even be a cost/benefit calculation that will justify the effort to build such a system. But chances are that the final result will be an order entry system that still involves the same people and the same basic business processes; the only thing that will have changed is the replacement of a traditional Windows-based application with a new application that runs under a Netscape or Microsoft browser. Indeed, such an effort may be nothing more than putting lipstick on a pig; the cosmetic exterior may hide the ugliness of what lies beneath, but it doesn't eliminate its basic piggish nature.

Why does BPR take place; or to put it another way, why would an organization want to use Internet-based technology to change its business processes? In rare cases, an organization will embark upon such a project simply because it's new and interesting. This corresponds to the market segment referred to as innovators in Figure 1.3 of Chapter 1, but that only represents 3–5% of the overall marketplace, and it certainly does not describe the behavior of most organizations. Indeed, the only reason most organizations *do* change is because of extreme pressure for improvement in profitability, sales, efficiency, productivity, customer satisfaction, or some other measure of business performance.

Such a change could be initiated by a new leader within the organization; for instance, if a new CEO is hired in from the outside. But most often, it's caused by *external* factors such as:

- Intense competition in global markets
- Radical opportunities to introduce new products and services
- Social/political change (e.g., privatizing of public enterprises)

Thus, a company in a highly competitive industry (e.g., banking, airlines, insurance, etc.) may discover that one of its competitors is able to generate the same revenues with only half as many employees, or that it has cut its overhead in half by eliminating regional warehouses and distribution offices, or that it has devised a business process whose cycle time is ten times faster—for example, the Loan Application Department in a competing bank is so efficient that they can approve or disapprove a loan application while the customer is talking to them on the phone, or while he or she is logged in to their Web site.

A competitor whose overhead is 10% lower, or whose employee headcount is 10% lower, or whose cycle time is 10% faster, may be cause for some concern, but this will typically result in an executive mandate that says, "We must all work faster and harder; from now on, everyone will work one hour of voluntary overtime each day!" But working faster, and volunteering an hour of overtime each day, are unlikely to succeed if the competitor's overhead is 5 times lower, or if its cycle time is 10 times faster.

If we imagine the management hierarchy as a pyramid, then the response to a competitive threat is likely to take the form shown in Figure 3.1. At the bottom of the pyramid, we find first-level supervisors in charge of groups of clerks, administrators, factory workers, sales representatives, etc. They typically have neither the inclination nor the authority to make fundamental changes in the business processes they supervise; instead, they typically look for ways to speed up the processes by a modest amount, or reduce the defects and errors associated with the process. Thus, they might be interested in an Internet-based system because it allows their clerical workers to retrieve documents in a PDF or HTML format, rather than getting up from their desk and retrieving hard-copy versions of the documents from a file cabinet in a corner of the office, but they typically won't bother asking why the documents exist in the first place, or why the clerical workers need to consult them.

So what? Well, if you're a project manager who has been given the assignment to build an Internet-related system that supports HTML/PDF retrieval of documents, you might console yourself with the knowledge that you're making a small, incremental improvement in the human race; maybe you're even saving a few trees, and maybe the global warming phenomenon will have been improved by a miniscule amount. But it's certainly not a significant improvement, and it's probably not worthy of the high-intensity effort that one usually associates with Internet-related projects. In simple terms: Can you see yourself trying to motivate the developers on such a project to work 16-hour days to do nothing more than put paper documents into an HTML format so they can be displayed on a Web browser?

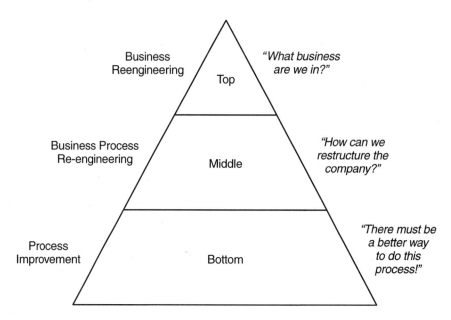

FIGURE 3.1 Where does BPR take place in an organization?

It's at the next level where things get interesting, and where the Internet really does support BPR. At this level, the project manager is usually interacting with a middle-level manager within a business unit, for instance, a vice president, a regional sales manager, a manufacturing plant manager, etc. Indeed, BPR *really* gets interesting when the project involves *several* vice presidents, or a combination of managers from the Finance, Sales, and Customer Service Departments. These are the managers who typically find themselves faced with the competitive pressures described above, and it is they who must find a way to cut overhead by 50%, or speed up a manufacturing process by 100%, or increase the profitability of each customer transaction by 50%. This is where you will find serious discussions about completely eliminating certain business processes, or using the Internet to streamline and speed up other business processes. This is where you will hear a business manager ask questions such as, "Why do *our* people have to enter all this data? Why can't we let the customer do it from a Web browser at home?"

Finally, the top of the pyramid in Figure 3.1 is where the "C-level" managers—for instance, the CEO, COO, CFO, and CTO—ask fundamental questions about the very business they are in. "Why should we be in the widget manufacturing business," they will ask, "when new technologies like the Internet make it a commodity business where nobody makes a decent profit? What kinds of *new* businesses are available to us, where we can use the Internet to leverage our strengths and increase our profits?" In most cases, questions like these are far more interesting and lead to far more significant results than the questions raised at the middle- and lower-level portions of the pyramid. But for reasons discussed in Section 3.3, IT project managers are often excluded from such discussions. We'll discuss the business strategy issues in Chapter 4, but the remainder of this chapter will focus on the BPR issues that most Internet-related project managers are likely to face in their projects.

3.2   Processes, core processes, and process interfaces

If the purpose of a new Internet-related system is to re-engineer a business process, then we'd better make sure we understand what a *process* is. It's not a computer, a Web server, a Java applet, a department, or a functional area of an organization. Here are some useful definitions of a process:

- "A collection of activities that takes one or more kinds of input and creates an output that is of value to the customer."[1]

- "A process is simply a structured, measured set of activities designed to produce a specified output for a particular customer or market."[2]

- "A process is thus a specific ordering of work activities across time and place, with a beginning, an end, and clearly identified inputs and outputs: a structure for action."[3]

---

1. *Reengineering the Corporation,* Michael Hammer and James Champy, New York: Harper Business, 1993.
2. See *Process Innovation: Reengineering Work through Information Technology,* Tom Davenport, Harvard Business School Press, 1992. Cambridge, MA: Harvard Business School Press, 1992.
3. *Process Innovation: Reengineering Work through Information Technology,* Tom Davenport.

Thus, a business process can be big or small, and it can contain embedded sub-processes. Depending on whether an Internet-related project is taking place at the bottom of the Figure 3.1 pyramid or at the middle portion, the project team may decide to identify hundreds, or even thousands, of little processes, each of which might be the subject of some improvement effort. But the improvements are likely to be more significant and noteworthy if we focus on a smaller number of basic or core processes that characterize the entire enterprise. Or to put it another way, improvement and re-engineering of tiny business processes are low-risk activities, and they will usually have only incremental benefits; thus, they are usually not the focus of an Internet-related project.

Improvement and re-engineering of core processes usually lead to larger improvements, and interestingly, the greatest opportunity for improvements occurs in the interfaces, or hand-offs, *between* major business processes. Imagine, for example, an organization that has decided to create an Internet-based system to improve the core business processes of receiving, processing, and shipping customer orders. From the perspective of a high-level business user, those processes might appear to be as simple as those shown in Figure 3.2.[4]

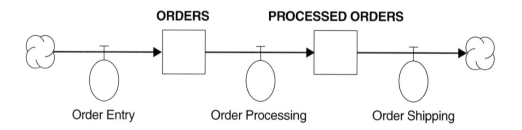

ORDERS   **PROCESSED ORDERS**

Order Entry   Order Processing   Order Shipping

FIGURE 3.2 A simplified view of the customer-order business process.

---

4. The notation used for Figure 3.2 was taken from a system dynamics modeling tool called iThink. The "clouds" on the extreme left and right side of the diagram represent the external world from which orders arrive and to which orders are shipped. The rectangular boxes can be loosely regarded as databases, or storage areas where unprocessed orders and processed orders are queued before being sent downstream. And the double-headed arrows can be thought of as pipelines through which data moves.

But before we get involved in a detailed discussion about which processes might be, could be, or should be improved with Internet-based technology, it's useful to take a closer look at what's really going on at the business process level. One can imagine a situation in which the three main activities of order entry, order processing, and order shipping have been assigned to three separate departments, each of which has a legacy computer system to carry out the required work; thus, a more detailed view of the situation might look like Figure 3.3.

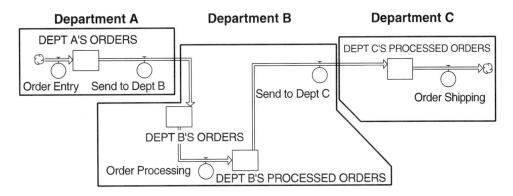

FIGURE 3.3 A detailed view of the business processes.

Not only is there likely to be a great deal of redundancy in this situation (e.g., redundant databases), but since Departments A, B, and C are likely to have entirely different computer systems, the data moving between the departments has to be converted from one format to another. And errors are likely to be introduced along the way because of faulty technology and error-prone workers who are involved in the processes. Thus, the *real* situation is likely to be something even more complex, along the lines of Figure 3.4.

Indeed, even this doesn't approach the ugliness of what really takes place in many organizations today. Note that Figure 3.4 is further complicated by various inquiry processes that are inserted to help business users (on behalf of irate customers) try to track lost orders that somehow disappeared after being received, or are merely taking an extraordinarily long time to be routed all the way through the system.

One can easily imagine an Internet-related project that focuses on one small part of Figure 3.4—for example, someone might say, "Why don't we make it possible for customers to access our mainframe database via their Web browser so they can find out why their order has been lost within our factory for the past six months?" or "Why don't we connect the computers in

Departments A and B via the Internet so we can ship the data via TCP/IP rather than writing it on magnetic tape and shipping it through the Post Office?" But questions like these ignore the more fundamental question: "What can we do to 'explode' the mess in Figure 3.4 and replace it with a cleaner, simpler, streamlined model like the one in Figure 3.2?" Bottom line: If you're running a project where fundamental questions like these have *not* been asked, chances are your project team will end up doing nothing more than rearranging deck chairs on the Titanic.

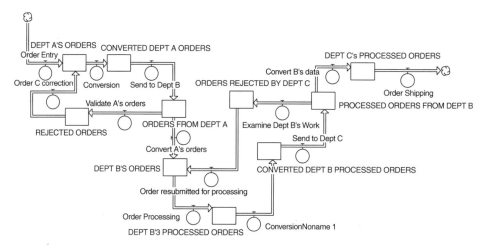

FIGURE 3.4 An even more detailed view of the business processes.

Which core processes should we be focusing on? The example of order processing, discussed above, is a natural one.

A great deal of research took place throughout the 1980s and 1990s to identify the most fundamental core processes in typical organizations. MIT Professor John Rockart proposed that there were only three: developing new products, delivering products to customers, and managing customer relationships. And researchers at Harvard suggested that there were only two: managing the product line and managing the order cycle.

The notion of reducing an entire business to only two or three fundamental processes is probably too radical for most organizations, but there is certainly a lot to be gained from a consolidation of legacy business processes that have evolved over a period of decades down to a smaller number of rational processes that make sense in today's business environment. For example, IBM identified approximately 140 processes across the organization in the 1980s, but simplified them to 18 broader processes in the 1990s.

Most large organizations end up with approximately 10–20 core processes that they focus on. As management consultant Ken Orr puts it:

- "The objective of a business or enterprise is to add value, and core business processes are the mechanism by which value is added.

- In every business, there is *at least* one core business process that represents the main-line flow of business activity.

- Business process reengineering attempts to clear away the underbrush of organizational history, clear/rebuild the main arteries of the system, and focus on the ultimate customer."[5]

As noted above, the most significant opportunity for improvement in a BPR project involves the interfaces, or hand-offs, between core business processes. And if we extend that idea a little further, it usually turns out that the very biggest opportunity of all involves the interfaces at the boundary between the *entire* business process and the outside world. This is illustrated in Figure 3.5, which suggests that the IT project team should be asking questions like these when they look for opportunities to use the Internet to improve business processes:

- How long does the business process take from the customer's perspective? How many errors occur during the performance of the process?

- How many hand-offs does the customer have to endure with other processes in the organization?

- How many times does the customer have to call back—and talk to a different individual within our company—to get his or her transaction carried out?

- What percentage of "top ten questions" can be answered the *first time* a customer interacts with our company?

- What percentage of "top ten objections (or complaints)" can be answered the *first time* a customer interacts with our company?

---

5. See "How Real is Business Process Reengineering Really?", Ken Orr, *American Programmer*, Nov. 1993.

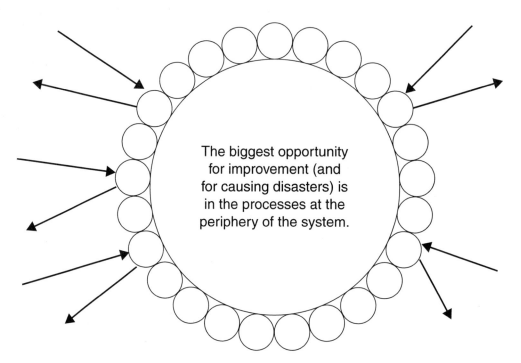

The biggest opportunity for improvement (and for causing disasters) is in the processes at the periphery of the system.

FIGURE 3.5 The biggest opportunity for improvement in a BPR project.

In many cases, a detailed analysis of a business process will demonstrate that the customer has to endure something like the situation shown in Figure 3.6. Indeed, almost all of us have had this experience at one time or another: being put on hold, being transferred to a different phone number where we have to explain our problem again (and recite our name, date of birth, 14-digit account number, and other details for the Nth time), being put on hold again and forced to listen to stale Muzak, and finally being told that the one individual within the company who might be able to solve our problem is, unfortunately, on vacation for the next three weeks. Marketing surveys in many industries indicate that every time a customer is told, "Call back tomorrow and maybe we'll be able to solve your problem, if Joe is back from vacation…", his or her loyalty drops by 10%, and his or her willingness to transact business with a competitor increases by 10%.

Obviously, there are many situations where an Internet-based version of a business process would be a great improvement. Instead of forcing customers to call on the phone (but only between 9 a.m. and 5 p.m., except for lunchtime, and not on whatever bizarre holidays our company happens to celebrate), we could allow them to interact with the company via the Web.

Instead of writing a letter, they could send us an email message. Indeed, before they even had a chance to become unhappy (e.g., because they realized that interest rates dropped and the mortgage loan they had with our bank is now outrageously non-competitive), we could send *them* an email message. In fact, even if there wasn't a situation that would make them unhappy, we could operate proactively to send them email to make them aware of opportunities that would make them *more* satisfied with our products and services.

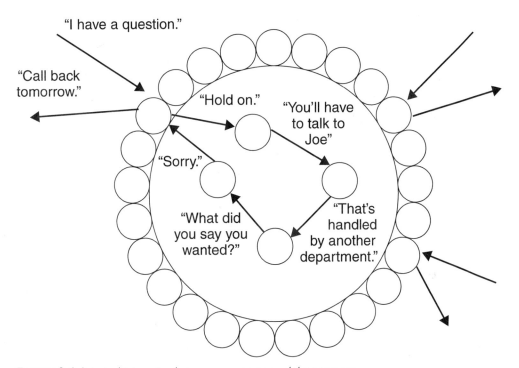

FIGURE 3.6 A typical interaction between a customer and the company.

In many ways, the scenarios suggested above sound like nothing more than common sense, but as the humorist Will Rogers once remarked, "Common sense isn't common." There's a common tendency for business users and IT project teams to become enamored with the technology of the Internet, and to lose sight of the more fundamental questions: What business processes are involved here? How can we eliminate some of those business processes entirely? How can we dramatically improve the hand-off between one business process and another? How can we reduce the number of questions, errors, defects, and problems associated with these processes?

3.3   The role of IT in a BPR project

The discussion throughout this chapter implies that IT should play a leading role in analyzing the business processes, recommending changes and improvements, and then installing appropriate technology to help support re-engineering a business process. But there are two fundamental problems: first, IT project managers rarely, if ever, have the authority and responsibility to change the business processes; and second, even if they did have the putative authority to do so, the political culture of the organization would typically resist the change.

We'll deal with the latter problem a little later in this chapter, but first, let's tackle the problem of authority and responsibility. One might assume that because Internet technology is new, esoteric, and complex, that IT managers *should* have the leadership role in determining how that technology will be employed for BPR. But the reality in many organizations is that IT managers play a passive role, or are even ignored completely. Why?

One possible answer comes from Rick Swanborg and Mary Silva Doctor, who have studied the way IT organizations organize and run their *own* business processes, the results of which have a noticeable impact on the rest of the organization. Swanborg and Doctor identify five key business processes, as shown in Figure 3.7, and argue that not every IT organization does a competent job at performing those processes. Indeed, the organizations at Level 1 on their scale[6] *are perceived by their business users* as doing a mediocre-to-incompetent job of providing IT customer support; for example, their help desk is disorganized, they can't respond to questions and problems, and they can't be counted on to create a new email account in a timely fashion for a new employee.

Level-2 organizations *are perceived by their users* as doing a mediocre-to-incompetent job of data center operations and/or IT component delivery/evolution. Competent operation of the data center was typically not such a visible issue 10–20 years ago because the data center was a mainframe environment that business users didn't interact with directly. But in today's environment, there are likely to be 10–20,000 desktop PCs interacting with a complex environment of servers, networks, and databases that are expected to be available on a 24-by-7, continuous basis. If the network is down, everyone (including external customers, who complain to their business represen-

---

6. Note that this scale has nothing to do with the famous five-level Capability Maturity Model scale promulgated by the Software Engineering Institute.

tatives) knows about it immediately, and the IT department is perceived as doing an incompetent job.

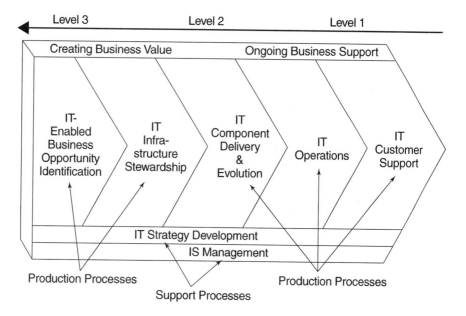

FIGURE 3.7 The Ernst & Young IT leadership model.

As for IT component delivery and evolution, the complaint is a familiar one: "You IT folks were six months late in delivering our last system to us, and it takes forever to get you to make any changes to the system. Why should we trust you to build a mission-critical Internet system for us? We've got an IT outsourcing firm talking to us now, and they claim they can revolutionize our business by building a new system at a third what it would cost if we let you do it."

Bottom line: It's only if your business users consider the IT department to be at Level 3 on this scale that they will entrust it to be the steward of an IT infrastructure on which their business processes depend, and it's only at Level 3 that they will listen to proposals from the IT department about new business opportunities (e.g., e-business or e-commerce initiatives) that involve advanced computer technology. In other words, Level-3 IT organizations have earned the credibility to initiate BPR projects based on IT opportunities they can see.[7]

By contrast, Level-2 IT organizations are typically regarded as partners in the BPR, along with user groups, but they don't have the authority to impose any BPR solutions on a unilateral basis. And, Level-1 IT organizations have little or no credibility in this area; they need to concentrate on getting their own house in order, if not for any other reason that their business users don't trust them and perceive them to be part of the problem rather than part of the solution.

If you are part of a Level-1 or Level-2 IT organization on the scale shown in Figure 3.7, be prepared to play no more than an equal role, and possibly a passive role, when it comes to re-engineering the users' business processes. If you don't know where you are on the scale, ask senior management, or get an objective, credible outside assessment.

3.4 Critical success factors in BPR

While this book does not focus on BPR *per se*, our assumption is that the IT project manager will be involved in the BPR effort that accompanies the development of an Internet-related system. Thus, whether the IT project manager plays a passive or active role in the BPR effort, it's important to understand the critical success factors associated with BPR—for if the BPR effort itself fails, then the technology associated with the Internet system is likely to be irrelevant.

Here are the key success factors for a BPR effort:

- *A vision of the re-engineered environment*—People whose jobs and day-to-day lives will be affected by a BPR effort won't participate voluntarily if they don't have a model of what is to be achieved. We must be able to tell them a story about the new post-BPR world. A broad-based, horizontal dissemination of this story is crucial, too (e.g., via email, video conferencing, etc.). The vision must define the re-engineered outcomes, processes, and behaviors that can be measured, reinforced, and practiced.[8] Note that much of this also involves the (unspoken) concerns about the impact of the BPR on everyones' jobs, power, salaries, etc. (More on this later!)

---

7. Typically, this means that the IT organization understands its own business processes well enough to have created a formal model of those processes, to institutionalize, refine, and improve them. Thus, it usually turns out that they have reached Level 3 on the SEI-CMM process maturity scale. Interestingly, even Level-3 IT organizations may need to revise their internal processes to accommodate the demands of e-business; for more on this, see "IT's Role in Transitioning to E-business," Geoff Dober, *Cutter Consortium Business-IT Strategies Advisory Service*, Vol. 4, No. 1, and "Ensuring IT is E-Business Ready," Ian Hayes, *Cutter Consortium Business-IT Strategies Advisory Service* Executive Report, Vol. 3, No. 4.

- *A re-engineering methodology*—There must be a step-by-step plan that addresses all areas of the organization impacted by the BPR project. It must compel people to work in teams for the long-term benefit of customers and the organization. It must deliver clearly defined, executable, and trackable implementation tactical plans. And it must demonstrate, through the BPR work itself, the new behaviors expected in the new environment.

- *Partnership participation from all levels of the organization, including executives and managers*—It's crucial to avoid the impression that "BPR is one of those crazy things IT is doing." Ownership in the re-engineering decisions is crucial to operational success. If the BPR "problem" is pushed down to the level of bottom-level workers, it's usually impossible to solve the issues that cross departmental boundaries.[9]

- *Flexible, temporary teams*—Re-engineering is not a lifetime career! Initial work should be spearheaded by temporary cross-organizational, cross-functional, and multi-level teams who report to the BPR project executive sponsor. Different teams will be needed at different stages in the BPR project, depending on whether the emphasis is on technology development, organizational redesign, etc.

- *Continued quality improvement*—This may be the focus anyway, if the process innovation turns out not to be radical, but merely incremental improvement. In any case, the dramatic BPR changes need to be followed up with continued improvements, because customer and production needs will continue to evolve as time goes on. Ongoing quality improvement should be done by the people in the re-engineered work units, not the BPR team. The big challenge in many BPR projects is avoiding a degeneration back to the old ways of doing things—that is, a "crash diet" syndrome in which the initial results are very impressive, but the long-term situation is the same as it was before.

- *Team training*—Because the BPR team is a new group of cross-functional people, they probably don't know how to work together—this is especially common with Internet-related/e-business projects, which

---

8. As Tom Davenport puts it, "A process vision consisting of specific, measurable objectives and attributes of the future process state provides the necessary linkage between strategy and action. Unless such a vision is shared and understood by all the participants in a process innovation initiative—before redesign begins—the effort will all too easily slip from innovation to improvement." *Process Innovation: Reengineering Work through Information Technology*, Harvard Business School Press, 1992 .

9. As an IT consultant colleague of mine likes to say, "Unless your project pisses off at least three vice presidents, it's not really a BPR project, and it won't really get rid of the 'silo' empires within the organization."

tend to be much more multi-disciplinary than traditional IT projects. Team members typically don't know what their roles will be during and after the BPR effort; hence, miscommunication and political infighting are some things to watch out for. Team-building work and training exercises are often necessary and more important than technical skills training. For the technical/IT members of the BPR team, it may be necessary to provide training in modeling techniques (e.g., UML, object-oriented analysis, data flow diagrams, etc.), simulation techniques, interviewing techniques, basic analysis techniques, etc.

- *"Systemic" thinking*—The team should make its decisions based on numbers and facts, not politics, hunches, and intuition. (Failure to do this is probably one of the big reasons for the failure of many dot-com companies!) It's also important to think outside the box and to remember that every system is a component of a bigger system. There is a common tendency in BPR teams to ignore feedback loops and focus instead on simple cause-and-effect situations, which may ultimately backfire.[10]

- *Visible, active leadership*—There is a common tendency for senior management to initiate a BPR project and then get distracted by ongoing crises. This can sometimes occur if too many BPR projects are initiated; for example, the U.S. Defense Department had 230 BPR projects underway in the 1990s, and it's hard to imagine that senior management was able to focus on more than a few at a time. Management must focus on helping to articulate the problem and root causes, and not preach a predefined solution. Particular emphasis is needed on the value system and support system components of the BPR project, which will be discussed later.

---

10. A classic example of this is the utility company that decided to improve its cash flow and accounts receivable situation by removing the payment due date from the electric bills that it sent to millions of its customers. The theory was that if there was no date on the invoice, customers would assume that the bill was due *immediately,* and would thus pay more quickly. Indeed, they did so, and cash flow did improve; but what the BPR team failed to realize is that customers were also confused and irritated by the absence of a due date, and the number of complaints and phone calls to the Customer Service Department skyrocketed. Since the manager of the Customer Service Department never spoke to the manager of the Accounting Department, a long time went by before anyone realized that the benefits of faster cash collection had been swamped by the extra costs of hiring additional customer service personnel to deal with all the complaints.

3.5 A BPR management plan

As Dorine Andrews and Susan Stalick discuss in an excellent book,[11] a BPR project affects several different areas of an organization. The areas of impact are illustrated in Figure 3.8.

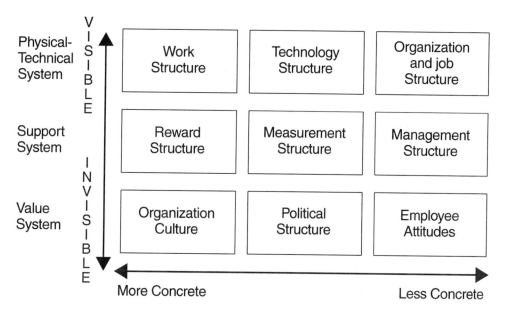

FIGURE 3.8 Organizational impact of a BPR project.

In many BPR projects, IT professionals concentrate on the top row of Figure 3.8 because it is the area they know best. Senior management may be seduced by the top row because it is the most glamorous—after all, they've heard that the Internet is going to revolutionize their business, so that's where they tend to focus. Indeed, *everyone* focuses on the top row because it is the most visible. IT has difficulty dealing with the bottom two rows of Figure 3.8 because they involve issues outside their political turf, and because they often lack the negotiation and assertiveness skills to work with the business departments.

The top row of Figure 3.8—the so-called "physical-technical system"—is where we see the BPR-initiated changes in the work structure, technology structure, and organizational/job structure.

---

11. *Business Reengineering: The Survival Guide,* Dorine C. Andrews, and Susan K. Stalick, Prentice Hall/Yourdon Press, 1994.

- *Work structure*—This is where we ask questions such as: "What inputs and outputs are produced by this process? What steps must be carried out, and how must they be done?" On Internet-related projects that are contemplating large, complex changes to the work structure, it's often useful to develop *models* of both the current work structure and the proposed post-BPR work structure. A decade ago, it was common to see structured analysis models used in this area, and they continue to be used in some organizations today.[12] But in organizations where the technology plays a dominant role, it's more common to see object-oriented modeling techniques, such as use cases and other UML-based models.

- *Technology structure*—This is obviously where we see discussions and proposals about various Internet-related technologies, ranging from Web servers to wireless technology to whatever new gadgets vendors are unveiling this season. Unfortunately, the Internet has not changed one of the fundamental practices in the field: Vendors tend to push their proposed *solution* before anyone has even figured out what the problem is; indeed, they will work hard to redefine the problem, if possible, to make it more amenable to the solution they are trying to sell. Thus, it's far better to look for appropriate technology structures *after* we have a good idea of the required work structure and re-engineered work processes.

- *Organizational/job structure*—Changes in the work and technology structures inevitably change job definitions and organizational structures. This is where we see changes to reporting hierarchies (including the elimination of middle levels of management, in some cases) and workgroup relationships (e.g., the redefined work structure may facilitate people working on a more individualized basis, or perhaps in more of a group/team fashion). It also changes the accountability of the work, that is, who owns the process, and who is responsible for seeing that it is carried out properly? It's likely to change the job content, knowledge requirements, and required skill levels.[13] All of these

---

12. Whenever you hear people talking about "business process modeling," there's a good chance that they're using traditional structured analysis techniques such as data flow diagrams to model the user's processes.

13. It's common to assume that a post-BPR environment will require higher skill and knowledge levels—for example, an Internet-based system will require at least a modicum of computer literacy skills, such as an ability to interact with a Web browser. On the other hand, a well-designed system may eliminate the need for less-skilled workers to carry out difficult computations, or to make complex decisions in a real-time fashion. On a more subtle level, it may reflect the preference of a younger generation of clerical/administrative personnel for *visual* representations of information, rather than text-based displays of the same information.

issues are visible, which is why we've put them at the top level of Figure 3.8; but they have an immediate impact on less visible areas of culture and employee attitudes, which we'll discuss below.

The middle level of Figure 3.8—the so-called "support system"—is where we see BPR-initiated changes in the reward structure, measurement structure, and management structure. Or to put it another way: If you *don't* change the reward structure, the manner in which people's work is measured, and the manner in which they are supervised on a day-to-day basis, you're likely to find that all of the visible changes implemented in the top layer of Figure 3.8 have no impact. This was true when mainframe computers were introduced in the 1970s, when PCs were introduced in the 1980s, when client/server systems were introduced in the 1990s, and when sexy new Internet-based systems are introduced today. No doubt it will be true in the next decade and the decades beyond that.

- *Reward structure*—Rewards can motivate individuals and teams in a variety of ways; but as many BPR teams have learned, changes to the reward structure are tricky, because they may lead to unanticipated consequences! In general terms, though, people do what they are paid to do and what they are recognized for, and they don't bother doing the things for which there is no apparent reward, benefit, or recognition from their employer. Obviously, politics or culture may make it difficult to make radical changes in the reward structure to accompany radical changes in other parts of BPR project; indeed, idealists may argue that it's impossible to develop a reward structure that will guarantee ideal process performance. But it's evident in many cases that *any* change in the reward structure would be an improvement over an existing situation that virtually guarantees dysfunctional behavior because of the way it penalizes people for doing more work or better work.

- *Measurement structure*—Note that we want to measure *outcomes* and processes rather than the length of time a clerical worker spends logged in on their terminal or the number of times they visit the ESPN Web site to see if the Yankees are winning.[14] Measurement, when implemented properly, should help reduce randomness and unpredictability in behavior and processes. A common problem in an old

---

14. Various corporate requirements may mandate that the BPR team introduce a number of "Big Brother" measurements to keep track of unauthorized use of the Internet to download MP3 music or to visit joke-of-the-day Web sites. However, such efforts usually ignore the fact that the *current* environment provides similar opportunities for employees to indulge in occasional unauthorized activities. In any case, all of these onerous measurements do little to improve the overall performance of the business process being re-engineered, and can actually backfire in terms of motivation and morale.

pre-BPR business process is that nobody measured anything, and failure to institute a measurement structure as part of a BPR effort often leads to disastrous results in new business processes.

- *Management structure*—The management structure involves things such as whether people are included in business decision-making, availability and support for personal growth and development, and how workers are treated (orders vs. consensus). It can also include other changes that reinforce people's behavior on a day-to-day basis. (Can they use the new Internet-based system to telecommute, or work from home? Are they still required to punch time cards to prove that they are working?)

Finally, the "value system" involves BPR-initiated changes in the organization's culture, political structure, and employee attitudes.

- *Organizational culture*—The organizational culture involves the rituals, myths, symbols, and language of "how we do things around here." Tasks are carried out in a certain way because they have become rituals over time; for example, it's common to hear remarks like, "I learned how to do things this way, before you IT whippersnappers were even born!" The older the culture, the more difficult it is to change. Dealing with these issues is often entirely beyond the ability of the IT professionals, especially because their culture may be perceived as being different from the rest of the organization.

- *Political structure*—An organization's political structure includes formal and informal organization leaders, including unions, special interest groups, etc.; it also includes informal relationships among key members who play golf together or who congregate at the local bar after work each day. Political leaders promulgate and reinforce organizational values and beliefs; and as many BPR teams have learned, an entrenched political structure may not wish to lose its power. Thus, BPR teams in the 1990s were often heard to exclaim, "Obliterate, don't automate," for they were more concerned with changing an entrenched political structure than they were with the details of the new technology they were trying to introduce.

- *Employee attitudes*—Aside from organizational culture and political structure, employees have their own mental model and beliefs that affect their attitude and behavior in the organization. This involves cultural characteristics like impatience, skepticism, openness, control, rigidity, and flexibility. Employee attitudes *can* be changed, but it's usually a slow process, and it requires active leadership "walking the talk" (i.e., demonstrable evidence that the organization's leaders are exhibiting new attitudes), etc. In some cases, it requires throwing out the old guard, and bringing in a fresh new generation of employees.

3.6 Conclusion

Many IT professionals have little or no interest in the various aspects of BPR that we've discussed in this chapter; they're impatient to begin building Web servers, writing Java code, and exploring new wireless gadgets. Project managers may be similarly impatient, for they feel they have a relatively narrow technically defined charter. On the one hand, they may be correct: The immediate judgment of success or failure will be focused on whether the team was able to write 100,000 lines of Java and get it working within six months. But it's a shame to win the battle and lose the war, and ultimately, the war depends on changing the business processes, not just substituting yesterday's technology with today's new gadgets.

Throughout this chapter, I've noted that similar BPR issues existed a decade ago, when client/server technology was being introduced, and it existed two or three decades ago, too, when earlier generations of technology were being introduced for the first time. But the Internet *does* bring one revolutionary change that we typically did not see in earlier technologies: It changes the relationship between the company and its external customers, suppliers, and partners. In the past, we typically used information technology to improve *internal* business processes, but we continued to interact with the external marketplace through telephone, snail-mail, and other traditional devices.

Obviously, the Internet has made it possible for customers to interact with us via email, and for them to view our company's products and services on a Web site. *But the change is more fundamental than that: Among other things, customers can now talk to each other about our company's products and services, and they can aggregate their individual purchases, using the Internet, to negotiate better prices through volume purchases.* As we'll see in the next chapter, this is one of several examples of how the Internet is causing many organizations to consider making fundamental changes in the way they do business.

‌‌‌‌‌‌ ‌‌ ‌‌ ‌‌ ‌‌ ‌‌

E-Business Strategy

Amid a multitude of projects, no plan is devised.

Publius Syrus, Maxim 319.

As we discussed in Chapter 3, the most irrelevant kind of Internet-based project (aside from an utter failure) is the "lipstick-on-a-pig" project that uses Web browsers, TCP/IP, Java, and other Internet technologies to provide a faster implementation of a fundamentally obsolete business process. Thus, at the very least, you should be looking for projects where your developers can make *substantial* improvements to the existing business processes, either by eliminating some of them altogether,[1] or by finding entirely new and innovative ways to carry them out.

An even more exciting type of project is one where the overall business strategy is changed or substantially improved to take advantage of Internet

---

1. The most common opportunities for eliminating existing business processes usually involve situations where the old business processes did nothing more than *transport* data from one place to another, *convert* it from one format to another, or *validate* the data to eliminate manual errors. Data can often be transported directly and automatically from source to destination via the Internet, thus eliminating intermediate processes; it can also be converted automatically; and if manual processing is eliminated, many of the sources of errors will disappear, too.

technologies. As we pointed out in Chapter 3, IT is often excluded from technology-related business strategy planning sessions because of its poor reputation at managing its own internal business processes. But this only works if senior management believes that it has a sufficient grasp of technological possibilities to make the necessary decisions; and for at least the next few years, the Internet is still new enough and mysterious enough that senior managers recognize that they need to have IT representatives involved in the planning sessions. It may turn out that it's the CIO, or some other senior technical manager, who is invited to participate. But it may also turn out that *your* project is the one that will revolutionize the very nature of your company's business, in which case, you may find yourself sitting in a conference room alongside the CEO, COO, CFO, CIO, and CTO. You may find yourself playing a somewhat passive role in such meetings, and you may only be asked to comment on what's technologically possible with the Internet and how soon it can be developed, but you should understand the nature of the planning process because you may have an opportunity to make some suggestions, comments, and observations that would not have occurred to the senior business leaders.

4.1   Developing a business strategy

Strategic planning is obviously not a new idea, and most medium- and large-sized companies were developing business strategies for many decades before the Internet arrived on the scene. Throughout the 1960s, 1970s, and 1980s, it was common for organizations to review and update their strategic plans every five years (with or without an IT component to the strategy), and to then derive annual tactical plans based on those five-year forecasts. In the 1990s, though, strategic planning fell into some disfavor because of the rapid pace of technological change, organizational/managerial change, global competition, and regulatory change.

Just because strategic planning is a familiar concept, it doesn't mean everyone does it effectively; a century ago, for example, Western Union was offered patent rights to the telephone for $10,000 but turned it down—because they thought they were in the "telegraph" business rather than the "communication" business. Similarly, U.S. railroads failed to see the competitive threat offered by the nascent airline industry because they thought they were in the "railroad" business rather than the "transportation" business.[2]

For better or worse, a recent survey indicated that 68% of organizations *do* have a formal business strategy, and 81% have a formal IT strategy. Interestingly, an e-business strategy is included in 49% of business strategies, but only in 32% of IT strategies.[3] These statistics lend greater credence to the suggestion in Chapter 3 that senior business managers feel that IT has not even got is own house in order, and is thus not ready to be included in high-level strategic planning sessions.

Figure 4.1, taken from Michael Porter's classic *Competitive Strategy*,[4] shows a simple sketch of the strategic planning process. Note that the first activity in Phase 1, calls for identifying the company's current strategy. A couple decades ago, this might have involved nothing more than dusting off the previous version of the strategic plan, looking at it quickly, and confirming, "Yep! That's it! That's the plan." But in today's business environment, you may find yourself attending a planning session in which none of the individuals in the room was involved in developing the last official strategic plan. Indeed, the last published strategic plan may have no resemblance to what the company is currently doing, and the senior officers, if asked, may have great difficulty articulating the company's business strategy. So this first activity may prove to be more educational and illuminating than one might think, as the various participants in the planning session ask themselves, "What the heck *are* we doing, and why are we doing it?"

The latter part of this question—"*Why* are we doing it?"—is crucial because it requires the senior managers to identify and articulate the assumptions upon which the strategy is based. These assumptions may involve customers, competition, government regulations, technology, organizational culture, and the fundamental nature of the products and services that the company offers. Thus, you might hear comments like:

- "Our customers would *never* be willing to get out of their car and fill up their own gas tanks." (Take a look at the 1985 movie *Back to the Future* to see Michael J. Fox's reaction to this assumption.)
- "Our whole strategy is based on the assumption that our competitors don't have access to the raw materials and parts with which our products are built."
- "We assume that the government would *never* let us do X..."

---

2. On the other hand, some of the railroads *did* understand that the most valuable asset associated with their business was the real estate that they acquired when the government granted them the right-of-way to build their railroads. By contrast, breweries in England were frustrated by the difficulty of running their pubs at a decent profit and failed to realize that the most valuable part of their business was the real estate on which the pubs were built.
3. See "Business-IT Strategies in Practice," Chris Pickering, *Cutter Consortium Business-IT Strategies Advisory Service*, Vol. 4, No. 5.
4. *Competitive Strategy*, Michael E. Porter, Free Press, 1980.

- "The whole strategy is based on the assumption that our computer technology will last for seven years before we have to replace it. It would be a disaster if we had to replace that equipment every two years."
- "Whatever else happens, we can always assume that our people will rise to the challenge, and will willingly volunteer for pay cuts, postponed vacations, and 16-hour workdays if it's necessary to meet a competitive challenge."
- "Our products are built to last for 10 years. It makes no sense to assume that our customers would use them once and then throw them away."

In some cases, the assumptions are so deep-rooted that they are unconscious; the most difficult thing may be realizing that they *are* assumptions. We're all guilty of this behavior, but some of us are guiltier than others, and we're guilty in different ways than others. Some of the assumptions are generational in nature, and this can lead to serious problems if the senior executives are of a different generation than the customers to whom they sell their products and services. Some of the assumptions are ethnic, religious, national, or regional in nature, and this can obviously lead to problems if the company is now selling its products and services in a global marketplace. And some of the assumptions are based on long experience with technology that has always behaved in a certain way ... until a "disruptive" technology comes along.

There may be opportunities for an IT project manager to make some valuable contributions and observations about organizational, cultural, generational, or ethnic/national assumptions that the rest of the business planners take for granted. If so, such contributions should be offered carefully, with full appreciation for the politics that may be involved. But situations like this are outside the scope of this book, and I can offer no advice other than "Good luck!"

On the other hand, IT project managers *can* play a useful role in identifying, articulating, challenging, or confirming any fundamental assumptions about computer-related technology in such planning sessions. Indeed, that is likely to be the very reason they were invited to participate in the first place. Thus, you should listen carefully for both direct and indirect statements about technological assumptions. These statements may reflect both good and bad experiences with the organization's existing computer technology, and the statements may also reflect assumptions about what's possible or impossible with newer technology. Thus, you might hear statements like:

- "We've always had a policy of requiring our customers to give us their credit card numbers in person or over the phone because everybody knows that it's impossible to achieve adequate security over the Internet."

- "The strategy we've followed for the past three years is based on the prediction from the XYZ market research firm that COBOL is an obsolete technology, and that within five years, all existing COBOL programmers will have died of old age. So we can't depend on any of our legacy applications, and if we decide to enter the ABC marketplace, it will require us to write 10 million lines of new code in Java."[5]

- "We've deliberately avoided going after the XYZ business because it would require twice as much network bandwidth as we currently have available."

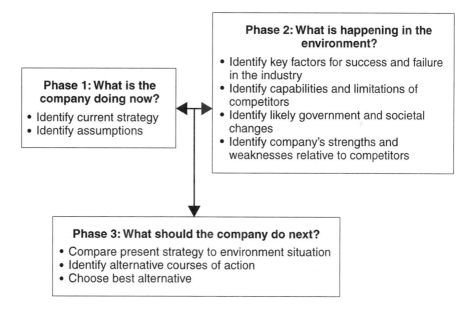

Phase 1: What is the company doing now?
- Identify current strategy
- Identify assumptions

Phase 2: What is happening in the environment?
- Identify key factors for success and failure in the industry
- Identify capabilities and limitations of competitors
- Identify likely government and societal changes
- Identify company's strengths and weaknesses relative to competitors

Phase 3: What should the company do next?
- Compare present strategy to environment situation
- Identify alternative courses of action
- Choose best alternative

FIGURE 4.1 The strategic planning process.

5. Ironically, an article appeared shortly after I wrote the first draft of this chapter, indicating that as of early 2001, "Applications managing about 85 percent of the world's business data are written in COBOL." There were 200 billion lines of COBOL in existence as of 2000, with an estimated annual growth rate of 5 billion lines of new COBOL per year; and there were 90,000 COBOL programmers in North America as of 2000, a figure expected to decline at an annual rate of 13% because of retirement. See "From the Dustbin, COBOL Rises", Stephanie Wilkinson, *E-Week*, May 28, 2001.

Assuming that the existing strategy and assumptions behind it can be adequately documented, it's likely that the strategic planners will spend most of their attention on Phases 2 and 3 of Figure 4.1. Again, there are many issues involved in such an analysis, and much of it—for instance, issues involving marketing, finance, and evolving government regulations—is likely to be outside the expertise of IT project managers. But to the extent that those conversations involve technology, either directly or indirectly, then IT project managers may be able to contribute some valuable insights and recommendations.

4.2   The impact of the Internet on business strategy

An important element of strategic planning is to analyze the *competitive forces* that the company is currently facing, and is likely to face in the near future. As Michael Porter suggests, and as Figure 4.2 illustrates, there are four major factors to consider: potential entrants into the competitive arena, the behavior of buyers, the behavior of suppliers, and the possibility of substitute products or services. Aside from whatever else might be influencing these four areas, it's obvious that the Internet represents a potentially enormous influence. Consider, for example, the following possibilities:

- The Internet makes it possible for competitors *anywhere in the world* to offer their products and services to your customers, via an e-business Web site. In many cases, it's no longer necessary for competitors to create a physical presence with a store-front and live marketing representatives. Of course, the converse is also true: Your organization now has the possibility of offering its products and services on a world-wide basis, thus allowing entry into marketplaces that were previously too expensive to reach. As we'll see later in this chapter, the possibility of new entrants is even more subtle and complex than this.

- The Internet gives buyers more power than they had before; in many cases, they can no longer be considered a captive market. Prior to the Internet, the cost and inconvenience of driving from your store to a competitor's store might have diminished the effective bargaining power of a buyer; now, all the buyer has to do is click on a Web browser to find an entire list of competitive offerings. But again, the change is even more fundamental and profound: *Buyers can now talk to other buyers via the Internet.* In the past, companies often benefited (either consciously or unconsciously) from the fact that buyers were isolated from one another, and made their purchasing decisions in a state of relative ignorance (i.e., based on whatever advertisements and marketing propaganda they received from the company). Today, they can share information with one another,[6] offer and receive unsolicited recommendations for or against particular products, and even pool their individual orders to achieve collective bargaining power.

- Suppliers also have greater bargaining power because of the Internet. They, too, can shop around to see if they can get better prices from other competitors in the same industry. And, within the limits posed by government regulations, they can also compare notes with other suppliers to make more intelligent decisions.

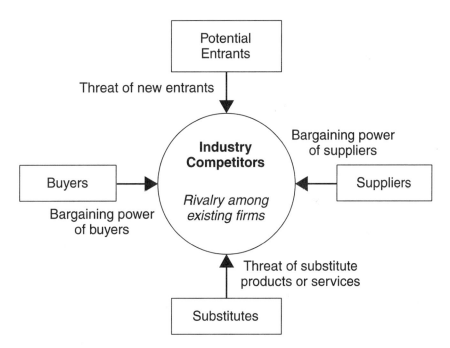

FIGURE 4.2 Forces driving industry competition.

- For information-intensive products and services, the Internet provides *substitutes* for traditional offerings. An obvious example of this situation is the publishing industry: When the Web first became popular in the mid-1990s, many newspaper publishers felt compelled to offer an electronically accessible version of their publication to avoid what they

---

6. A good example of this phenomenon can be found on the amazon.com Web site, where individuals offer their unsolicited opinions about books they've read. The same is true in the software industry. I regularly consult www.versiontracker.com before purchasing a new version/upgrade of a software product to see what other customers think of it.

perceived as devastating competition. By contrast, book publishers are obviously aware of "e-books," but as *this* book was being written in the spring of 2001, there was still considerable doubt as to when—or even *if*—the marketplace would abandon traditional hard-copy books for their electronic equivalent. On the other hand, the music industry was clearly blindsided by the competitive threat associated with the Internet; while they were presumably aware of the technology of MP3 digitized music, they didn't seriously consider the possibility that a college dropout would create something like Napster in January 1999, and that a significant percentage of college-age customers would prefer the substitute form of digitized music over the traditional CD/cassette form.

One of the most significant aspects of the Internet is that it allows an organization to separate the physical, tangible "atoms" associated with its products from the information-related "bits" *and distribute them separately*. In the past, most business organizations embedded the information about their products into the product itself, or into a user manual or associated technical documentation that was packaged with the product. But in many cases today, a competitor can grab the (profitable) information and market it separately, without being stuck with the (less profitable) product itself.

This is particularly evident when the essence of the product itself is information, for example, newspapers, magazines, books, music, business software, and computer games. The reason why Napster succeeded so quickly is that the marketplace saw little or no value associated with the atoms of plastic and paper with which the music industry had packaged an artist's songs. It's nice to be able to look at a colorful picture of your favorite band, and it's occasionally nice to have the album liner to read the lyrics of songs that are unintelligible when sung by the band, but the marketplace made it abundantly clear that it wasn't willing to pay the price for these atoms that the music recording industry had been charging.[7]

While the argument is an obvious one when we're dealing with information-intensive products, it may also be true in more traditional industries:

---

7. Note that I'm avoiding any commentary or opinion about the legal issues associated with the downloading of "free" music. It's worth noting that several surveys conducted during the height of the Napster controversy suggested that most consumers would have been willing to pay a "reasonable" cost for the luxury of downloading individual songs, but they didn't want to pay $10–15 to buy an entire album, which contained a number of songs they weren't interested in, along with physical "atoms" which apparently had no value to them. In any case, I think it's fair to suggest that the strategic planning activities within some of the music companies failed to anticipate the willingness of the marketplace to flout existing copyright laws and aggressively seek a substitute form of music, made available via the Internet.

Information related to purchases, transactions, customer preferences, and supplier behavior may be more valuable than "owning" those customers and selling products to them. Commercial airlines, for example, could be considered a financially risky industry, and the profits are often marginal, but the information associated with reservations and ancillary purchases (rental cars, hotel rooms, etc.) could be quite valuable.[8]

These concepts may seem obvious in the abstract, but they can have profound implications. Because of the Internet, some companies may decide to give up their traditional business of selling atoms+bits and sell *only* atoms or *only* bits. But this is a risky proposition, and most traditional companies are understandably reluctant to go so far. Any decision to do so needs to be made with an accurate and realistic understanding of the possibilities and limitations of Internet technology, and that's where technically literate IT project managers can play an important role during the planning sessions.

Indeed, even if an organization decides to continue its traditional business of manufacturing information-embedded widgets, it still needs to separate the business processes associated with the manufacturing of the widget atoms from the business processes associated with the widget bits, and then streamline those processes. IT project managers may not be involved in the strategies for streamlining manufacturing processes, but they will surely be involved in any streamlining that may be associated with the widget-related information. This may seem like obvious advice, and it's easy to follow when a company is building information-intensive products, but for more traditional industries, senior managers typically focus on economies of scale to optimize the manufacturing, production, and distribution of the atoms associated with their products. Thus, they can find ways to manufacture cars, refrigerators, or shoes at a lower cost and higher quality, but they tend to downplay the bits associated with those products, thereby leaving themselves vulnerable to competition from upstarts.

4.3 Basic types of business strategy

Every company develops its own kind of business strategy; but in general, they fall into three categories:

---

8. Indeed, American Airlines recognized this point years ago and spun off its SABRE airline reservation operation into a separate business. For several years in a row, the airline made more profit from its airline reservation business (which outsourced reservation services to other airlines) than it did by flying passengers on its airplanes.

- Customer-focused
- Operations-focused
- Product-focused

4.3.1   Customer-focused business strategies

If a company's products and services are essentially a commodity in the marketplace—readily available from multiple sources at approximately the same price and quality—then it makes sense to devise a business strategy that emphasizes the relationship with the customer. This may seem like an obvious point, but it requires that the organization acknowledge that it *is* providing commodity-style products and services. That may not have been true in the past, when there were few alternative suppliers or when the company had a proprietary technology that allowed it to build products of substantially higher quality than those offered by competitors.[9]

Because the Internet makes customers more powerful than they were before when shopping for commodity-style products and services, it makes sense to focus on value propositions that *emphasize the relationship with the customer*, and determine how best to supply that value. In some cases, this can be accomplished by optimizing an existing value proposition—"We used to be able to process your order in 10 seconds over the phone; now we can process it in 5 seconds over the Internet!"—but in most cases, a better strategy is to look for *new* value propositions that help optimize the customer's buying experience.

A good example of this point is the large U.S. clothing retailer that recognized that in the real world, many of its customers enjoyed shopping with a friend or family member. So when they built their e-business Web site, they incorporated a virtual facility to support the concept of "shop with a friend" via instant messaging and shared access to common Web pages. Note that this did more than just make buying the company's products a little cheaper and faster; it allowed customers to do something that, for all practical purposes, they had been unable to do before: shop with a friend or family member located in a different geographical area. One would like to think that it was an IT professional who proposed this concept, but if not, at least we

---

9. It's also important to realize that fashions, styles, and lower prices may affect the consumer's perception of what is a commodity and what isn't. When I was a child, for example, most household appliances were expected to last for several years; today, they're often so cheap that if they break, we merely throw them away and replace them with a newer, cheaper appliance that has more functionality and is designed to appeal to the latest fashions and styles.

would want the IT professional in a strategic planning session to say, "Yes! Of *course* we can do that! What a clever idea!"

Note that this example does something on a social level that has nothing to do with the official purpose of selling products and services: it fosters communities of users and customers. As the authors of *The Cluetrain Manifesto*[10] observe, "Marketplaces are conversations"; in other words, the shopping activity is a social experience, and the actual purchase of goods and services is almost a secondary by-product. Indeed, even if the purchase of goods and services is the primary activity, consumers typically enjoy talking, gossiping, and kibitzing about the product, and about the experiences associated with buying it, using it, owning, and getting it serviced and repaired. This is true for clothing, automobiles, computers, books, and a wide variety of other consumer products—and the Internet is a natural medium for supporting this concept of a community of like-minded consumers.

Unfortunately, this is an alien concept in most organizations. Since the advent of mass marketing through newspaper, radio, and television, many organizations have built their advertising and promotional messages on the theory that: (a) the company can craft an offer that will entice customers to buy the product; (b) there are so many customers, and they are generally such a nuisance, that communication *from* the customer *to* the company should be discouraged whenever possible; and (c) the customers are isolated and never talk to each other.

IT project managers are unlikely to get involved in discussions about assumption (a), but they will be instructed to incorporate graphic artists, advertising specialists, and various other non-IT personnel on the project team that builds the company's e-business Web site. Assumption (b) has an interesting corollary in the e-business world: If customers visit our Web site, how will we make it possible for them to contact us? It's amazing to see how many Web sites provide *no* telephone number, fax number, or postal address,[11] and after searching laboriously through the entire Web site, all we can find is an obscure footnote, set in 6-point type, that says, "For questions or comments, please send email to info@ourcompany.com." Who is "info"? Why would anyone want to send an email to an anonymous entity known only as "info"?

---

10. *The Cluetrain Manifesto: The End of Business As Usual* Christopher Locke, Rick Levine, Doc Searls, and David Weinberger, Perseus Books, 2000.
11. The opposite situation is equally frustrating, that is, the organization that says, "Even though you have visited our Web site on the Internet, we won't give you any mechanism to contact us via email. If you have any questions or complaints, you can bloody well send us a snail-mail letter through the post office."

More important: What business processes are being designed into the system to ensure that the customer who went to the trouble of sending an email message will actually get a response during his or her lifetime? With many Internet-based systems, incoming email disappears into a black hole somewhere, and the customer doesn't get a response until three months later, by which time, he or she has completely forgotten what the message was all about.

If you really want to see how politically sensitive this area is, try confronting assumption (c), that is, the assumption that, on the Internet, customers are *not* necessarily isolated from one another, and that perhaps they would actually like to talk to one another before, during, and after they purchase a product or service from the organization. Suggesting that an uncensored, unregulated customer-oriented discussion forum be attached to the corporate Web site is like discussing religion or politics (or, in some companies, like discussing incest): It provokes a hostile reaction that is likely to cause the IT project manager to be disinvited from future strategy meetings.

In situations like this, it may help to do a little homework before the meeting begins. If your company name is XYZ, use your favorite search engine to conduct a Web search for "I Hate XYZ," or "XYZ sucks," or equivalent phrases. If you're lucky, you won't find anything at all; but it's more likely that you (and your senior managers) will be stunned to learn that there are one or more active Web sites, populated by hundreds, if not thousands, of irate customers and ex-customers. It doesn't make much sense to concentrate on building an e-business strategy that "optimizes the customer experience" if you deny that such customers exist, if you deny that something about the company's products or services has made them irate, or if you deny the reality that they're going to talk to each other whether you want them to or not.

4.3.2   Operations-focused business strategies

Another strategy for commodity producers is to become the lowest-cost, highest-quality, most hassle-free supplier of the products or services. This will typically involve re-engineering business processes behind the scenes, with the customer only being aware that the company produces a high-quality, competitively-priced product in a reliable, dependable fashion.

Depending on the nature of the existing business processes, there may be numerous areas for improvement, and numerous opportunities to deploy Internet-based technologies to accomplish those improvements. One of many popular strategies today is using the Internet to help optimize the supply chain between various suppliers and partners who provide raw materials and parts for a company's products. Properly executed, an Internet-based supply chain system can achieve dramatic reductions in inventory levels, costs, and the amount of time that raw materials spend traveling through the supply chain from the component/part producers to the company.

Another strategy involves "disintermediation," which is the removal of wholesalers, distributors, or middlemen who occupy the space between your company and the ultimate customer. These intermediaries served a number of valuable functions in the past, and in some cases, they continue to do so; but if the product/service is indeed a commodity, then it may be practical to find a way to allow customers to place their orders directly with the manufacturer. For example, when PCs first appeared in the early 1980s, I found it useful to visit a computer store and talk to a sales representative to decide which computer to buy. But I gradually discovered that: (a) the sales representatives didn't know very much; (b) I was able to acquire all of the necessary information on my own; and (c) it was more convenient to order the PC directly from the manufacturer, via phone or Internet, and have it arrive at my home a day later. From that perspective, many retail stores are in danger of being disintermediated, as are airline travel agents, and even auto dealers.

Amazon.com is obviously a good example of an Internet-based company trying to compete through disintermediation, that is, eliminating the need to visit a bookstore to purchase a book. But Amazon has also done just the opposite: "re-intermediation" is a potential strategy for businesses to take advantage of a large number of enthusiastic "fans" who are willing to promote the company's products and services in return for a small sales commission. Amazon is only one of thousands of companies exploiting this strategy today, but they were one of the first, and continue to be one of the more innovative. They make it extremely simple for individuals, non-profit organizations, and other companies (including MSN, AOL, and Motley Fool, at the time this book was written) to place a banner on their Web site that enables visitors to click through directly to Amazon to purchase a recommended book. The effect is to create a massive "sales army" (Amazon has over 50,000 associates providing this kind of click-through capability) at almost no cost.

Actually, there is one significant cost associated with the creation of such a "sales army," and it involves a concept discussed in Section 4.3.1: building an Internet-based community. As already noted, it makes sense to recognize that one's customers represent a community that can be nurtured and supported; but an army of volunteer sales associates is also such a community. While many conservative organizations shun the idea of supporting a community of their customers ("What?!? You want us to *help* our customers get together and complain to each other? Are you crazy?"), it's hardly a radical idea to suggest devoting some resources to support a community of volunteer sales associates.[12]

4.3.3 Product-focused business strategies

A third business strategy may be appropriate for companies building high-tech products that involve frequent upgrades, revisions, technical documentation, and customer support. Computer hardware and software companies are one obvious example, but so are companies that manufacture digital cameras, automobiles, televisions, stereo systems, and many other appliances and high-tech products.

Using the Internet to provide technical support is one of many business strategies that can be pursued; rather than forcing customers to ask questions by telephone (for which the company typically incurs a cost of $50–100 in salaries, overhead, etc.), customers can be encouraged to log in on the company's Web site and search for answers to their questions. Here again, the community idea can be quite valuable: Some customer problems are so obscure that the company technicians may not be familiar with them, but other customers may be familiar with them, and may be able to offer solutions.[13]

An Internet-based business strategy can also help customers optimize the process for upgrades and revisions, as well as notify the marketplace of new versions of the product and bug fixes to older versions. An important characteristic of this kind of product is *rapid change*: Rather than bringing out new versions of their product on an annual basis (the way automobile manufacturers do), high-tech companies are typically creating upgrades, updates, revisions, and bug fixes on a monthly, weekly, or even daily basis. It's difficult for customers to stay up-to-date with this degree of rapid change if they rely on traditional communications mechanisms like phone, fax, and snail-mail; and it's both expensive and cumbersome for the com-

12. As an example of this concept, visit Amazon's "community" page for its "associates," located at http://www.amazon.com/exec/obidos/subst/partners/associates/associates.html/107-3989913-7498900.
13. A particularly common example of this situation involves interfacing the company's product with *other* products that the company is not familiar with, or operating it in an unfamiliar environment. Thus, one will sometimes hear a customer ask, "Why doesn't my XYZ software product work when I run it on my old Intel 386 computer? Could it have anything to do with the fact that I'm simultaneously running programs ABC and PQR on the same computer, and that I'm using a third-party hard disk drive manufactured in Afghanistan?"

pany to *proactively* notify its customers of such changes using older communication mechanisms.

4.4 Implementing the business strategy

Figure 4.1 illustrated a strategic planning process that had been used for decades in many organizations. In a stable business environment, such a process typically only had to be revisited every five years; and because there was plenty of time available, the steps shown in Figure 4.1 could be carried out in a sequential, waterfall fashion. Not only that, the *implementation* of the plan could usually be delegated to mid-level business managers without much risk of trouble. And finally, as we have already discussed, it often turned out that key representatives of the IT department were excluded from the strategic planning activity.

But all of that changes with the e-business strategies based on today's Internet technology. A more appropriate process is suggested by Ravi Kalakota and Marcia Robinson,[14] and is illustrated in Figure 4.3. Because the competitive environment and technological landscape are changing so quickly, many companies find that they need to carry out *all* of the activities in Figure 4.3 in parallel. And, as most software development organizations have also discovered, the old waterfall model is no longer effective. The rapid changes require more feedback and iteration than ever before (e.g., the initial evaluation of the changing environment, shown on the left side of Figure 4.3, can be rendered obsolete tomorrow by a competitor's new product announcement or the passage of a new government regulation).

Also, many companies have discovered that implementation of an e-business strategic plan cannot simply be delegated to mid-level managers; the implementation details must be supervised directly by senior management, and it is thus represented in Figure 4.3 as part of the planning process itself. There are two key reasons for this:

- The development of new Internet-based e-business systems often requires difficult re-engineering of legacy IT architectures. This is both expensive and operationally risky to accomplish, and it thus needs senior management involvement.
- The time-to-market pressure of e-business often requires politically difficult business prioritization, which also requires senior management involvement.

---

14. *e-Business: Roadmap for Success,* Ravi Kalakota and Marcia Robinson, Addison-Wesley, 1999.

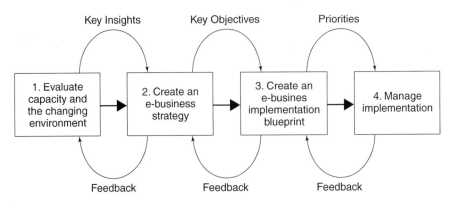

FIGURE 4.3 A strategic planning process for e-business.

4.5 Conclusion

As already discussed in this chapter, it may turn out that IT representatives are excluded from strategic planning sessions. But this is relatively uncommon for e-business planning sessions, and there's a good chance that the CIO, or the CTO, or other senior technical managers will be involved. Of course, that doesn't mean that *you* will be invited to attend; you may find that your role is limited to box number 4 in Figure 4.3, that is, the management and supervision of an Internet-based project that will implement the company's e-business strategy.

Nevertheless, it's important for you to be aware of all the earlier planning activities, because if they haven't been carried out, it puts your project at great risk. This may seem like an obvious statement, but a substantial number of IT project managers in recent years have found themselves assigned to projects that made no business sense to them. And when they ask, "What's the business justification for this system? How are we going to make a profit with this system?", they get nothing but silence and a blank stare. "Just *do* it!" they're often told, in exasperated tones, by senior management. "It's essential that we have a presence on the Internet!"

Whether or not it's "essential" for companies to have a presence on the Internet is a philosophical question beyond the scope of this book. But it's reasonable for a project manager to ask, "Why are we doing this? How does this Internet system help us accomplish our business strategy? For that matter, what *is* our business strategy?" And if the project manager doesn't get answers to these questions that he or she understands, believes in, and can articulate to the project team, then it's quite possible that the entire project will become what was described as a "kamikaze project" or a "suicide mission" in Chapter 2.

Internet-related projects tend, by their very nature, to be high-intensity projects that involve lots of overtime and stress; it hardly makes sense to sign up for a project requiring 80-hour work-weeks if senior management can't explain how it will achieve a worthwhile business objective. Forewarned is forearmed.

❧ ❧ ❧ ❧ ❧

Managing the Software Process 5

Method goes far to prevent trouble in business: for it makes the task easy, hinders confusion, saves abundance of time, and instructs those that have business depending, both what to do and what to hope. ∎

William Penn, *Some Fruits of Solitude,* no. 403, 1693.

5.1   Introduction

Let me begin with a fairly radical suggestion: It's possible that you should ignore this chapter altogether and simply skip to Chapter 6—at which point, you may reach a similar conclusion about Chapters 6–9 and skip further ahead to Chapter 10. This may seem like heresy, coming from someone who has spent most of his professional career teaching, consulting, and writing books about software processes, but since our objective in this book is achieving success with high-intensity Internet projects, sometimes heresy is appropriate.

Here's why: as a manager, you are responsible for the *results*—typically expressed as outputs or outcomes—of one or more individuals who report to you. You may also be responsible for the manner in which those individuals carry out their work—that is, the associated methods or processes—but for most high-intensity Internet development projects, the ends are considered more important than the means. We won't go so far as to suggest that the ends *justify* the means in such projects, but the message from senior management (sometimes explicit, often implicit) seems to be, "As long as you don't break any laws, and don't violate any basic ethical principles that we believe in, you're free to use any means necessary to get the project done on time and within the budget constraints."

If the assignment is simple enough, small enough, and of sufficiently short duration, then one of the most obvious managerial strategies is: Hire good people, get out of their way, and devote your energy to keeping them from being distracted and interrupted by the organizational bureaucracy. For a software development project, that usually means that it needs to be small enough that a small group of 1–3 people can finish the assignment in a period of 1–3 months. It also implies that the owners, investors, and users have a vague idea of what they want the system to do, and that they agree on the criteria for successful completion of the project.[1] It further implies that the manager is able to find experienced, competent developers who are familiar with the technology required to build the system, who have used that technology on at least one previous project, and (ideally) who have worked together at least once before, or (at a minimum) on at least one other project within the same organization.

I mention all of this because it's important to realize that, in many situations today, any discussion of, or investment of effort in, methodologies or processes is irrelevant at best, and counter-productive at worst. If you've got good people, especially people who have worked together on previous projects, chances are *they already have a process for building systems.* They may not be able to articulate that process, and they may be annoyed at the suggestion that the process should be documented and formalized; indeed, they may even reject the suggestion that they *do* have a process.

Even if their software development process is imperfect (in addition to being informal and undocumented), the high-intensity Internet project can benefit from another characteristic of the small, short, simple project: *brute-force effort*. I'm not recommending or encouraging massive amounts of unpaid overtime, but having been a typical workaholic, anti-social, unmarried techno-geek myself once upon a time, I know that software developers are likely to become sufficiently enthusiastic about new, exciting, leading-edge technology that they *want* to work nights, weekends, and holidays. In a perfect world, all of that extra effort would make it possible to finish the project ahead of schedule, or deliver it to the users with higher quality and additional functionality. But in a moderately successful world, all of the extra

---

1. Recall the discussion in Chapter 2 of the various players in the systems development process, and the importance of defining the criteria for success at the beginning of the project.

energy is at least sufficient to help them recover from whatever mistakes are associated with an imperfect or informal software development process.

Of course, things could be even better if the project team *did* have a well-documented, highly formalized development process that had been refined and optimized to meet the needs of an Internet development project. But if no such process exists, or if the existing IT culture refuses to acknowledge its existence,[2] or if it has not been updated since the era of punched cards and magnetic tapes, then the project manager has to decide which of the following three options is most appropriate, given all of the other pressures and risks associated with the project:

- Ignore the issue of software development processes altogether and depend on the talent, skill, and motivation of the team.
- Create an appropriate software development process to avoid the anarchy that would otherwise exist.
- Modify an existing software development process to make it more suitable to the pressures and realities of an Internet project.

During the heady days of the dot-com era, the first choice was by far the most common one. It wasn't always clear that the project managers consciously recognized the choice they were making, but if confronted, they would usually articulate the same kind of argument that I've presented in this section. But gradually, it became apparent that many of the Internet development teams *had no previous IT experience whatsoever*, and could not be trusted to follow a reasonable development process out of raw instinct. And perhaps equally important, the relatively short, simple Internet projects of the late 1990s have evolved into much larger, longer-lasting, complex projects today, that is, projects for which the inadequacies of an informal, incomplete process cannot be overcome as easily by vast amounts of unpaid overtime.

Thus, the details of this chapter are likely to be relevant and useful to project managers who find themselves in any of the following circumstances:

- A project team whose members don't know each other, and have never worked together before.
- A project team whose members have little or no formal background, education, or experience with software engineering principles, or traditional software development life-cycle activities. Such individuals

---

2. This is not a flip statement. In many IT organizations, there *is* an "official" software development process created by a group whose official name is "Process Improvement" or "Quality Assurance Department" or "Development Methodology Group," but whose unofficial name is "Methodology Police" or "Process Nazis."

may be highly intelligent, highly motivated, and extremely talented in skills that are crucial to the success of the project—user interface skills, application domain skills—but they have no idea how to carry out the *process* of testing in a methodical fashion, nor do they know how to document user requirements, nor have they ever seen any of the common modeling notations for representing a logical database design.

- The project is large enough that it requires more than one level of supervision; for example, there are teams of teams, with first-level team leaders reporting to a second-level manager who has no direct supervisory oversight of the people writing code.

- The project is complex enough that no single person can hold the entire design in his or her head. Everyone understands his or her little piece of the system, but nobody understands how it all fits together.

- The project lasts long enough that people get burned out after months of overtime and constant pressure. Voluntary turnover increases, and a mood of jaded cynicism sets in. If the project is sufficiently intense, this mood shift can occur in as little as six months; it's more common to see it after the first anniversary of the project. Only a few projects are able to maintain a high-intensity culture for more than two or three years, and by then, most of the developers are like zombies from *Night of the Living Dead.*

5.2   Heavy processes

For the remainder of this chapter, we'll assume that you've decided that you *do* need to have an official software development process for your Internet-related project. But what should it look like? What should it consist of? Before we talk about the details (which will occupy the next several chapters of this book), let's talk about the basics: should it be formal or informal? Or, to use more colloquial terms, should it be heavy or light?

Many IT professionals who entered the industry in the 1970s and 1980s know from experience where the term "heavy process" came from: They were obliged to follow a set of formal, step-by-step activities that filled a dozen thick manuals sitting on their bookshelf. Each activity had to be documented in excruciating detail, which produced even more ponderous documents; and if the creation of the first version of such documents was painful, the prospect of revising them was a nightmare.[3]

Throughout the 1990s, the notion of heavy processes gradually became associated with the efforts of a well-intentioned group at the Software Engineering Institute (SEI) to develop a so-called *Capability Maturity Model*, or CMM. The SEI-CMM included an assessment mechanism to determine when an organization had no formal, documented software processes, in which case it was deemed to be at the "initial level" (or Level 1) on a scale of process maturity. Level 2 was reserved for organizations that had formalized some, but not all, of the key software development practices, such as requirements management, configuration management, project planning, and project tracking. Organizations at Level 3 also had developed formal processes for peer reviews (sometimes known as walkthroughs or inspections), and had not only *documented* their processes to ensure consistency and repeatability, but had also institutionalized the processes to make them part of the formal IT culture. Meanwhile, Level 4 included processes for *measuring* the development processes themselves; and Level 5 included processes for continuous process improvement. The five levels are illustrated in Figure 5.1.[4]

Interestingly, the SEI-CMM does not mandate *how* the various processes should be carried out; it does not dictate, for example, that object-oriented methodologies such as the UML be used for systems analysis or design, nor does it dictate that object-oriented programming techniques be used for the implementation of a system. Nevertheless, there is a widespread belief and

---

3. In my textbook *Modern Structured Analysis* (Chapter 7), I relate the sad tale of a major New York City bank that encountered this problem in one of its projects in the mid-1970s. Embarked upon a typical "Mongolian horde" application development project, the project team interviewed dozens of users throughout the bank and gradually developed a Victorian novel specification of mind-numbing size. Typing the document occupied the typing pool for two weeks, and all available photocopy machines were commandeered for several days to make enough copies to distribute to the users. The user community was given a week to read through the entire functional specification and indicate any desired changes or corrections; somewhat to their surprise (but to their immense relief!), the systems analysts received no comments from the users by the appointed deadline. So the functional specification was declared "frozen" and work commenced on design and programming. Three weeks later, six members of the user community announced that they had finally managed to read the entire specification—and, yes, they did have a few small changes. A small panic ensued: What should be done to the specification? After two angry meetings at which users and systems analysts eloquently insulted each other's heritage and intelligence, a decision was reached: The changes were not put into the typewritten specification (for that would be too difficult), but they would be incorporated into the system itself. Or, to put it another way: The project team found that it was easier to change COBOL than it was to change English.

4. This brief description obviously does not do justice to the SEI-CMM and should not be considered an adequate explanation for the uninitiated. There are numerous Web sites (such as www.sei.cmu.edu) and textbooks (such as *The Capability Maturity Model: Guidelines for Improving the Software Process*, Mark Paulk, Charles V. Weber, Bill Churtis, and Mary Beth Chrissis, Addison-Wesley, 1995) that describe the SEI-CMM in more detail.

assumption that an IT organization attempting to gain Level-3 certification will, of necessity, find itself burdened with a heavy process that brings back painful memories of the "bad old days" of 17-volume methodology manuals.

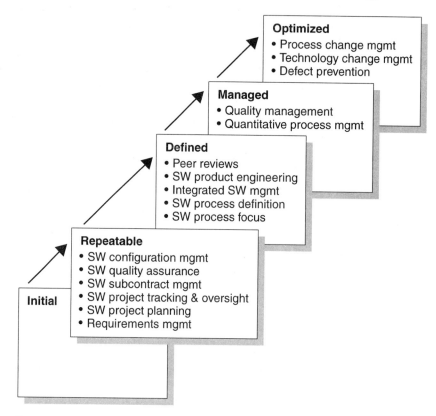

FIGURE 5.1 The SEI Capability Maturity Model (CMM).

Ultimately, then, the question is whether you want to impose a Level-3 (or higher) degree of formality, discipline, and rigor on your project team as they work on a high-intensity Internet project. Recognize what this means: Not only should you be able to ask them, "Are you folks carrying out peer reviews of every requirements statement, every design document, and every piece of code?" with the expectation that you're going to get something more substantial than a blank look and a shrug of the shoulders from your developers, it also means that you should be able to say to them, "Can you show me a written document describing the peer review process that you're following?" with the expectation that they'll show you the generic process description, together with an explanation of how (and why) they've customized it for this project. Indeed, this latter part should be unnecessary: If you're managing an SEI Level-3 project, the peer review process (and all of the other required processes) should have been identified, discussed, customized (if necessary) and agreed upon before any technical work began. *You* should know what those processes are, and so should your developers; all that should remain is a periodic confirmation that they're still performing those processes.

I chose peer reviews for this example because: (a) almost everyone who has worked in traditional IT organization knows what they are;[5] (b) almost everyone believes that such reviews are time-consuming and laborious; and (c) in Level-1 IT organizations, emotional arguments about the merits and benefits of peer reviews are common. If the development team has worked together before, and if it has really jelled, then it may not need a formal document describing the process it uses for peer reviews; everyone does it because "that's the way we do things around here." But in an organization whose culture is heavily oriented toward doing things in a formal, disciplined fashion, not only is there a formal process for peer reviews, but that process entails checklists, pre-review homework assignments (i.e., to familiarize oneself with the product about to be reviewed), and post-review documents, reports, and statistics.

Such a heavy approach to peer reviews (or any other software development process) is terrific if the team knows what it's doing, and if it has done the same thing before. And to the developer who says, "Yeah, that's great, but we're under a lot of pressure on this project, and we don't have time for it," the standard response comes from the original leader of the SEI-CMM project, Watts Humphrey, who says, "If a process can't be used in a crisis, it shouldn't be used at all." Unfortunately, many Internet projects not only operate under deadline-imposed pressures, but they are carried out by teams who have never worked together before, and some of whose members have never heard of the concept of a peer review. Not only that, they may be dealing with entirely new tools and technologies, and working on a project for whom the end-users can't even articulate their requirements.

There's another factor that mitigates against the heavy process approach, but it's one that the official corporate culture finds difficult to discuss openly and realistically: the conflict between short-term and long-term economic benefits. One of the main reasons for investing resources in a formal soft-

---

5. If you're not familiar with the concept of peer reviews, walkthroughs, and/or inspections, then this whole discussion about formal, heavy software engineering processes is probably over your head. Take a look at books such as *Software Inspection*, Tom Gilb and Dorothy Graham, Addison-Wesley, 1993 and *Project Retrospectives: A Handbook for Team Reviews*, Norman L. Kerth, Dorset House, 2001.

ware process during the development phase of a project is that it increases quality *over the lifetime of the system*, which has traditionally been 5, 10, or even 20 years for the IT systems we've developed in the past. Thus, one could usually make a fairly good economic argument in favor of investing an additional 10% in the development cost for a system (which might also extend the development schedule by 10%), to reduce defects and maintenance costs by, say, 50% over the 10-year lifetime of the system once it went into production.

Unfortunately, in today's fast-moving, rapid-obsolescence technological environment, there's no guarantee that a new system will last for more than a couple of years before it needs to be replaced completely. And if the investment in building a higher quality system *does* extend the development schedule by 10%, the company runs the risk of missing the market window for introducing a new product before its competitor. And finally, the political reality for most companies is that managers and developers are rewarded for achieving results *this* year, and in *this* financial quarter—and if their short-term decisions lead to expensive consequences five years down the road, chances are they will have already moved on to some other job. In a corporate culture that provides significant rewards and punishments for short-term results, but no rewards or punishment for long-term consequences, it's not surprising that behaviors and associated software processes will be oriented toward the short term. And that, quite simply, means that the corporate culture in many IT organizations will be predisposed against heavy processes and in favor of light processes.

But that doesn't justify the complete *absence* of processes, and it should not be used as the basis for allowing anarchy within a high-intensity Internet development project. While some processes, for instance, those associated with identification and documentation of user requirements, may be performed in a light fashion, the project team and its manager need to decide whether various other processes will be carried out in a more rigorous, heavy fashion. Configuration management (sometimes referred to as change control) is one good example of a process that probably should be formalized; testing and defect-tracking are additional examples.

As a practical matter, there's no point mandating the use of a particular software process if it's going to be ignored by the team. That's what happens all the time with the corporate-level "Process Police": They publish an official software development process with the blessing of a high-level IT manager who wouldn't recognize a software process if he or she fell over one ... and then they just assume that every project team will instantaneously begin using that process on their next project. Occasionally, the Process Police will swoop in to audit a project, and will write a critical report about the team's unwillingness to follow approved process activities ... but the manager has already figured out that the only thing that *really* matters is delivering a good enough system to the business users on time within the prescribed budget. So the Process Police are ignored and nothing changes.

If you want a particular software development process to be followed on *your* project, then one of two things must be true: either the team must sincerely believe in that process and must sincerely agree to follow it, or you have to impose it in a dictatorial fashion, and you must be prepared to mete out appropriate punishments to those who ignore or violate the process. In the latter case, it usually means that you have to write a memo or deliver a persuasive speech to the team at the beginning of the project, which says something like this: "I think we should be using UML models to document our design, but I'm not going to insist on it. On the other hand, we *will* use Microsoft SourceSafe for version control of our source code, and every developer *will* have a distinct user ID for logging and tracking all of the code that we check in and check out. I *will* review the log on a regular basis, and I *will* fire anyone who fails to use SourceSafe for his or her coding activities."

Obviously, it's preferable not to have to threaten such dire punishment; at the very least, the project manager should identify those processes that he or she intends to carry out in a formal, rigorous fashion, and should make it clear to prospective members of the project team that adherence to those formalized processes is a mandatory condition for joining the project. "If you're violently opposed to Microsoft SourceSafe, or if you don't think you can maintain the discipline of keeping all of your source code in a controlled environment, then it's probably better if you don't join our team" is a reasonable way for the project manager to announce his or her intentions.

But as a practical matter, it's usually a disaster to introduce a new, unfamiliar process into a high-intensity project *unless* it's so obvious and so straightforward that it requires no training and very little behavior modification. It's one thing if the project team members say, "Oh, yeah, we know about SourceSafe ... and we agree it's a good idea to use it. We've haven't been as disciplined about using it as we should have been, but we understand that *this time* we're going to use it religiously." But if the project team members say, "SourceSafe? What's that? It comes from Microsoft? Oh no, we hate Microsoft and we refuse to use any of their products! Anyway, we've never, ever, *ever* worked on a project where the manager expected us to keep our source code under a centralized control environment. After all, it's *our* code, and we prefer to keep it in our own private directories."

5.3   Light/Agile processes

If you're building software to control a nuclear reactor, or a guided missile, or an air-traffic control system, chances are that you'll be following a heavy software development process. And for some Internet-related projects, you probably *should* be using a heavy process because the cost, risk, and complexity are great enough to warrant the additional time, effort, and investment.

But for the majority of high-intensity Internet projects that are likely to take place in the coming years, we will see a predominance of light or agile processes. There are many buzzwords for these processes: "iterative," "spiral," and "prototyping" were popular names in the 1990s. In the early 2000s, XP, Scrum, Crystal, and "adaptive software development" were popular terms.[6] Among the differences between the light and heavy processes are these:

- *Volume of documentation*—For example, a heavy software development approach might insist that user requirements for a new system be documented with a full set of UML object-oriented models, including detailed business rules for each of the methods in each object; a medium approach might stipulate that each user requirement be documented in one paragraph of narrative text; and a light approach might merely request that each user requirement be documented in a single sentence that begins: "The system shall …"

- *Frequency of reviews and approvals*—A heavy process might insist that *every* artifact produced by the team (user requirements, design models, code, test cases, user manual, etc.) be subjected to a formal inspection. It might also insist that several, if not all, of the work products produced by the team be approved by the Quality Assurance Department, as well as senior managers from the User and IT Departments. A medium approach might stipulate that a limited number of such artifacts and work products be reviewed on a more informal basis. And, a light approach might rely entirely on demonstrations of interim prototypes of the system during development.

- *Degree of decision-making authority*—As Jim Highsmith points out, this concept has been borrowed from the Japanese "lean manufacturing" approach and adapted to IT systems development. In a heavy project,

---

6. For more details, see "Extreme Programming," Jim Highsmith, *e-Business Application Delivery*, Feb. 2000; "Put Your Process on a Diet," Martin Fowler, *Software Development*, Dec. 2000; "Retiring Lifecycle Dinosaurs," Jim Highsmith, *Software Testing & Quality Engineering*, Jul./Aug. 2000; and *"The Light Touch,"* Ed Yourdon, *Computerworld*, Sep. 18, 2000.

the project manager and members of the team typically have little or no independent decision-making authority about *anything* in their project; decisions are made by committees, review boards, or higher echelon managers who work in a different geographical area. In a light project, all decisions that impact the team are made by the team itself, or by higher level managers who are nearby and immediately accessible when a decision needs to be made.

In the past, light processes were typically advocated because the business users weren't certain about their requirements. Since the traditional, heavy processes associated with requirements analysis were time-consuming and laborious, the preferred alternative was to invest a minimal amount of time identifying high-level requirements and then build a prototype to solicit meaningful feedback and commentary from the user. That scenario continues to be valid in today's environment, but now there is an added incentive for light processes: the turbulence and unpredictability of the external business/competitive environment. Thus, even if the business users know *exactly* what they want the system to do, their plans are likely to be completely upset by unexpected news from competitors or government regulators anywhere in the world.

Another argument in favor of light/agile processes is that they encourage the project team to demonstrate intermediate versions, releases, or prototypes of a system at regular, frequent intervals. Such demonstrations of *tangible* evidence of progress are politically important in a high-pressure project, and they also create the opportunity for releasing less-than-final versions of systems for productive use. This may not always be possible when releasing a commercial product for an external marketplace, though software companies have often taken advantage of releasing beta versions and preview versions of their products to get early feedback and marketing exposure.

For Internet-related systems, the ability to release interim versions of a system are less common today than they were in the late 1990s, partly because the systems themselves are becoming more complex, and partly because the marketplace is becoming more sophisticated and demanding. In the early days of the dot-com era, an Internet system sometimes began as a simple Web site with static HTML pages, and then slowly evolved into a more elaborate system. While the evolution was taking place, visitors and customers would tolerate broken links and Web pages that displayed nothing but a little icon that said "Under Construction." Today's marketplace typically expects something more complete, more sophisticated, and less error-prone from the very beginning; hence, the Internet project team is less likely to be able to get away with an "extra-light" approach.

Marketplace expectations are certainly one key consideration for determining whether a project should follow a light or heavy process approach. We could generalize this statement by replacing the phrase "marketplace expectations" with "risk assessment"—that is, the project manager (along with the business user, owner, and investor(s)) needs to assess the consequences of defects, errors, and system failures when deciding how formal, rigorous, and disciplined the system development approach should be. Traditionally, the IT industry has used a heavy approach whenever building safety-critical systems, or whenever the financial/legal/marketing consequences of a failure were significant. For Internet systems, there may still be many situations where the external marketplace is tolerant and forgiving, but there are more and more situations where the company's Web site *is* the business and/or the only way of accessing the company's products and services.

The other common parameters of risk assessment involve project cost, project duration, and the size of the project team. As suggested at the beginning of this chapter, a project that can be carried out by a team of 1–3 people in 1–3 months is more likely to follow a light process, and a project involving dozens of people and a development schedule of 2–3 years is more likely to follow a heavy process. A short-term, small-staff project is also likely to have a small budget, so senior management may be more willing to accept the financial risk of doing the project all over again if it fails. Conversely, a project with a $10 million budget is likely to endure much more scrutiny, and will need to demonstrate that it is proceeding in an organized, controlled fashion.

5.4   A recommended light process

The details of the development process will vary from one organization to another, and from one project to another. In the spirit of light processes, I will avoid the temptation to provide a ponderous, detailed description of a recommended development process for high-intensity Internet projects; instead, I've summarized it simply with Figure 5.2.

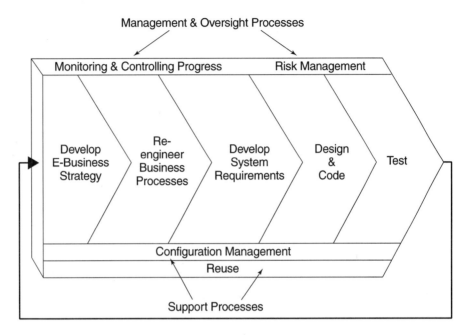

FIGURE 5.2 A recommended light development process for Internet systems.

Here are the key points to keep in mind with such a development process:

- The five process activities in the center of the diagram are intended to be repeated iteratively, for example, on a quarterly, monthly, or even weekly basis. The number and frequency of the iterations will depend on the overall duration of the project, the political pressure for demonstrable results, the perceived volatility of the business environment, and the fickleness of the user/customer. On projects lasting a year in a reasonably stable environment, we might see as few as four iterations delivered to the user on a quarterly basis. On a six-month project in a more turbulent environment, we might see iterations on a monthly basis. Kent Beck, developer of the XP (extreme programming) movement,[7] advocates a two-week release cycle, and there are a number of Internet-related projects for which this is a desirable approach.

- The e-business strategy and re-engineered business processes involve the activities discussed in Chapters 3 and 4 of this book. Since the development of an e-business strategy is typically regarded as more of a business planning activity than a technology-related activity, it is

---

7. See *Extreme Programming Explained: Embrace Change*, Kent Beck, Addison-Wesley, 2000 and *Planning Extreme Programming*, Kent Beck, Martin Fowler, and Jennifer Kohnke, Addison-Wesley, 2001.

usually documented more in the form of a business proposal than a series of technical documents. By contrast, the BPR activities discussed in Chapter 4 are more likely to be documented with technical models (e.g., data flow diagrams or UML use cases) that illustrate the nature of the new business processes. In any case, the key point here is that in a light process, the documentation produced by these first two processes is presumed to be relatively succinct, *and it is assumed that the processes will be revised, refined, and re-examined on each iteration through the overall process.*

- Identification and documentation of user requirements are more traditional IT-related system development activities; we'll discuss them in Chapter 6. A heavy development process would require detailed documentation in the form of UML object-oriented models, structured analysis models, process descriptions, and/or business rules; in the light environment articulated by Kent Beck's XP approach, requirements are elicited and articulated by conversations with the user.

- In traditional IT development projects, designing and coding were considered separate activities; indeed, many organizations distinguished between high-level design (sometimes known as systems design or architectural design) and low-level design (also known as program design or module design). That may still be appropriate for some of today's Internet-related projects, and you're welcome to modify Figure 5.2 accordingly. More often, though, designing and coding are integrated into a single activity, and such an approach is supported by development tools such as Rational ROSE and Togethersoft's Together/C++ product (and, to a lesser degree, Microsoft's Visual Studio environment and other visual development tools).

- Testing remains a separate process, but the visual representation in Figure 5.2 implies that testing takes place after design, in an old-fashioned, sequential, waterfall fashion. While it still seems appropriate to imagine doing design and coding *after* some attempt is made to identify the requirements, many of today's light processes encourage that testing be done *concurrently* with design/coding activities. Not only does this speed up the process by overlapping activities, but it also provides more rigor to the requirements definition activity: If you can't describe how you're going to test the code (and its associated requirement), then you shouldn't be writing the code in the first place. We'll discuss this in more detail in Chapter 8.

- The processes shown at the top of Figure 5.2 are, in my opinion, the essence of what project management is all about. While the developers are busy doing the productive work of analysis, design, coding, and testing, someone needs to watching over the activities to ensure that progress is being made at a reasonable rate, and that the combination of technical, business, and team-related risks is being monitored and managed. We'll discuss these activities in more detail in Chapter 9.

• The processes shown at the bottom of Figure 5.2 are support processes that can be carried out with as much, or as little, formality as required. Configuration management involves coordination and management of the *changes* that are being made to the various artifacts and work products created by the development team—the code, test cases, user manuals, design models, and descriptions of user requirements. In addition, reuse is described as a process here, for it involves activities on the part of the development team to identify opportunities to reuse pre-existing components, as well as opportunities to create new components for future reuse. Configuration management and reuse are fairly traditional concepts in the IT field; we won't discuss them in detail in this book.

5.5 Conclusion

Discussions about software development processes are almost like discussions of religion or politics: They often require a great deal of faith, and they can become very emotional. Unfortunately, they share other common attributes with religion and politics: They tend to be articulated in a dogmatic fashion, and they tend to be advocated by zealots who view any deviation as heresy punishable by excommunication, if not execution. In a turbulent environment with fast-changing technology, the trick is to find a process that provides the right balance between agile, flexible innovation and orderly, predictable, repeatable procedures.

As a project manager, you should consider yourself lucky if you work in an organization that recognizes the need for establishing such a balance and provides helpful guidelines, advice, and support for achieving the necessary balance in *your* project. All too often, though, project managers find themselves working in organizations whose processes and procedures are enforced with a heavy hand, even though they no longer apply to the circumstances of an Internet-related project. In a situation like this, you need to ask yourself one fundamental question: Will you be punished more severely for violating the official process but delivering a successful system, or for following the official process but failing to deliver a successful system? The answer to that question will help you decide what to do about software processes, or it will illustrate the existence of such a fundamental conflict that your best bet may be to seek employment elsewhere.

🐸 🐸 🐸 🐸 🐸

Managing the
Requirements Process

6

The necessary has never been man's top priority. The passionate
pursuit of the nonessential and the extravagant is one of the chief traits
of human uniqueness. Unlike other forms of life, man's greatest
exertions are made in the pursuit not of necessities but of superfluities.■

Eric Hoffer, The New York Times, July 21, 1969.

6.1 Introduction

Requirements analysis has long been a source of great conflict in IT development projects, and it continues to be so with Internet-related projects. On the
one hand, it's almost impossible to plan and organize a project if you don't
know what you're supposed to deliver; as the old proverb says, "If you
don't know where you're going, any road will do." On the other hand, if the
user doesn't understand the requirements, or isn't able (or willing) to articulate those requirements, how can the developers document them properly?
And if the requirements are subject to constant change, why bother spending a lot of time and energy documenting them?

Unfortunately, the reaction to this dilemma has typically vacillated between
two extremes. One extreme could be called "requirements overkill," and it's
practiced by organizations who feel that the best way to deliver successful
results is to document the user requirements in excruciating detail, using all
the latest methods and tools. An additional incentive, according to this
group, is that a sufficiently detailed statement of requirements can be trans-

lated into working code automatically, with the use of CASE tools or code generators.

The other extreme is represented by the requirements anarchists, who argue that any time or effort invested in documenting user requirements is wasted. The arguments in favor of this position are familiar to almost every IT developer: Users don't know what they want, they're not good at explaining their needs, and they change their minds. The extreme form of the anarchist school of thought goes so far as to say that the requirements for an IT system are not only unknown, but *unknowable*, that is, it is *never* possible to identify and document the requirements before a system is built. Instead, one should follow an emergent approach, and simply allow the requirements to emerge from an evolving set of prototypes and interim versions of the system.

Presumably one can find an existence proof to justify either one of these extreme positions. But for the vast majority of IT organizations—and for the vast majority of Internet-related projects, no matter how intense they may be—it's more realistic and practical to find a compromise somewhere between the two extremes. Because most projects are required to operate within the broad constraints of a schedule and budget, it's simply not practical to avoid any consideration whatsoever of the requirements during the initial planning stage of the project. But since the details of an IT development project, especially one involving new technologies associated with the Internet, are indeed likely to be unknowable, it doesn't make sense to waste a lot of time and energy documenting those details.

The trick is to find the proper level of detail, and to defer consideration of as many details as possible until the last possible moment. But that doesn't mean ignoring *all* efforts to identify and document the requirements of a system; this chapter, as you will see, is not a defense of the anarchists' position. Indeed, we'll begin by summarizing—primarily for the benefit of the project manager—why well-documented requirements *are* so important. Then we'll discuss the three separate aspects of system requirements: elicitation, documentation, and prioritization. Particularly for high-intensity projects, where there never seems to be enough time to accomplish everything that the user has asked for, a cold-blooded form of prioritization known as *triage* is essential for success.

6.2 The importance of requirements

Why are requirements such an important part of the IT development process? Because numerous surveys and studies have indicated that between 40% and 80% of IT project failures can be traced back to a misunderstanding of, or incorrect specification of, the system requirements. But it's important to recognize that not all such failures take the form of an outright rejection by users who say, "Ugh! This isn't what we wanted! This system doesn't do what we need it to do!" That's probably the most extreme kind of failure, and it was more common 10–20 years ago, when the IT project team interviewed the users *once* to identify the requirements and then disappeared for a year or two to build the system without any further contact with the user community.

Such extreme situations still do occur from time to time, especially in outsourcing situations where the requirements form the basis of a legal contract between two hostile parties. But even in situations where there is a cooperative, continuous set of interactions between the developers and users, there are still numerous opportunities for a requirements-oriented failure at the end of the development effort. Perhaps the most frustrating form of failure is the case where the users say, "We can see that you gave us what we asked for, but it turns out that it's not what we need. This system doesn't do what we really need it to do."

For the project manager, it's important to think about a scenario like this from a risk management perspective. What are the chances that your users will ultimately say to you, "This system would be terrific, if only it didn't have so many bugs!"? Yes, some projects could fail because of coding bugs or inadequate testing, or because the hardware vendor went bankrupt, or the programming language didn't work, or any one of a number of other technical problems. But it's far more likely that a failed project will be associated with a profound dissatisfaction by the users with the requirements (or lack of requirements) that have been implemented in the system.

What about the situation where the users say, "This system does exactly what we need it to do ... but you're six months late in delivering it to us, and we've lost the window of opportunity that we would have had if the system had been available when you promised it to us!" In this case, the obvious question is: *Why* was the project six months behind schedule? Again, there are a number of possibilities that the project manager should be thinking about from a risk management perspective. Maybe all the programmers came down with bubonic plague and had to be replaced with new programmers. Maybe the programming effort turned out to be more complex than anticipated, or the programmers turned out to be less productive than anticipated, so that all of the plans and estimates turned out to be too optimistic. More likely, the plans and estimates were hysterically optimistic to begin with, because they were based on an outrageous deadline that was imposed on the project before anyone even started thinking about requirements.[1]

Optimistic estimates of programmer productivity and schedule problems associated with unanticipated illnesses have little or nothing to do with the issue of requirements. But the phenomenon of outrageous deadlines *does* have something to do with requirements, and it can be fatal for the project manager to ignore the associated risks. In its simplest form, the problem is this: Even though the user is unable (or unwilling) to articulate the requirements in detail, we have enough information about the "gross" requirements to determine that it's mathematically impossible to implement those requirements within the constraints of the schedule and deadline that have been imposed on the project. The more complex and subtle form of the problem is this: The initial assessment of the rough description of requirements indicates that the team *might* be able to get everything finished before the deadline (but usually only if we assume high levels of productivity, no illnesses or absences, and substantial amounts of "voluntary" overtime); unfortunately, the users add new requirements through the development process, they change their minds about the details of the requirements, and the details turn out to be substantially more complex than we originally believed them to be.

In either the simple version or the complex version of this scenario, the outcome is the same: When the deadline arrives, we're not finished. But this frustrating state of affairs could take several different forms, including these illustrative examples: In one case, the project team has finished 90% of *all* the requirements, but *nothing* works completely. The project team is desperately coding and testing, is on the verge of collapse from several weeks of round-the-clock death march activity … and the project manager begs the users: "Give us just one more week, and we'll be done!" Unfortunately, after the week has transpired, it turns out that the team is now 93.75% finished … but

---

1. This often leads to a phenomenon known as "backwards wishful thinking." That is, the project manager says, "We've been told that we *must* finish this project by December 31, even though we don't know exactly what it is we're supposed to develop. And that means we have to finish coding by September 30, so we'll have three months to test whatever it is we're supposed to be doing. To finish coding by that date, we'll need to wrap up the design by July 31, and that means we need to get the requirements documented by tomorrow afternoon!"

nothing works completely. "Just one week more!" begs the project manager. "That's all we need!"

An alternative scenario is one in which the deadline arrives, and 90% of the user requirements are *completely* finished, while 10% have not received any attention at all. "That's outrageous!" cry the users. "You promised that *all* of the system would be done!" To which the project manager replies, "Actually, we only promised that we would *try* to get everything done, and it turned out to be impossible. But the requirements that *are* done are the most important ones, and it should give you enough functionality to begin using the system now. We hope to get the rest of the requirements finished in the next couple of weeks."

There's much more to say about this, of course, and we'll discuss the details in Section 6.5. But the main point to emphasize here is that well-articulated requirements can form the basis for rational negotiations regarding schedule, budget, resources, deliverable functionality, and quality. And, in the common situation where the available schedule and budget are inadequate for delivering *all* of the required functionality of the system, then a set of well-articulated requirements can form the basis of intelligent, pragmatic *triage* decisions.

There is one more reason why requirements have been considered an important element of systems development: Traditionally, requirements errors have been the most expensive kind of defect to fix. Of course, *any* defect (or bug) can be either simple or complex, but the experience of the IT industry from the 1960s through the 1980s was that, in general, coding errors were relatively simple to fix, and requirements-oriented errors were difficult and expensive to fix. The reasons were quite straightforward: The technical resources (i.e., time and effort) that had been expended for design and implementation had to be un-done and re-worked when the "true" requirement was identified. And in many cases, the user and systems analyst who first negotiated and documented the initial (incorrect) set of requirements were no longer readily accessible for discussions when the testing effort uncovered the requirements-oriented defect.

Today, the situation is likely to be somewhat less severe. With high-level prototyping and development tools, a developer can build a crude skeleton version of the implementation of a requirement, and show it to the user for feedback; if it turns out that the developer misunderstood the requirement (or, equally likely, the user changes his or her mind about the requirement), only a small amount of time and effort has been lost. Indeed, it may take less effort to build a quick-and-dirty prototyped implementation of a requirement than it would to write a detailed description of the requirement, review it with the user, and then produce a revised document. Not only that, the same individual is likely to perform both the systems analysis activity of documenting the requirements *and* the subsequent activity of implementing those requirements—in contrast to the common situation in older projects, where different individuals were assigned to the analysis, design, coding, and testing efforts. Also, the entire life cycle of analysis, design, coding, and testing is likely to take place within a matter of weeks or months in today's projects, instead of months or years in older projects. Thus, if it does turn out that the requirements were improperly understood or improperly documented, it's much more likely that the project team will still be able to find the responsible user, and that user is much more likely to remember the details of the previous set of discussions about the requirements.

Thus, it's probably not as important as it used to be for the project manager to exhort his or her team, "Get the requirements documented right the first time, because we may never see this user again—and if we make a mistake, it's going to be incredibly expensive to correct it later on!" Instead, the more relevant exhortation will be, "Let's identify and enumerate as many of the requirements as possible because we're not going to have enough time to implement them all before we run out of time—we've got to make sure that we know which ones are the most important ones!"

While project managers are likely to agree that it makes sense to identify requirements as the basis for planning, it's important to remember that the developers on the project team—that is, the people who actually *do* the work of identifying and documenting requirements—are likely to resist. Also, if you're dealing with business users who are over-worked, over-scheduled, and too busy to spend much time talking to you about the details of the system you're building for them, they too may resist the suggestion of spending time to identify the requirements. Here are the most common objections you're likely to hear:

- "Prototyping eliminates the need for requirements."
- "This stuff takes too long, and we don't have time for it."
- "The users don't know what they want…"
- "…and even if they did, they would change their mind…"
- "This system is only going to be used once or twice…"

6.2.1   "Prototyping eliminates the need for requirements."

Indeed, prototyping *may* be a cost-effective way to model some aspects of the requirements, especially the user interface and all of the details about fonts, colors, and placement of windows and icons on the end-user's computer screen. Indeed, it's quite difficult to document this aspect of requirements in any other traditional form, and since many users do care about it so much, prototyping makes a great deal of sense.

But prototyping doesn't provide a good way to capture requirements for issues such as security, error-handling, performance, scalability, and other important non-functional characteristics of a system. In some cases, a prototype may perform sluggishly because of the programming tools that were used to build it; but in most cases, the user will see an unrealistically fast version of the system, because it will only be supporting one individual user rather than the production-level environment of dozens, hundreds, or even thousands of users. And the prototype doesn't provide a good way of discussing and validating functionality issues involving complex, detailed business rules. Obviously, the business user can look at a prototype to confirm simple business calculations (e.g., *gross salary equals hourly pay times number of hours worked*), but if the system is required to make complex decisions or complex calculations (e.g., withholding tax on a paycheck), the prototype is rarely an effective mechanism for ensuring that the requirements are well-understood.

In the best case, the prototype can serve as a document of the requirements, especially for the look-and-feel aspect of the user interface. But the prototype is usually *not* a good after-the-fact document of the functionality requirements. And the reality is that most project teams don't save the prototype for subsequent review and discussions; so if anyone asks, "How do we know that this final version of the system actually includes all of the user interface issues that we agreed to when we saw the prototype?", there may not be a prototype available for anyone to look at.

6.2.2   "This stuff takes too long, and we don't have time for it."

This is likely to be an emotional argument on the part of software developers who are more comfortable with Java than English, and have unpleasant memories of previous projects that required them to produce hundreds of pages of turgid prose before they were allowed to write any code. The key point that needs to be made to these people is that modeling and documentation of the system requirements do not have to be an all-or-nothing proposition.

If the user actually does understand the requirements, and *if* the user's business environment is relatively stable, and *if* the consequences of misunderstood requirements are serious (e.g., risks involving human life or safety, or the risk of a multi-million-dollar lawsuit), *then* it makes sense to document the requirements in considerable detail, using the methods that will be summarized in Section 6.4. There are still many such systems being built today, and we're likely to see more and more Internet-related projects falling into this category as the Internet becomes part of the infrastructure and fabric of *all* systems.

But if the user has only a general idea of what the requirements are, or if he or she is concerned that some of the requirements may change over the next few weeks or months, then perhaps it makes sense to articulate and document each requirement in a paragraph of narrative text. In some cases, it may also make sense to use a UML use case diagram to identify the actor responsible for interacting with the system in a certain area of functionality (e.g., is it the sales representative or the sales manager who interacts with the system to override the standard volume discount terms offered to a customer?). And it probably makes sense to identify the basic inputs and outputs, as well as the required databases, associated with each area of functionality; we can often identify the *fields* of data associated with these inputs and outputs, even if we can't specify the syntax and validation rules associated with each field.

In the extreme case, the project team can articulate and document each requirement in a single, imperative English sentence. Thus, we might see a project in which the requirements have been identified in the following fashion:

- "The system shall allow customers to place orders by mail, fax, phone, email, or via a Web browser."

- "The system shall allow customers to modify their orders at any point prior to shipment from our warehouse."

- "The system should allow customers to place orders during evenings and weekends, as well as during normal business hours."

- "The system may allow customers to describe the details of their telephone orders via voice input and voice recognition, in addition to standard touch-tone data entry."

Notice the use of "must," "should," and "may" in these examples. As we'll discuss in Section 6.5, this kind of qualifier is enormously helpful in prioritizing the requirements, even if we don't fully understand the details of each requirement.

One can easily understand why developers *and* business users would balk at the effort required to write a full-blown, detailed description of each requirement in their system. Indeed, they might balk at the approach suggested here; but it's hard to argue that you don't have enough time to write a paragraph of text to describe a requirement ... unless there are thousands of such requirements, and the project team is under enormous pressure to begin developing working software as quickly as possible. Even in this extreme situation, it's hard to argue that you don't have enough time to write a single English sentence for each requirement.

The reason why we want the users and developers to document the requirements in English sentences is not to practice their Shakespearean skills, but rather to *capture* that information in an automated tool and use it as the basis for planning, scheduling, and (if necessary) negotiating *which* of the requirements will actually be implemented. Again, we'll discuss this in more detail in Section 6.5.

6.2.3   "The users don't know what they want..."

Again, the key point here is that the users' understanding of their requirements should not be perceived as an all-or-nothing situation, unless, of course, they are indulging in pure, whimsical research and experimentation. In an "awareness-lite" situation, the users should be able to articulate broad areas of functionality, even if they don't know the details. In the example above, our users know that they want to allow customers to place orders through various channels, and they have a broad understanding that customers must be allowed to modify their orders. They may not be prepared to discuss all of the details and exceptions (e.g., Can orders be transmitted via Federal Express or other courier services?), but even the high-level identification of requirements is sufficient for some useful conversations with the development team (e.g., Are customers allowed to *cancel* orders? Are they allowed to return orders, once they have been received?).

In an "awareness-medium" situation, we would expect the users to be able to articulate details of the functionality, including most of the required business rules, even if they don't know much about the details of the preferred user interface. Thus, we could have some useful conversations with our users to determine whether the order entry system will only accept orders from existing customers, or whether we must also accept orders from new (unknown) customers; can orders be modified only once by a customer, or can they be modified as many times as desired before the order is shipped from the warehouse; do orders and modifications have to be approved by anyone, or is the customer the *only* actor involved in these transactions?

Obviously, the "awareness-heavy" situation is one in which the users know so much about their requirements that they can stipulate *all* of the details; unfortunately, they often go further, and begin stipulating *solutions* to their requirements, which is likely to be distracting and counter-productive. But there is also the danger that they may consume a great deal of time and energy describing requirements that subsequently turn out to be wrong, either because the user had not really thought about all of the ramifications and exceptions to the various business scenarios, or because the business environment changed during the course of the development effort. If *all* of the requirements could be documented in exhaustive detail in the course of a single day of work, it would be hard to argue that it's a waste of time; but if it consumes a full month of effort out of a three-month project, then it's more understandable that the developers and business users might worry about the possibility of wasted effort. And if a full year transpires while everyone works laboriously to document the requirements before any software is developed ... well, nobody is recommending that kind of extreme approach, at least not for the kind of high-intensity Internet projects being discussed in this book.

There is one aspect of the requirements documentation effort that requires special discussion: the distinction between *detailed* requirements and the kind of business process/business strategy requirements discussed in Chapters 3 and 4 of this book. That is, before we get involved in such discussions about whether customers should be allowed to modify their orders, cancel their orders, or return the goods they've ordered, we should be asking much more fundamental questions like: Why are we even thinking about the Internet for this project? What's our business strategy for using the Internet to acquire more customers, or service them more effectively, or process their orders more quickly, or persuade them to order more profitable items from our inventory? *How is our company going to be better off if we build this system than it is now?*

Similarly, we should be asking BPR questions like these: How is the business process for accepting and processing orders going to change with this new system? Do we still need to have order entry personnel, or will the orders be placed completely and directly by the customers, and thus go straight into our computer systems without being touched by human hands? Does it still make sense to have sales representatives, and if yes, how are we going to measure them, manage them, and compensate them? Can we use wireless technology to allow our sales representatives to place orders directly from the customer site, or out in the field, without going back to the office to type the orders into a desktop PC, and if so, which of our existing business processes can be eliminated completely?

Each of these questions will lead to a collection of detailed, specific system requirements—but there's no point documenting the details until we get a clear understanding of the business strategy and corresponding business processes that are going to be affected by the new system. Of course, the business users might not know the answers to all of these questions; they might say, "We're not really sure if we want to equip our sales representatives with wireless, hand-held computers for order entry, but we *do* know that we have to reduce the overall order entry and order processing time to something under an hour because otherwise we'll be wiped out by our competitors." Such a comment makes it clear that careful analysis of the existing order entry and order processing *business processes* are required, but it's also clear that the development of a wireless, hand-held order entry capability is a *business experiment*, which may have to be cancelled if the initial results are unsatisfactory.

6.2.4   "...and even if they did, they would change their mind..."

As my colleague Tom DeMarco once remarked, "If the users are operating a bank, but think they might want to turn it into a discotheque, then there isn't much justification for modeling the existing system." DeMarco made the comment in 1978, when the example seemed so ludicrous that it was highly amusing; today, it's not altogether impossible that the senior executives at some bank, somewhere, are seriously contemplating transforming their financial institution into a musical entertainment conglomerate.

But common sense argues that the project manager, developers, and business user will ask themselves just how tentative and uncertain the requirements are. The most obvious aspect of change is the user interface; it's virtually inevitable that the user will want different fonts, different colors, and a different arrangement of information on the display screen. Assuming that the Internet-related system has a Web browser front-end, they may want different combinations of video, graphics, sound, and hyperlinks to entertain, amuse, or assist the end-user who will be visiting the site. But even with the user interface, there are likely to be some fundamental requirements that won't change; for example, there may be a requirement to adorn every Web page with an icon representing the corporate logo, and there may be a basic requirement that every Web page have a "help" hyper-link, or a hyperlink back to the top-level page of the Web site. But yes, other details can be postponed, and can be explored with the user through proto-types; common sense suggests minimizing the amount of effort invested in documenting the audio-visual/multimedia aspects of the user interface.

What about the *functionality* associated with a system? If this is the organiza-tion's *first* Internet-related system and/or if it involves major changes in the organization's business model or business process, then the project team should indeed be prepared for the possibility of major changes and unex-pected resistance from affected users.[2] And it's quite likely that the require-ments associated with editing, validation, error-handling, backup/recovery, security, and other operational details will change during the course of sys-tem development. In this case, the strategy should be to build a *minimal* sys-tem, with no commitment to, or implementation of, low-level details. Even if the details are omitted, broad areas of functionality are likely to remain intact, and they can be identified and documented with either the require-ments-lite (i.e., one sentence per requirement) or requirements-medium (i.e., one paragraph per requirement) approach mentioned earlier.

It's also important for the project manager to remember that an even more common form of change will be *changing priorities* of the requirements. Such changes may be caused by external circumstances, for instance, a new announcement from a competitor, or a decision by high-level executives to reduce spending for the next fiscal quarter. In addition, the reality of an approaching deadline may also change the perception of priority. Require-ments that had once been described as "essential" may be allowed to slip to a subsequent release of the system to ensure that *this* release is delivered on time. As we've already discussed, rational discussions about re-prioritizing, or re-negotiating schedules and budgets, require at least a minimal list of requirements, along with a minimal, rough estimate of the time and resources required to implement each of those requirements.

---

2. A good example is the "backlash" associated with the introduction of wireless technology in some companies. A wireless device can be used to allow remote employees to communicate with, and send information to, the home office. It can also be used to track remote vehicles, remote products, and remote employees. This can help reduce the likelihood that valuable parts, components, and products will be pilfered and stolen as they are being transported from the factory to the customer; and it can be used to dynamically re-schedule and re-route delivery vehicles. But the remote employees are likely to realize that such devices also allow their supervisors to track *them*, if their hand-held device has a GSM capability. For obvious reasons, they may object to what they perceive as "Big Brother" surveillance.

6.2.5   "This system is only going to be used once or twice..."

The theory, of course, is that if a system is only going to be used once or twice, then it's not worth the effort to provide extensive documentation about the requirements, the design, or the code. And it's easy to imagine a business user making such a statement about a new Internet-related system: "Just throw something together quickly, okay? We need to have *something* as quickly as possible, so that we can tell the marketplace that we have Internet support for our products and services. Our Strategic Planning Department is developing a long-range plan to integrate our old legacy systems with a new e-business architecture, and when they get that finished next year, we can scrap this interim system and rebuild everything from scratch."

Statements like this may be entirely sincere, and they may even be accurate. But it's not the first time that IT groups have been told "don't worry" about the consequences of building a quick-and-dirty system; indeed, many of the Y2K problems would have disappeared long before December 31, 1999 if all of those quick-and-dirty systems had vanished when they were supposed to. Admittedly, the rapid pace of technological change—which *is* more rapid than it was 10–20 years ago—means that today's new IT systems are likely to be decommissioned and replaced more quickly than the applications developed in the 1960s, 1970s, and 1980s. But this still means that they're likely to last at least 2–3 years, instead of the 5–7 year lifetime that we used to see. And during that brief 2–3 year timeframe, it's highly likely that the original developers and the original users will have moved on to greener pastures; thus, ongoing maintenance will have to be performed by a new generation of maintenance programmers, interacting with a new generation of users, none of whom know exactly what the system is supposed to do because nobody bothered documenting the requirements.

None of this changes the politics of the situation. It's highly unlikely that you'll be able to persuade the responsible business user to stipulate *in writing* that the system is going to be decommissioned on a "certain date" (unless, of course, the business user is already in the process of updating his or her resume and looking for a new job). And it's unlikely that you'll be able to find a user, system owner, or investor who will commit the necessary funds to keep the original statement of requirements up-to-date. Bottom line: The system that your team is building *will* last longer than anyone is prepared to admit today, and the documentation associated with requirements, design, code, and test data *will* become obsolete sooner or later. Your budget and schedule probably won't include any resources to slow down the rate of obsolescence, and your company's reward/punishment system probably won't take these long-term quality issues into account.

Still, there *will* be long-term consequences if your team doesn't document the requirements associated with the system. Even if those long-term consequences don't affect you or your developers personally, I believe that you have a professional obligation to do the best you can in this area, simply because it's the right thing to do. For obvious reasons, you may find that you cannot afford to make the investment to document the requirements in as much detail as you would like to, but it's hard to argue that your developers don't have enough time to at least write a sentence or two about each of the system requirements.

6.3   Eliciting requirements from the user

Interestingly, most of the articles, books, training courses, and conference presentations on the subjects of systems analysis and requirements are concerned with *documentation* of the requirements, that is, using popular modeling techniques such as UML or older techniques such as structured analysis. But there's no point focusing on documentation techniques if we can't get the users to tell us what their requirements are. This presumes that the users do know—at least to some extent—what their requirements are, and that the task involves dragging those "fuzzy thoughts" out of the users' brains and into the open.

Note that this essentially involves a conversation between two alien races: *business users*, who are usually not expert in computer technology, and *IT professionals*, who are usually not expert in the subject domain that is to be automated. The problem today is not quite as severe as it was 10–20 years ago because the current generation of business users is much more likely to have acquired at least a superficial level of computer literacy, and the current generation of IT professionals is somewhat more likely to have been exposed to general topics of business, finance, and management in their educational studies. Still, it's a non-trivial discussion, especially when new technologies are being used to conduct new business activities in a new way.

We must also remember that politics are involved whenever an IT project team starts talking to business users. For example, the project team is likely to encounter the so-called "loser user," whose stature, reputation, salary, and employment status may be diminished by the introduction of a new system; in the extreme case, the loser user will be fired as soon as the system is installed, which obviously diminishes his or her enthusiasm for helping the IT project team! This is particularly common when the new system is associated with a BPR initiative that seeks to *eliminate* business processes, for instance, allowing customers to enter transactions directly into the system from their Web browser rather than talking to a telephone sales representative.

In other situations, the project team may encounter a business supervisor who says, "My people are far too busy to talk to you—that's why we need a new system! I'll tell you what they need from the system." But the supervisor's perceptions may be based on obsolete memories of what he or she used to do, back in the "good old days" before being promoted into a supervisory position. And in any case, the supervisor is likely to want functionality that will increase efficiency, productivity, and operational oversight of the clerical/administrative users;[3] the users themselves may be more interested in a user-friendly system that allows them to customize the details of their user interface, and that provides meaningful error messages and help screens.

Notwithstanding the potential political problems, there are numerous techniques for eliciting requirements from the user. For the most part, these techniques remain as useful and relevant for Internet-related systems as they did for earlier generations of technology. If your project team is unfamiliar with these techniques, there are several textbooks and sources of information that can be consulted;[4] for the sake of brevity, I'll merely summarize them here.

- *Interviewing*—Interviewing is a practical technique when most of the subject knowledge is in a few individuals, when it's practical and cost-effective to meet with them face-to-face, or when it's impractical to gather all stakeholders in one place. On the other hand, it can backfire if the IT project team interviews the wrong people at the wrong time, or asks the wrong questions and gets the wrong answers, or somehow causes bad feelings between both parties.
- *Questionnaires*—This is a widely used approach in which a pre-defined set of questions is sent to relevant stakeholders. It's a practical approach if the IT project team is dealing with a large base of geo-

---

3. The use of wireless technology to track remote employees and make sure they aren't goofing off, is a good example.
4. See, for example, *Software Requirements*, Karl E. Wiegers, Microsoft Press, 1999; *Mastering the Requirements Process*, Suzanne Robertson and James Robertson, Addison-Wesley, 1999; *Software Requirements*, Al Davis, Prentice Hall, 1993, *Exploring Requirements—Quality Before Design*, Donald Gause and Gerald Weinberg, Dorset House, 1989; *Modern Structured Analysis*, Ed Yourdon, Prentice Hall, 1989; and *Structured Analysis & System Specification*, Tom DeMarco, Prentice Hall, 1979.

graphically dispersed individuals, or if the developers need specific answers to well-defined, specific questions. It presumes, of course, that the developers *can* determine the relevant questions in advance; this may be difficult if entirely new opportunities are being explored with the users. Unfortunately, questionnaires sometimes give misleading results because the questions are phrased (either consciously or unconsciously) in such a way that the interviewee interprets them in a particular way. And the results of questionnaires sometimes appear to be more authoritative than they really are. The statement that "73.8% of users believe that their most important requirement is X..." may not identify the fact that 90% of the users refused to answer the question, and that only three relevant responses were recorded at all.

- *Brainstorming*—This is particularly useful in situations where innovative, creative solutions to an unfamiliar problem are needed. The most creative, innovative ideas often result from combining multiple seemingly unrelated ideas. Brainstorming involves both idea *generation* and idea *reduction* (or prioritization). The idea generation process usually involves the following guidelines, whose purpose is to generate as many new ideas as possible: Criticism and debate are discouraged during idea generation period; typical limits and constraints are suspended (e.g., "Pretend that the law of gravity doesn't apply; what new strategies would that give us?"); mutate and combine ideas whenever possible.

- *Storyboarding and role playing*—Passive, active, or interactive storyboards can be created to help identify different actors or players in a new system, explain what happens to them during various system interactions, and describe how those interactions work. Its primary purpose is to elicit, "Yes, but..." reactions from the user community. Storyboards are *not* intended to be prototypes, but rather rough, sketchy, easily modifiable, "unshippable" mock-ups of some aspect of the system. Storyboards are particularly useful when new or innovative functionality is involved, when requirements, actors, roles, and use cases are poorly understood, when the *sequence* of interactions between actors is poorly understood, and when user interface issues need to be discussed without an expensive, time-consuming investment in prototypes.

- *Prototyping*—The basic concept of a prototyping effort is to build a quick-and-dirty mock-up of the system that the user seems to want. As such, the prototype typically leaves out detailed consideration of input validation, error-handling, backup, recovery, performance, and scalability. It's important to emphasize that a prototyping effort does not have to preclude other requirements approaches. Sometimes, a prototype is the only way to engage the user in a discussion of requirements that would otherwise seem too abstract, and the experience of operating the prototype will sometimes elicit requirements that would otherwise be unknowable. As mentioned earlier, a prototype also has the political benefit of providing tangible evidence of (or at least the illusion of) progress, and in some cases, it may even support a limited production capability. Unfortunately, the real-world experience with prototyping is that it usually precludes any formal documentation of requirements; hence, the only statement of requirements is in the code. Significantly, this means that the details ignored by the prototype (error-handling, backup, performance, etc.) may *never* be explicitly stated as requirements.

- *JAD sessions*—JAD, an abbreviation for joint application design," was first introduced by IBM Canada in the late 1970s.[5] While it sometimes appears similar to the brainstorming idea discussed earlier, its primary objective is to get key stakeholders in a room for a concentrated session of 1–3 days of rapid, intense identification, documentation, resolution, and prioritization of requirements, and thus avoid sequential interviews with different stakeholders and user constituencies that would otherwise take weeks or months to complete. The success of JAD sessions depends heavily on the skills of the facilitator who leads the sessions—this person must be politically neutral, and needs to be reasonably familiar with the application domain associated with the development effort. It also depends on commitment from the key stakeholders and decision-makers, and a sufficient degree of cooperation to overcome disagreement and achieve consensus. JAD can be used in conjunction with modeling and a limited degree of prototyping.

- *Modeling*—By "modeling," we mean the creation of visual paper models, using such well-known techniques as data flow diagrams, entity-relationship diagrams, UML class diagrams, or even old-fashioned flowcharts. The basic assumptions are that such models are easier to build than the real system and that "a picture is worth a thousand words." The relative cost and effort required to build a visual model, versus an operational prototype of the system, are constantly changing and should be re-evaluated periodically. In some cases, it's cheaper and easier to build a prototype, and in other cases, it's cheaper and eas-

---

5. For a good discussion of the JAD concept, see *Advancing Business Concepts in a JAD Workshop Setting*, Anthony Crawford, Prentice Hall/Yourdon Press, 1994.

ier to create some visual models to show the user. Indeed, prototyping and modeling are not mutually exclusive concepts (particularly when one remembers that a prototype *is* a model of the ultimate system). Similarly, it's important to remember that modeling is not an all-or-nothing proposition. One can create simple high-level models to illustrate certain features or properties of a system, and one can also create *extremely* detailed, formal, rigorous models to investigate as many properties of the system as possible before implementing them in code.

6.4   Documenting requirements

As mentioned earlier, *documentation* is the topic that usually gets most of the attention in discussions about system requirements. As such, most IT professionals are familiar with the topic, and there are numerous sources of information to explain the latest techniques and methods. This book takes the position that in all but the most extreme cases, there is some benefit to documenting the requirements as they are elicited. The challenge for the project manager is to find a cost-effective middle ground between "extreme" documentation and *no* documentation; both extremes are likely to cause trouble, sooner or later.

Interestingly, IT professionals tend to focus on *functional* requirements and *data* requirements. But non-functional requirements—performance, reliability, user-friendliness, scalability, etc.—can also be crucial, especially if they ultimately become the criteria by which the success or failure of a project is judged. This point is often ignored for traditional in-house projects, performed by an IT organization for its business users; it becomes more evident in outsourced projects, where the agreement between the business users and the external development organization takes the form of a legal contract.

Since the details of requirements documentation techniques are discussed in so many other textbooks, I won't dwell on them here. Suffice it to say that if the system requirements are complex, with many details and interdependencies, then *visual models* (e.g., object models, UML diagrams, data flow diagrams, etc.) can be extremely helpful. But particularly in situations where the project team does not have the time, resources, or patience to generate voluminous documentation of the requirements, it often turns out that succinct narrative sentences are sufficient.

6.5   Managing the requirements

While the discussion in Section 6.4 focused on documenting the *technical details* of system requirements, there is another form of documentation that is essential for the project manager: itemizing the requirements succinctly, with appropriate information about the priority, risk, and estimated development effort associated with each requirement. A non-trivial project, that is, one that really does require conscious management effort, will typically have hundreds, if not thousands, of discrete requirements. And requirements are likely to be dynamic during the course of development; the technical details will change, and various other attributes—risk, priority, status, estimated development effort—will also change.

Because of the volume of requirements, because of their volatility and dynamic nature, and because the requirements form the basis of day-to-day project management decisions, it's highly advantageous to use automated requirements management (RM) tools. A number of modestly priced tools are available today, including the following:

- Caliber-RM, from Technology Builders
- DOORS, from Quality Systems & Software
- Requisite Pro, from Rational Software
- RTM Workshop, from Integrated Chipware
- Vital Link, from Compliance Automation

Unfortunately, the vast majority of development projects do *not* use such tools, and those that do are more likely to use home-grown tools based on readily available spreadsheet or database products. The advantage of using the more sophisticated tools is that they can provide the basis for estimating the impact of a change in requirements (e.g., a new requirement that the user has just introduced, or a change in the priority of an existing requirement) on the schedule and budget. They can also provide the basis for impact analysis, so that the project manager can estimate the consequences of adding more people to the project team, or deferring the deadline by an extra week.[6]

---

6. At the time this book was written, most of the commercially available RM tools operated either in a stand-alone fashion or with import/export capabilities for interacting with other software development tools. As time goes on, we should expect to see more and more *integration* of such tools, so that we can have interfaces between RM tools and traditional project planning tools like Microsoft Project, as well as interfaces between RM tools and other CASE tools, interfaces between RM tools and testing tools, and interfaces between RM tools and defect-tracking tools.

Thus, you should have an automated RM tool that allows you to create a report along the lines of that shown in Table 6.1. This puts you in a position for dealing with the inevitable scheduling conflicts and negotiations on a more rational basis.

TABLE 6.1   A typical report from an RM tool.

ID	Requirement Text	Estimated Development Effort (Person-Days)	Technical Risk	Priority	Release
1	The program shall run on the Windows 95 platform.	40.00	1	High	Version 1.0
2	The program shall allow the user to produce customizable reports.	24.00	8	Low	Version 1.1
3	The program shall allow the user to display three views.	10.00	3	High	Version 1.0
3.1	The "Requirements" View shall contain a list of all of the requirements to be included in the project.	40.00	7	High	Version 1.0
3.2	The "Probability of Finishing On Time" View shall display the likely probability of completing the project on schedule.	20.00	5	High	Version 1.0
3.3	The "Probability of Finishing with Budgeted Resources" View shall display the likely probability of completing the project within budget.	20.00	5	High	Version 1.0
4	The program shall allow the user to import and export features to/ from text files.	25.00	3	Medium	Version 1.0
5	The program shall run on the Macintosh platform.	100.00	10		Version 2.0
6	The program shall come with an online help file.	15.00	2	Medium	Version 1.0
7	The program shall allow the user to save their view configuration.	10.00	2	Low	TBD
8	The program shall provide a way to view requirements that have been deleted.	5.00	2	Low	Version 1.1

The point to remember is that many of today's high-intensity Internet projects have schedules that are so aggressive that they're not just optimistic, they're downright unrealistic. But since the deadline and budget are usually fixed because of political, legal, or competitive constraints, the only negotiable variable is the amount of delivered functionality, that is, how many requirements will actually be implemented by the deadline?

Unfortunately, politics, pride, naiveté, and over-optimism often prevent this issue from being discussed in a responsible fashion at the beginning of a project; instead, the problem rears its ugly head *late* in the development project, when the deadline is looming a few days or weeks ahead. At that point, political tensions are usually higher, making it more difficult to negotiate a rational compromise; for better or worse, the stakeholders often dig in and defend their position with great emotion and rancor. And from the project manager's perspective, the great tragedy is that by the time this negotiation takes place, irreplaceable resources (e.g., peoples' time) have been invested in analyzing, designing, coding, and testing requirements that ultimately turn out to be non-essential. Sadly, those resources often turn out to be wasted.

Since the final deadline is often preceded by several interim milestones (a.k.a. versions, releases, deliverables, or prototypes), the project team can plan which features will be included in which milestone. *Triage*, as we use the term in this book, is the art of selecting the "right" requirements to be included in the next release; note how the requirements shown in Figure 6.1 have been annotated to indicate the version for which they are being planned.

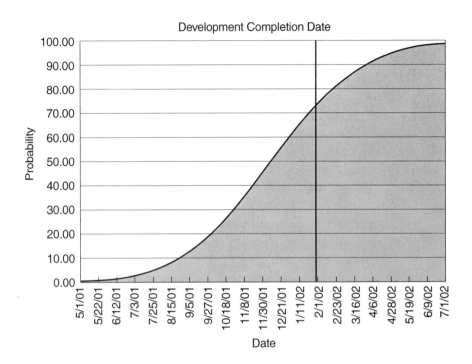

FIGURE 6.1 Probability of finishing on time, from OnYourMarkPro.

Obviously, this decision should be made as part of a negotiation with key stakeholders. But politics and experience are important elements in successful negotiations. Naïve users, or those who believe that negotiation means yelling louder and appearing more hostile than the other party, may argue that *all* of the requirements they've identified are essential. In the extreme case, that may be true, but it's more likely that the user can be coaxed into admitting that some degree of benefit can be achieved with a system release that has only *some* of the most essential features. ·

Thus, negotiation consists of balancing two different views of the project:

- *The project team's view*, which involves balancing a certain amount of delivered requirements against the constraints of schedule, development cost, and risk.
- *The business user's view*, which involves balancing the benefits of delivered functionality/features (market share, revenues, fame, fortune, etc.) against the available schedule, cost, and resources that can be provided to the project team.

It's important to emphasize that this negotiation does not just take place once, at the beginning of the project. It takes place periodically throughout the project, especially if the business users decide that they need additional functionality, or that the relative priorities of existing requirements have changed. In these cases, they typically want the project team to change existing requirements or add new ones *without changing the budget or schedule*, and without relaxing whatever quality constraints they imposed. If such changes are requested fairly late in the project schedule, it's not worth considering the possibility of adding more people to the project team. By this point, the project team is probably working so much overtime already that it won't help for the users to pound their fists on the table and shout, "Work harder!" About the only rational basis for negotiation involves re-prioritizing the existing requirements to determine which ones will be de-emphasized to provide resources for the new/modified requirements that have suddenly appeared.

The other reason for periodic re-negotiations is that the original schedule may turn out to be flawed. It may have taken longer than anticipated to hire the required developers for the project team, or unexpected illness or turnover may have reduced the available development resources. The technical work may have turned out to be more complex than anticipated, or the programming productivity may have been lower than had been hoped. Unexpected technical problems or delays may have occurred ... and the list goes on. Some of these problems can be handled by the project manager without affecting the schedule, by rearranging tasks, juggling assignments, or performing various other feats of magic. But it's also possible that the manager will conclude, long before the official deadline has arrived, that progress is not being made at the required rate, in which case, there are two choices: miss the deadline or perform another triage negotiation.

In many cases, these negotiations take place in all-or-nothing terms. For example, it's common for the project team to exclaim loudly, "If you add these five new requirements, it will be absolutely *impossible* to meet the deadline you've given us!" Perhaps this is so, but it's probably more accurate to point out to the users that the *risk* of meeting the deadline will increase substantially if five new requirements are added to the workload, or alternatively, the probability of meeting the deadline will decrease by some amount. When presented in this fashion, the rational response from the users will be, "*How much* will the risk increase? What's the probability that you'll be able to finish the job on time if we add these requirements?"[7] With estimating tools such as SLIM (from QSM Associates), Checkpoint (from SPR), or OnYourMarkPro (from Omni-Vista, Inc.), the project manager should be able to provide a quantitative answer to this question. And while the answer may be a rough estimate, subject to all the usual caveats, it's better than an emotional, all-or-nothing response.

For example, Figure 6.1 shows an output report from OnYourMarkPro,[8] indicating that, with a given set of requirements and resources, the probability of delivering the system on an arbitrary deadline of Feb. 1, 2002 is approximately 75%. If the users suddenly decide that they want to add five new requirements, it allows the project manager to say something along the lines of, "If we add these features, our probability of finishing on-schedule changes from 75% to 25%. Are we all willing to accept that risk?"

6.6   Conclusion

Traditionally, software development has been viewed as a combination of frantic coding and desperate debugging. More recently, it has come to be viewed as an ongoing exercise in prototyping to allow a system to emerge from a gradual recognition of the users' true requirements. Almost everyone today understands that prototyping is a valuable approach to systems development, and hardly anyone today would recommend that substantial time and energy should be spent developing a "Victorian novel" version of the user requirements.

But the reality is that project managers must *manage* their project, which means that they have to decide *which* people will be assigned to work on *which* tasks to maximize the chances that an acceptable system will be delivered within the constraints of a negotiated schedule and budget. The act of prototyping does not eliminate the reality of deadlines and budgets; in the best case, the delivery (or demonstration) of interim prototypes may facilitate a more rational and civilized renegotiation of what was initially a com-

---

7. Unfortunately, the project manager may not get a rational response at this point. In a highly political environment, where negotiations are adversarial in nature, the business user might say, "We don't want to hear about your problems—we have problems of our own! It's *your* job to figure out how to incorporate these five new requirements into the system without spending any more money, and without extending the deadline!" Sometimes miracles occur, and sometimes the project team (and/or the manager) can find a way to accomplish the additional work, but the problem with this kind of confrontational negotiation is that it prevents a *realistic* assessment of the situation from being discussed openly and honestly by the responsible parties. And then, if it turns out that a miracle does not occur, the relationship between the parties tends to degenerate into finger-pointing and blame-casting.

8. *Caveat emptor*: I'm a member of the Technical Advisory Board of Omni-Vista, and am thus favorably disposed toward the company's product. But, a similar kind of rational negotiation can be carried out with other available estimating tools in the marketplace.

pletely unreasonable deadline and budget. But in many cases, the deadline and budget are affected by external parameters, such as the activities of competitors or a governmental decision to impose new regulations on a certain date. If the deadline and budget are essentially fixed, then it's only a matter of time before the resources are fixed;[9] and if we further assume that the quality constraints are also fixed, then the only variable in the project management equation is the amount of delivered functionality. And you cannot make intelligent decisions about *what* functionality will be delivered *when*, if you haven't made at least a high-level identification of the system requirements.

Thus, the bottom-line advice for managers of high-intensity Internet projects is this: Don't allow your developers to use prototyping (or any of the popular buzzwords that serve as synonyms for prototyping) as an excuse for extemporaneous coding. *Do* identify the requirements, *do* ensure they are documented, even if it's in a "light," summarized form, and *do* use the requirements as the basis for your project negotiations, and for the inevitable triage negotiations that will address the frustrating reality that the users will want more functionality in less time, and for less money, than is realistically possible.

🙣 🙣 🙣 🙣 🙣

---

9. In the early stages of a project, there may be some negotiating flexibility in terms of personnel resources, even if the budget is fixed. For instance, the project manager may decide to outsource the development effort to an offshore company whose labor costs are lower than in the manager's "home" country. Or the project manager may argue that if he or she is allowed to offer twice the standard salary, he or she can hire "super-programmers" whose productivity is 10 times higher than the average programmer. But in any case, once these negotiations are concluded at the beginning of the project, it's difficult to change them midstream.

Managing the Design and Coding Processes

7

Design in art, is a recognition of the relation between various things, various elements in the creative flux. You can't *invent* a design. You recognise it, in the fourth dimension. That is, with your blood and your bones, as well as with your eyes.   ■

D. H. Lawrence, *Phoenix: The Posthumous Papers of D. H. Lawrence*, pt. 4, "Art and Morality" (edited by E. McDonald), 1936.

7.1 Introduction

This will be a mercifully brief chapter because most of what a project manager does with regard to the design and programming of a high-intensity Internet project is monitor and control the *progress* of these activities. Indeed, the topic of monitoring and controlling the progress of *all* the technical activities is the main thing that keeps the project manager occupied on a day-to-day basis, and I've devoted Chapter 9 to a more complete discussion of the topic.

In the IT profession, it often turns out that project managers are former practitioners who have been given the dubious honor of promotion to a more exalted status. Thus, the managers of today's Internet-related projects can probably describe all the gory details of the client/server system they developed in PowerBuilder back in 1995, or the COBOL system they built for an IBM mainframe in the 1980s, or the assembly-language program they wrote in the 1970s, or the Autocoder program they created for the IBM 1401 in the 1960s. But they haven't written any Java programs; they haven't personally used any of the development tools from vendors like Broadvision and ATG, or the early versions of .Net tools from Microsoft; and they haven't agonized over such TCP network details like trying to decide when and how to disable the Nagle algorithm.

There are exceptions, of course, especially for small Internet-related projects where the project manager is a "player-coach" who not only supervises the rest of the team, but also does some of the analysis, design, coding, and/or testing activities. On the other hand, there is also the exception that takes the form of a *non-technical* project manager, for instance, a person representing the business/application area, who knows how to send email and manipulate Microsoft Project, but who has never written a line of code in *any* programming language.

If you're a technically oriented player-coach, you probably have some good experience, and some strong opinions, about how best to carry out the process of design and coding. You may have some questions about the best way to do the job in a particular environment—for example, for a system using Visual Basic in a Microsoft environment, or a system using Java in a Linux environment—in which case, there are numerous resources available on the Internet, from various vendors, and in technical book stores. For the remainder of this chapter, I'll avoid any further discussion about *doing* the design/coding activities, and focus instead on *managing* the activities as they are being carried out by other developers on the project team.

7.2 Design issues

Assuming that you've got a reasonable description of the requirements for your Internet-related system, along the lines of what we discussed in Chapter 6, then what should you be focusing on when your developers tell you that they're ready to start designing and coding? Fundamentally, these are the management issues you should be concerned with:

- How should I allocate and assign the work to different individuals on the team?
- How do I know if they're doing *good* work?
- How do I know if they're making sufficient progress to meet our schedule and deadlines?

As mentioned earlier, the issue of monitoring progress is sufficiently important that we'll devote a separate chapter to it. The other two questions are discussed in more detail below.

7.2.1 Assigning and allocating work

Obviously, some of your managerial decisions are going to be based on the technical nature of the work to be done; for instance, if a database needs to be done, you'll assign it to your Oracle wizards, while the network design will be assigned to the geek who has actually read all of those obscure manuals from the Internet Engineering Task Force. Note that there's a subtle assumption here: At the beginning of most projects (both prior to the arrival of the Internet and in today's world), there are usually some *a priori* design decisions that could theoretically have been deferred, but have nevertheless been made and frozen. Who decided, for example, that the system was going to require a database, and that the database would be implemented in Oracle? Indeed, we could discuss the philosophical aspects of this situation at great length, but it deserves a separate book of its own; suffice it to say at this point that certain technological design decisions *will* have been made, either for political reasons or because of *a priori* assumptions about the form and shape that the implementation was likely to take, and the allocation of technical design work will almost certainly be based on those decisions.

To some extent, the assignment and allocation of design work will also be based on the *magnitude* of the work, as estimated in the early phases of the project. For example, we noted in Chapter 6 that when the requirements are identified, it's common to provide some helpful attributes such as risk and priority; and it's also common to provide a rough "guesstimate" of the amount of work required to implement each of the requirements, to facilitate the inevitable triage decisions that will determine which requirements actually get built into the various system versions that will be built. Thus, if it appears that the requirements entail a total of 40 person-days of effort, and if the system has to be delivered in two calendar months, it's quite likely that the project manager will allocate two developers to the project, and divide the work more or less equally between them.

Aside from these basic issues—which involve project management tasks that were just as relevant for the IBM 1401 systems of the early 1960s as they are for the Internet-related systems of today—the main principle is that *the requirements should drive the design process*, and *the requirements should drive the allocation and assignment of work*. These principles involve some additional basic software engineering principles: The requirements should be decomposed to the point where it makes sense to assign them to either a single individual or perhaps a small group of 2–3 individuals, and the requirements should be sufficiently discrete and independent that they can be assigned to individuals who can carry out the work on a more or less independent basis.

On many Internet-related projects, the most difficult part of allocating and assigning design tasks is associated with the "infrastructure" in which the application programs will operate—e.g., the network, the database, the security system, the servers, the interfaces and connections to other external systems and servers, etc. These infrastructure elements may not be mentioned at all in the "official" list of requirements, or they may be mentioned only indirectly. And while the infrastructure typically *does* exist for the older mainframe and client/server systems within the organization (and can thus be taken for granted by each new project team), it often does *not* exist for Internet projects, simply because there were no predecessor projects to cause them to be created.

7.2.2 Determining and monitoring the quality of the work

How does a project manager know whether his or her developers are creating a good design, especially if it involves technology with which he or she is not familiar? While the manager wants to be able to ask this question on a day-to-day basis throughout the project, we have to begin by asking the same question about the *final* design of the system. If a project team of 10 people spends 6 months writing 100,000 lines of Java code, how would we know whether the design, upon which the code was based, was a good one? How would we distinguish between a good design and a bad design?

In a particularly intense Internet-related project, you're likely to find that nobody really wants to talk about something that seems so abstract and philosophical. If you ask the key stakeholders—that is, the people who are paying for the project and/or the people who have to entrust their business operation to the system—you will find that they will merely shrug and say, "Well, the most important thing is that it has to *work*. If it does that, and if it implements the requirements we've identified, and if it's delivered to us on time and within budget, then it must have been a good design!"

If a project is small enough that one or two people can build it within a month, then it may be reasonable to assert that "a good design is one that works," and bring the conversation to an end. But as organizations begin building more and more mission-critical business applications to run in an Internet environment, they *should* be willing to identify, and help quantify, such "goodness" criteria as these:

- *Performance*—The system can handle X users, or Y transactions/second, or Z hits on the Web server, with an average response time of T seconds. Unlike many of the older generation systems, which were typically developed to support a *known* community of users, with a known volume of daily transactions, many Internet systems are accessible by the entire global population. Thus, depending on its visibility and popularity, it may receive a thousand transactions on its first day of operation, a million on the second day, and 10 million on the third day.

- *Scalability*—Since the user load is completely unpredictable for many Internet systems, a related "goodness" criterion may be the ease with which it can be scaled to handle more users, more transactions, or more data. For instance, if a new server can be plugged in *while the system is running*, that's good; if the system has to be shut down and completely reprogrammed every time the number of users increases by 10%, that's bad.

- *Reliability and availability*—Since the community of Internet users is likely to expect access to the system on a 24-by-7 basis, it's likely that a high level of reliability will be seen as one criterion of goodness. And if the system *does* fail (because of power outages, hardware failures, network glitches, or a software crash), the speed with which the system can be restored to operational capacity (either by fixing the bug, switching over to backup equipment, or re-routing around the problem area) is another criterion of goodness.

Note that these are *non-functional requirements* of the system—requirements in the sense that if they are not met, the system will be unacceptable to the user. But because they do not have anything to do with the features or functions of the system, they may or may not have been explicitly identified during the analysis/requirements phase of the project. Indeed, it may not become evident that they are even relevant until the project team begins focusing on the high-level architectural design of the system. At that point, someone on the team might remark, "You know, if we program this employee timesheet system in Visual Basic, it's going to run like a pig. It may be okay as long as we don't have to support more than 10 simultaneous users in the Accounting Department, but if they decide to open up the system and allow *every* employee to enter his or her own timesheet data from a Web browser, the system will collapse!"

Bottom line: The criteria that determine whether or not the design of a system is good should be traced back to the criteria that determine whether the user (or the owner, the investor, or other key stakeholders) thinks the system is good. And while those issues should have been articulated and documented during the systems analysis phase of the project, chances are that many of them won't surface until the team is deeply involved in the design of the system. At that point, the manager should be able to ask the team periodically, "Can you explain your design to me? Can you show it to me? Can you point to the elements of your design, or the design decisions, that determine whether or not the design will achieve the necessary degree of performance, scalability, reliability, and availability?"

In many cases, the team will respond with some hand-waving and verbal mumbo-jumbo: "Don't worry about it, boss; we've got it covered. We've got a four-tier architecture that's fully scalable and totally fault-tolerant!" To which the manager should respond, "Show me."

This will typically lead to more hand-waving, more mumbo-jumbo, and more assurances that the team is using the latest, greatest technology from the best vendor in the industry. But if the manager continues to respond to each such barrage of mumbo-jumbo with the simple request of "Show me," it will eventually become clear to the developers that some *documentation* is being requested, and that the manager wants to invoke a process that would normally be called a design review.

The developers may balk at this for reasons that have been discussed in previous chapters. They may regard documentation as a bureaucratic waste of time, and they may view design reviews as non-productive, political activities that do absolutely nothing to help them accomplish what they see as their *only* priority: building a working system. The more intense the project, the more emotional the resistance will be against documentation and design reviews. Thus, it's important for the manager to avoid the trap of the following "all-or-nothing" dialogue: "Okay, boss, if you really want to delay this project by three months, we can sit here and churn out a thousand pages of design diagrams. But if you really want this system finished on time, then leave us alone and let us start coding. We *know* what the design is going to be. We've talked it over, and we've got a totally clear understanding of what it is! You wouldn't understand it, because you're an old COBOL fogey, but trust us—we know what we're doing!"

As discussed in Chapter 6, it's possible to talk about both the process and the supporting documentation from a light, medium, or heavy perspective. If the project team is building a system that has safety-critical consequences and a budget of a hundred million dollars, then it's not unreasonable for the manager to say, "Sorry, team, but there are human lives and vast fortunes riding on the decisions you're making in your design. We have no alternative but to produce detailed documentation of the design so that it can be carefully reviewed."

But in most high-intensity Internet projects, the users and stakeholders may be willing to risk the possibility of wasting millions of dollars on a bad design, if it appears to increase the chances of getting the system delivered earlier. Thus, they are likely to support the team when it balks at spending additional days, weeks, or months creating formal design documentation. But that doesn't necessarily preclude a medium approach to the task, which might include an object model (e.g., a class hierarchy model in UML) or a set of data flow diagrams and an entity-relationship diagram.

If even that is regarded as too time-consuming and onerous, then the manager should at least insist on a one-page, high-level architectural diagram that shows the major components and sub-systems. The developers may grumble about the effort required to produce such a document, but it usually requires no more than an hour or two of time. In the worst case, they're almost always willing to sketch such a diagram extemporaneously on a white-board or flip-chart; the manager can then find the necessary clerical resources to convert the rough sketches into a more formalized document for subsequent review and analysis.

The objective here, of course, is not to produce documentation for the sake of documentation, but to have something tangible to look at, point at, and talk about in a design review. And from the manager's perspective, the objective of the design review is not to indulge in a Dilbert-style meeting in which the "pointy-haired manager" berates and insults the terrified members of the project team, but rather to indulge in a risk management exercise by pointing to the design document and asking questions like:

- "Where are the weak spots in this design? Where are we vulnerable? From the way it looks on this design document, *everything* depends on access to the product database, which we're planning to implement in Version N+1 of the DBMS package from vendor X. But I just saw a news headline this morning indicating that vendor X is six months behind schedule, their CEO just quit, their stock has dropped by 90%, and all their programmers who are holding worthless stock options staged a mutiny and burned the corporate headquarters building to the ground! If we don't get that new DBMS product in time, how badly will it affect our design?"

- "What happens if the load on our system suddenly increases by a factor of 10 because every citizen in mainland China has suddenly discovered the existence of our Web site?"

- "How quickly can we add new servers if we have to increase capacity overnight? According to the design document, we're going to have servers in 10 different cities; what kinds of logistical problems are we going to have if we need to upgrade them?"
- "What happens if the network connection between our New York office and our San Francisco office, which I see *here* on the design diagram, stops working? What kind of backup, or redundancy, features do we have?

How often should such design reviews take place, and how formal should they be? That, too, is something that can be answered in a light, medium, or heavy fashion. Informal reviews involving the developers and project manager can be held on a weekly, or even daily, basis; in such cases, there may not be any formal notes or minutes, and there may not be a formal agenda for the topics to be discussed. However, if the overall development schedule involves periodic versions or prototypes of the system, demonstrated and delivered to the user community on a weekly or monthly basis, that provides an obvious opportunity to have a semi-formal design review meeting, in which there *is* a formal agenda, and in which notes/minutes are kept. It also makes sense, in many corporate environments, to invite at least a few outsiders to attend such review sessions, for example, members of the QA Department or technically savvy members of the user community. And, of course, the heavy approach would involve elaborately planned and orchestrated design review sessions, attended by dozens of people; these are far less common for today's high-intensity Internet projects, but they may still occur when the stakeholders (e.g., the venture capitalists) need to persuade themselves that the design is sufficiently robust to justify the investment needed to scale it up to a full-scale production model and roll it out to a large audience of customers.

There's one last point to consider in the area of design: how much time and effort should be invested in designing for the future versus the expedient approach of designing for *today's* requirements and being prepared to modify it tomorrow? This has been a philosophical question that project teams have grappled with since computer systems were first built half a century ago, and it continues to be a question for today's Internet-related project teams. One popular school of thought, articulated by Kent Beck as part of the extreme programming (XP) approach, suggests that *less* time and effort should be devoted to creating an initial design that can accommodate any number of unanticipated future changes, and *more* time should be spent revising, or re-factoring, the design on a continuous, day-to-day basis.

With today's high-level development tools, continuous re-factoring is a much more practical option than it was even 10 years ago, when the logistical effort and computer overhead of re-organizing, re-compiling, and re-building the software were significant.[1] And to the extent that Internet projects (and the supporting technology) are new, unfamiliar, and rapidly changing, it's probably not cost-effective to invest a great deal of time and energy to design a system that can accommodate whatever changes may or may not be required five years into the future.

On the other hand, there are some *fundamental* principles of design, particularly the modularity concepts of low coupling (interdependencies between components) and high cohesion (each component dedicated to performing one, single, well-defined test),[2] that can enhance the maintainability and flexibility of a system in both the short-term and the long-term, and the manager should continually ask the developers whether they are adhering to those principles. Arguably, the reason that the XP concept of re-factoring is even possible is that the fundamental design adheres to the basic principles of loosely-coupled, highly-cohesive, independent components (objects) with clean, well-defined interfaces. One common manifestation of that principle is the N-tier architecture in which the user interface layer of a system is separated, as completely as possible, from the data management layer, the application layer, and the transport, or network-related, layers.

7.3 Coding issues

Notwithstanding all of our discussion about the importance of design reviews and design documentation, the reality is that many high-intensity

---

1. "Significant" is a relative term, of course. For some projects, the effort was never very onerous, but to illustrate the opposite extreme, consider the circumstances of a 100-person project team whose work I reviewed a couple years ago. The team produced a system involving roughly a million lines of COBOL code, and it took nearly a week of non-stop computer time to re-compile and re-build a new version of the system. This sounds like a horror story out of the mainframe era of the 1970s, but the project involved reasonably current development tools and technology during the latter half of the 1990s.

2. These principles were espoused in early books on program design in the late 1960s and early 1970s, and became the basis for the structured design approach described in such books as *Structured Design*, Larry Constantine and Ed Yourdon, Prentice Hall, 1979. But if the manager mentions "structured design," he or she is likely to be labeled an irrelevant, obsolete old-timer by the younger generation of developers. Thus, it's appropriate to find current-generation gurus and textbooks that illustrate the same concepts. Indeed, most of the same concepts are discussed in the popular books on object-oriented analysis and design; but since those books are now nearly a decade old, they too might be considered old-fashioned!

Internet projects deliver nothing but code at the end of the development effort. Of course, one could argue that it's the project manager's fault that no design documents are produced, but the manager might well respond that the situation is similar to that of parenting unruly teenagers: You have to pick your battles and focus your energy on the things that *really* count. If you spend all your time forcing your teenage child to keep his or her bedroom neat and tidy, and then discover that he or she has become a drug addict because you ignored the tell-tale signs, well, then, you've won an irrelevant battle and lost a terribly important war. It's the same with managing software projects: It may turn out that insisting on detailed design documentation is the equivalent of forcing your teenager to make his or her bed every day.

There's no point belaboring the issue of documentation: If your developers can't be persuaded to document their design, they probably won't spend much time documenting their code, either. Or, they'll write the documentation once (e.g., an explanatory paragraph at the beginning of each source code module) and then forget to update the documentation when the code is changed. More likely, they'll give you an eloquent speech to persuade you that their code is "self-documenting," and that any competent programmer should be able to read their code *without* comments. There's no point telling them that you used the same excuses when you were a young programmer, and that one of the major selling points of COBOL, back in the Dark Ages, was that it was so self-documenting that even a business person could read the code.

So, what is it that really *does* matter when it comes to managing the coding process? More than anything else, *source code management* (SCM) is a critical part of the coding process. The more intense and chaotic your high-intensity Internet project, the more critical your SCM process. There are numerous commercial SCM products available today, for virtually every conceivable programming language; indeed, they are bundled into the high-end, enterprise versions of many popular development environments from vendors like Microsoft, Rational, and IBM. There are relative advantages and disadvantages of one SCM product versus another, but they are relatively minor; the main point is to make sure that the project team has an SCM product integrated into their development environment, and that they use it religiously. Taking a hard line on SCM usage is, in my opinion, the managerial equivalent of a parent taking a hard line on teenage drug abuse.

A second priority is the use of a development environment that will produce design-level documentation *automatically* from the code, and which guarantees to keep the code synchronized with the design-level documentation. As we have already suggested, it's difficult to get the designers to produce diagrams, models, and design documentation *while they are designing*, but it's also extremely useful to reverse-engineer that documentation once some code has been written, to carry out the kind of design reviews discussed earlier. And, although the software industry now understands that it's unrealistic to expect that *all* of the source code can be generated automatically from a CASE tool, it *does* make sense to use such tools to generate header files, skeleton programs, and various other support files associated with the programming effort.

Most of the visual development environments, such Microsoft's Visual Studio and IBM's VisualAge products, will generate skeleton code automatically. But the ability to generate design-level documentation, synchronized with the source code, is not as common. The Rational ROSE suite of tools has such a capability; so does the Togethersoft tool suite; and there may be others that your project team will find suitable for its efforts.

One last programming issue should be mentioned since it has a considerable impact on the way a project is managed: You should investigate, and strongly consider, the XP concept of *pair programming*. The concept is simple: Each programming assignment (and in most cases, the associated design effort) is allocated to *two* individuals, who are expected to sit together at a workstation or PC to develop the code. Though there were no readily available results from formal experiments available at the time this book was written, the informal feedback from many project managers indicates that— at least for small to medium projects—the productivity of such pair programming projects is at least as high as, if not slightly higher than, what would be true if the programming assignments were allocated in the more traditional, individualistic fashion. But the same informal feedback suggests that the *quality* of the code produced in a pair programming environment is much higher, because two individuals are looking at the code, on a moment-by-moment basis, and are more likely to spot bugs and problems than an individual programmer would.

The pair programming approach has a number of obvious cultural and sociological ramifications, and it was the subject of great debate in many organizations and computer conferences at the time this book was written. I am personally in favor of the concept, perhaps because it reminds me of an earlier era, when programmers were often forced to work together because of limited access to workstations and computer hardware. But, to use the earlier metaphor of choosing one's battles with a headstrong teenager, I don't think I would be willing to impose a pair programming work approach on a headstrong project team if it distracted the team from other practices—such as SCM or documenting requirements—that I felt were even more important. In any case, we should expect to see more and more discussion, statistical data, and case study reporting about pair-programming projects in the coming years; it's something that you should review on a regular basis.

7.4 Conclusion

Design and coding—*especially* coding—are what developers live for; everything else is typically considered "resting up" and getting ready for the real work associated with a project. Consequently, it's unlikely that you will have to motivate, prod, or nag your developers into focusing their best technical efforts on these activities. On the other hand, you do have a responsibility for ensuring that the right work is done by the right people, at the right level of quality. And that's likely to require some minimal degree of documentation, some degree of reviews (or walkthroughs, or inspections) of the technical work, and a constant monitoring of progress.

Of course, the most familiar form of quality review associated with the coding effort is that of *testing*. Traditionally, testing has been considered a post-coding activity that was concerned *only* with the code that was written. But as we'll see in Chapter 8, today's approach to testing is much broader in scope and begins at a much earlier stage in the development process.

🐾 🐾 🐾 🐾 🐾

Managing the Testing Process 8

The greatest blunders, like the thickest ropes, are often compounded of
a multitude of strands. Take the rope apart, separate it into the small
threads that compose it, and you can break them one by one. You think,
"That is all there was!" But twist them all together and you have
something tremendous.　■

Victor Hugo, *Les Misérables*, Part 2, Book 5, Chapter 10, 1862.

8.1 Introduction

For anyone who has worked in the IT industry, testing is like going to the
dentist: It's something you dread, but also something you dare not avoid. If
you've taken good care of your teeth, and if you're lucky, you might find
that you have no cavities and it's a short visit. Similarly, if you've followed a
good software development process, and if you're lucky, you might find that
the testing activity is short and painless. But just like you can't take the risk
of skipping the visit to the dentist just because you've been diligent about
brushing and flossing, so you can't take the risk of avoiding the testing process just because the developers are highly confident that everything they've
coded will work without problems.

This should, of course, be obvious. But I mention it at the beginning of this
chapter because one of the common experiences of managing high-intensity
Internet projects is that some (and occasionally *all*) of the developers have no
prior experience with software development projects. Thus, it's not uncommon for some of your developers to give you a puzzled look and ask, "Test-

ing? What's that?" Aside from providing an elementary description of what testing is all about, in the context of software development, it's obviously incumbent upon the manager to define what the *process* of testing will be for the project, what *categories* of testing will take place, and what the *criteria for completion* will be. If the developers continue to look puzzled and stupefied at the end of such an explanation, then it may be appropriate to outsource the testing effort to a different group, or even an outside firm. At the very least, it's highly recommended that the project team contain at least one or two developers who *are* familiar with testing; otherwise, the manager is likely to be in a position analogous to supervising children who have watched videos and read books about the fine art of brushing teeth, but who have never held a toothbrush in their hand.

8.2 Scheduling the testing activity

If you were offering advice on tooth-brushing and flossing, and you were limited to a single recommendation, what would it be? Professional dentists might or might not agree, but my advice would be: *Start early.* No matter how diligent and industrious your dental care activities might be, it doesn't help if you wait until you're 21 to get started. The damage will have been done, and will probably be irreversible.

Similarly, if you wait until a week before the deadline to start testing, you may find that it's too late, regardless of how powerful your testing tools are, and how sophisticated your testing procedures. This might not be the case if you have a relaxed development schedule, if you've allocated plenty of time for the testing effort, and if all of the pre-testing activities are completed on schedule. But none of those conditions is likely to be true for a high-intensity Internet project: The schedule is usually compressed to the point of being ridiculous, the time for *all* of the activities is typically compressed to make everything fit to the deadline, and chances are that at least some of the pre-testing activities will be late and/or behind schedule. Thus, if you're not careful, you're likely to find that the developers aren't even ready to start their testing activity until a week before the deadline, by which time it may be too late.[1]

---

1. Of course, it's theoretically possible that one week of testing effort will demonstrate that the system has *no* bugs and can therefore be delivered to the user. That's roughly akin to a 21-year-old who visits the dentist for the first time in his or her life to be told that because he or she had followed a sugar-free diet and drank fluoridated water, he or she is one of those rare people (at least in North America!) who reached adulthood without experiencing any cavities.

So how do we schedule the testing activity to avoid this problem? The answer lies, for the most part, in the *process* of testing, which we'll discuss in the next section. But it's based on three basic principles, which can be summarized here even if you don't pay any attention to the process discussion below:

- Testing can be done *concurrently* with other activities, rather than sequentially. This principle has been known since the earliest days of the IT industry, and it certainly applies to Internet-related projects. You don't have to wait until all of the code has been written before starting the testing effort; testing of individual components, modules, objects, or features can typically be done in an independent, stand-alone manner while other components are being programmed.

- Testing can be applied to development activities *prior* to coding. This, too, is a principle that has been known for a long time, but even veteran programmers act as if testing is something that only pertains to computer programs. Thus, it's not surprising that an Internet-related project team with neophyte developers would make the same mistake, and would fail to realize that it's extremely valuable to test the requirements and the design as soon as possible, rather than to wait additional weeks or months before the opportunity arises to test the code.

- Testing can be done incrementally, rather than in an all-at-once, "big bang" approach. Indeed, this is one of the benefits of the iterative, evolutionary prototyping approach discussed in earlier chapters: It forces some of the bugs and programming mistakes out into the open at a much earlier point than would be the case if the entire system was tested in one fell swoop. But as we'll see in Section 8.3, we can carry this concept even further with a strategy known as the daily build.

8.3 The testing process

Generally speaking, the process of testing an Internet system is essentially the same as testing any other kind of IT system. There may be different *categories* of testing (e.g., network testing, security testing, testing for broken URL links on a Web page, etc.) than one would find for, say, a mainframe COBOL system, but the step-by-step process of testing the two kinds of systems is likely to be much the same.

Here again, as in previous chapters, we're likely to see a conflict between the manager—who typically wants to impose at least a modicum of process discipline, to ensure that things remain under control—and the developers. Even if the developers are experienced IT professionals, they may still argue that their intuitive, *ad hoc* approach is sufficient, and that the time constraints of their high-intensity project do not allow for any bureaucratic activities that are unrelated to *doing the work* of testing. And as we've discussed in the previous chapters of this book, there are many reasonable opportunities for compromise between the extremes of utter anarchy (in which every developer tests whatever he or she wants, whenever he or she wants, in whatever fashion he or she wants) and overwhelming bureaucracy. Here's a fairly light description of the key processes that I believe a project manager should implement, with as much or as little formality as the occasion requires:

- *Derive test cases from requirements*—As my colleague Tom DeMarco likes to say, "The specification (i.e., the requirements statement) *is* the acceptance test." Whenever anyone suggests creating a test case, the manager should ask (if it's not obvious), "Which requirement are we testing with this test case?" More appropriately, the *creation* of the test cases should be driven by the requirements. Rather than creating them randomly, the project team should *begin* with the list of requirements (both the functional and non-functional requirements), and determine which test cases are required. As a side benefit, this process helps provide a quality check on the requirements themselves: If nobody (including the user) can figure out how one would go about testing the requirement (e.g., a nebulous statement like: "The system shall be user-friendly"), then it's not a very good requirement.

- *Automate the testing activity*—Manual testing is laborious, tedious, time-consuming, expensive, inefficient, and error-prone. Everyone knows this, everyone nods their head solemnly when the suggestion is made to acquire automated testing tools, and yet the majority of *all* software projects are still tested on a mostly manual basis. It may not be easy, or even possible, to test all of the features and characteristics of the system in an automated fashion, but more and more of the vendors of testing tools (e.g., Rational Software, Mercury Interactive, AutoTester, etc.) have sophisticated offerings for testing the front-end Web features and the back-end application logic of an Internet-based system. Every time you see a developer performing a manual testing activity, you should be asking, "Why can't we automate that activity?"

- *Perform regression testing*—A test that ran successfully yesterday won't necessarily run successfully today; whenever possible, you want to add today's test cases to the collected aggregate of all previous test cases and run them all again. The obvious scenario for doing this is the addition of new functionality to a system being developed, or a change to existing functionality, or a modification to existing code to correct an existing bug. Any of these activities may break some previously working component of software, including components that appear to be completely unrelated to the one being added/changed/fixed. Of course, it's not usually practical to carry out regression testing unless the overall testing process has been automated, at least to some extent. An automated regression test also eliminates the human tendency to ignore, or overlook, the very possibility that the introduction of new software may have broken something that worked perfectly yesterday; the automated regression test makes no such assumptions. This is a good example of a process that can be articulated, documented, and practiced in a very light fashion—all it requires is a firm statement from the project manager: "Whenever we change *anything* in the software under development, re-run *all* the tests."

- *Use a daily build approach*—A common flaw in the testing process is to add 10 new components to a partially developed system, and then run a thousand test cases (plus the regression tests covering all previously created functionality and their associated test cases). If one of those 10 new components has a bug in it, then any one of the thousands (or tens of thousands) of test cases may detect an error, and the error may be associated with a subtle interaction between *several* of the new pieces of functionality. Tracking down the source of the bug then becomes a nightmare, and the overall discipline of testing begins to degenerate. The ideal scenario is one in which only *one* new component (or module, or Web page, or piece of functionality) is added, and that incremental change is then subjected to the full battery of tests. But that may not be practical in a high-intensity project involving half a dozen people who are coding furiously and prepared to add new functionality to the existing system on an hour-by-hour basis. A reasonable compromise is to implement the following process: *Every day*, the entire system (including all of the new and/or modified code that has been added to the existing base of stable code) is compiled, linked, loaded, and then subjected to as many automated tests as can be run during the course of the night. If bugs are uncovered by the overnight testing, the presumption is that the newly added/modified code is to blame, or at the very least, something about the new/modified code caused the old code to misbehave. If the bugs can't be easily found and corrected, then a good SCM system (see Chapter 7 for a discussion of the importance of this approach) can be used to roll back the software to the previous day's version.

We'll discuss the daily build approach again in Chapter 10, as a mechanism for the project manager to monitor the progress of the project during the development phase.

- *Track and monitor the defect closure rate*—As noted in the previous bullet point, bugs that are detected by testing are not always found, fixed, and re-tested instantly. It's not always easy to identify the *location* and *cause* of a bug, and it's not always easy to determine an appropriate *correction* for a bug, especially if it appears that the correction might introduce various side-effects. Thus, some bugs may linger on for days, weeks, or even months as the developers try to track them down, while simultaneously adding new code to implement additional features. To ensure that un-fixed bugs do not become a time bomb of increasing significance, the manager should capture metrics data to track the *rate* at which detected bugs are tracked down and fixed. In many of the larger and more complex development efforts, these metrics are categorized according to the severity of the defect so that a higher priority can be placed on tracking and fixing the bugs with serious consequences.

8.4 Categories of testing for Internet-related systems

For those who ask, "What's so different about testing Internet-related systems?" one answer is: "In addition to testing the application functionality of the system you're building, there are a lot of other things you need to test, too." In many cases, there are direct correlations between the categories of Internet testing and the categories of testing client/server systems, online systems, or even batch systems—but the vocabulary is different, the tools are sometimes different, and the details are different. The categories of Internet testing include:

- *Code-level testing*—Here, HTML, Java, JavaScript, Visual Basic, C++, and other forms of code are tested for correct operation. Not only does this require testing to ensure that the correct outputs are generated for the appropriate set of inputs, but it also involves testing to ensure that the system will run on the full range of Web browsers that the system has promised to support (e.g., the last two or three versions of Netscape Communicator and Internet Explorer), as well as testing to ensure that the system handles images, image maps, fonts, tables, and style sheets.

- *Compatibility*—Here, the system is tested to ensure that it will function in the desktop/client environment that the end-user is expected to have. Thus, not only does the system have to operate properly with a designated range of Web browsers, but also with an appropriate set of plug-ins and helper applications that the user may have on his or her client machine. And the testers may need to ensure that the Internet-related system runs properly on a range of client hardware platforms, network bandwidth facilities, RAM/disk configurations, and operating systems.[2]

- *Navigation testing*—Here, the system is tested to ensure that visitors to the Internet system can successfully follow internal links, external links, and anchors to locations within a Web page. This level of testing also tends to deal with bookmarks, frames and framesets, site maps, internal search engines, site navigation diagrams, and "redirects" (where the external user accesses the system via a URL that is no longer the official home page of the system, but which needs to be supported anyway, rather than generating an error message). This may also be the area where the developers test the session management capabilities of the system, which involves a sequence of one or more interactions between the end-user and the Internet system to accomplish a transaction, which may be completed successfully or aborted prematurely because of inactivity, network connection problems, or the end-user's conscious decision to cancel the transaction.

- *Usability and accessibility*—These involve testing for things such as overall readability of information on the Internet system, support for multiple languages, screen size and pixel resolution, and personalization (either based on a user login procedure or on-the-fly responses to user activities and preferences, color combinations, and other forms of accessibility [e.g., support for people who are color-blind]).

- *Performance testing*—This typically involves fairly traditional testing for response time, as well as load testing and stress testing.

---

2.   Note that this problem is much easier to define and test if the system is being developed for a known community of users with a known range of client/desktop computing environments, for instance, the typical in-house corporate intranet system. By contrast, it's a much more difficult problem when the system is being developed for an external marketplace of users, who may be logging in from anywhere in the world, running on a wide range of old and new, familiar and unfamiliar hardware platforms, Web browsers, etc.

- *Reliability and availability testing*—Here, we test the system's ability to deal with scarce resources (e.g., about to run out of RAM or disk space on the server) and various forms of fail-over testing (e.g., for hot backup, warm backup, and cold backup situations).
- *Network testing*—This tests the system to ensure that connections, messages, and packets of data are not being lost. It also includes testing to ensure that the system can deal with dropped lines, noisy lines, overloaded or sluggish communication channels, etc.

8.5 Criteria for completion

Perhaps the most important managerial decision involving testing is: "When can we stop testing?" In many high-intensity Internet projects, the question is answered by default: Testing stops when the team has run out of time or the project has been canceled. But it's a question that *should* be answered in advance, and the answer should be somewhat more intelligent than, "We'll stop testing when we have used up the amount of time and resources that I have arbitrarily set aside for the activity."

In a perfect world, we would continue testing a new system until the testing was "complete," that is, until we had subjected the system to test cases for *every* conceivable scenario, as well as every conceivable incorrect, erroneous scenario. But everyone who has worked in the IT field knows this is impossible for anything other than the most trivial, uninteresting computer program. The only thing you need to remember as a manager is that some of the non-technical developers (i.e., those with no formal IT training or background) will actually believe that their testing activity is complete after they finish creating the two or three test cases that happen to pop randomly into their little brains. You may need to spend five minutes with them to demonstrate that the number of possible test cases is an extraordinarily large number, if not infinite.

Ultimately, then, the question comes down to this: "What level, or extent, of testing will be considered 'good enough'?" The phrase "good enough," which I discussed at length in an earlier book,[3] has been criticized in some IT groups as an attempt to justify mediocre software;[4] but the reality is that *every* project team, and every user, needs to determine what constitutes "good enough" for the particular project at hand. In some cases, the definition may be: "When you can provide statistically convincing evidence that

---

3.   See *The Rise and Resurrection of the American Programmer*, Prentice Hall, 1996.

the probabilistic number of undetected bugs is so small that we will have only one system crash ever 40 years." And in other cases, the definition may be: "When you've spent two consecutive days of diligent testing activity without finding any new bugs that crash the system or wipe out the database." It's interesting to note that the concept of "good enough" is particularly relevant for Internet-related systems, because the newly developed system is likely to depend on, or interact with, other externally developed Web sites and URL links, *which are not under the project team's control.* Thus, a URL link that worked fine yesterday might not work today; the destination page/site may have been moved, or it may simply be dead.[5] In any case, the overall effect is an awareness that the Web is *always* slightly broken, and the users' acceptance of the system typically depends on *what* is broken, and just how badly it's broken.

The most common criteria are things like this:

- *Test coverage*—The team may be required to demonstrate that it has created a sufficient number of test cases to exercise 99% (or perhaps 95%, 90%, or some agreed-upon number) of all possible logic paths through the code. There are commercially available testing tools that will calculate the test coverage represented by a sample of test cases; however, it's worth noting that this approach is used far less commonly for the client/server and Internet-related systems of the past 10 years than was the case for the batch-style, mainframe-based systems of the 1970s and 80s.

- *Successful testing of specific, agreed-upon test cases*—In this case, the user community may be responsible for creating test data that represents an acceptable selection of both correct and incorrect (erroneous) inputs to the system. Thus, the users will typically test the normal case, the high end, the low end, and a few typical bad inputs. Note that this criterion is not the same as the vague statement that, "We'll continue testing until the users tell us they're satisfied." As noted in Chapter 3, some users (especially the "loser users") don't want the system to succeed at

---

4.   This perception seems to be particularly strong in Europe, but it's also noticeable in some U.S. IT organizations, where the developers themselves or the "Process Police" have decided that it's *their* job to determine what constitutes an adequate level of technical quality for the customer, even if it means delaying the completion of the project by a significant amount. Remember, it's the users who ultimately determine what is good enough, and what isn't.

5.   This is yet another reason for doing regression testing: Even if you haven't changed anything in *your* software, some external resource on the Internet may have been changed, without anyone notifying you or asking your permission.

all, which means they'll *never* be fully satisfied that the testing efforts are complete.

- *Elimination of open bugs*—The presumption here is that an adequate effort has been made to expose the latent bugs within the nascent system, either by generating sufficient test cases (with an automated testing tool) to create the desired level of test coverage or by submitting a set of test cases that has been agreed upon with the users. Most of the bugs can be identified, tracked down, fixed, and re-tested relatively quickly; but in most projects, there is a residue of un-fixed, or "open," bugs that the developers and users know about, and which are in some stage of investigation or repair. And those bugs (as well as the ones that have been fixed, or closed) are typically categorized in terms of their severity: A Level-1 bug might cause a complete failure of the system, with irrecoverable loss of data; a Level-2 bug might cause the loss of some degree of functionality of the system; and a Level-3 bug might cause nothing more than an inconvenience, or a minor amount of additional work on the user's part. Thus, a criterion for stopping the testing effort might be that: (a) there are *no* open Level-1 bugs, (b) there are no more than X open Level-2 bugs, and (c) there are no more than Y open Level-3 bugs.

One of the reasons for emphasizing the collection of closure metrics in Section 8.4 is that the key stakeholders will typically want a credible estimate of the expected date when the number of open bugs will be reduced to an acceptable level. This might seem like a simple issue, but it's important to remember that in a high-intensity Internet-related project, where there may be a dozen developers coding as fast as they can and creating new daily builds every day (duh! That's why they call it a daily build!), there may be dozens of open level-1 bugs, and literally hundreds of open level-2 and level-3 bugs at the point in time when the users and key stakeholders ask the project manager, "Aren't you done yet? When are your developers going to get those bugs fixed so we can release the system? How about tomorrow? The day after tomorrow? Next week?" To answer such a question in a responsible fashion, the manager has to be able to draw a trend line that shows the rate of discovery of new (open) bugs and the rate of fixing (closing) existing bugs to extrapolate forward and predict the time when the residue of open bugs will have sunk below the agreed-upon threshold.

8.6 Conclusion

There is much, much more to say about testing; fortunately, much of it has already been said, in numerous textbooks that have been published over the years.[6] Most of the principles of testing are just as relevant for Internet-based systems as they are for any other kind of computer system; the differences are usually associated with the high-intensity nature of such projects, which tends to force the development team to operate on a schedule that would be unrealistic by any rational standard. Not only do such projects jettison analysis, design, and documentation processes that are perceived to be bureaucratic and non-productive, but they also tend to run out of time at the end of their development schedule. The inevitable consequence is that testing is sacrificed, or carried out hurriedly and superficially.

Because it *is* a high-intensity project, there may also be pressure from the users or stakeholders to terminate the testing activity in a more premature fashion than would have been tolerated in an older technology development effort. But this can be a disastrous decision. Because the system *is* connected to the world-wide Internet, there is a larger and larger chance of *immediate* exposure and embarrassment (not to mention financial loss and even legal consequences) than ever before if the system has too many bugs and flaws. Thus, it is ultimately in everyone's interest to subject the Internet-related system to as much testing as possible, within the schedule, budget, and resource constraints. And one of the best ways to accomplish that is to *start* the testing activity as soon as possible, rather than waiting until the end of the project, when the coding activity has been completed.

❧ ❧ ❧ ❧ ❧

---

6.   See, for example, *Black-Box Testing: Techniques for Functional Testing of Software and Systems*, Boris Beizer, John Wiley & Sons, 1995; *Software Testing in the Real World: Improving the Process*, Edward Kit and Suzannah Finzi, Addison-Wesley, 1995; *The Craft of Software Testing: Subsystem Testing, including object-based and object-oriented testing*, Brian Marick, Prentice Hall, 1995; and *Effective Methods of Software Testing*, William Perry, John Wiley & Sons, 1995.

Monitoring Project Progress

9

Progress everywhere today does seem to come so *very* heavily disguised as Chaos.

    Joyce Grenfell, *Stately as a Galleon*, "English Lit.," 1978.

9.1 Introduction

How do project managers spend their time and justify their existence once they have organized the basic project plan and allocated the work to the appropriate developers on the project team? If it's a good plan, and if the developers are competent, experienced, responsible individuals, why can't the manager just take a vacation and come back on deadline day?

In the ideal situation, this is not as crazy as it sounds: *Self-managed teams* don't require day-to-day supervision, nagging, or second-guessing as they carry out their assignments. If indeed they are competent and responsible, they'll re-allocate and reschedule their work as needed, and they'll cope with whatever problems come up on a day-to-day basis. Unfortunately, high-intensity projects often encounter problems that the team itself can't handle; not only that, those on the team are often working so hard that they don't have a chance to step back and assess their progress on a regular basis.

One of the key tasks of the manager is to monitor the progress of the project on behalf of the team. While doing this, it's important to maintain a proper degree of humility: Despite what you may think, you don't *know* the actual status of the project, and you don't *know* the actual delivery date—all you have is some degree of confidence in an estimate, based on various metrics and indicators. The more visible and tangible those indicators, the more confidence you and your team can have in them.

There's a related issue that I'll mention, but will largely leave for you to solve on your own: Even if you did know precisely what the status of project was at any particular moment, how would you communicate that to the team, and in what fashion would you use that information to change the team's behavior, if necessary? Some of this depends on basic styles of management (e.g., theory X, theory Y, or theory Z), and a lot of it depends on choosing team members with appropriate personalities. I'll make a few general comments on this situation in the paragraphs below, but in general, I'll assume that if you and your team come to the conclusion that you're a week behind schedule, you'll figure out how to handle the situation.

A valuable piece of advice in this area comes from Jim McCarthy,[1] who observes that if a project team is late delivering version N of their system, it's psychologically important for them to be on time for version N+1. If they miss their deadline on two or three consecutive versions, they are likely to lose faith in their ability to meet *any* schedule, and at this point, their energy and motivation drop, and they are likely to turn into programming zombies who work sluggishly from 9 to 5, and then stagger home to sit in front of the television to watch re-runs of *I Love Lucy*. Interestingly, a similar recommendation comes from Kent Beck, originator of the XP development approach.[2] He recommends guarding against the natural exuberance that comes from delivering version N on time, with all of the promised functionality for that version. In particular, Beck suggests, don't get cocky and over-promise when planning the details of version N+1 ("We managed to deliver 25 new features in release 2, so let's promise 30 new features in release 3! We can do it, team! C'mon! Let's have a team cheer! Rah! Rah! Rah!"); instead, base the extent of promised functionality for the next version on the actual productivity of what was delivered for the current version.

Because the time constraints of a high-intensity development project allow very little time for meetings and moment-by-moment supervision of each developer's activities, I'm a big believer in self-organizing projects. That is,

---

1. See *Dynamics of Software Development*, Jim McCarthy, Microsoft Press, 1995.
2. See *eXtreme Programming eXplained: Embrace Change*, Kent Beck, Addison-Wesley, 2000.

if the manager has appropriate measures and indicators of progress, and if he or she makes that information publicly visible (at least to the members of the team), they can easily see whether they're on target, ahead of schedule, or behind schedule. And if the team understands what features are required for the completion of an upcoming version/release, and if they understand the nature of the dependencies between their various components,[3] they will exert their own pressure upon themselves, rather than depend on the manager to beat them up and force the necessary degree of progress to occur.

This is an appropriate place to point out that one of the many reasons for recommending an iterative or prototyping-oriented kind of development process, as we did in Chapter 5, is that it provides the manager with a more trustworthy means of monitoring the progress of a project. In general, it's almost impossible to monitor the progress of a high-intensity Internet project if it's carried out in a classic waterfall fashion because the first few activities of e-business strategy development, BPR, requirements documentation, and design, provide very little *tangible* evidence of progress. They produce a lot of meetings and a lot of documents, but they don't produce any software that actually runs on a server or client workstation. Thus, it's essential that the team use some form of "time box" approach that obligates them to deliver a pre-negotiated extent of functionality upon a pre-negotiated deadline; the ability or inability to achieve that deadline is usually something that can't be faked, and is therefore very tangible.

It's also very important to make the metrics and indicators as *visible* as possible. As noted earlier, this allows the team to self-regulate many of the minor changes to priorities, assignments, or day-to-day schedules if necessary. It also prevents problems from festering in the background until a weekly status meeting brings them to the manager's attention. Jim McCarthy, the former manager of Microsoft's Visual C++ product, has an excellent piece of advice in this regard; as he suggests in his excellent book on managing soft-

---

3. The dependencies are typically visible in either the technical design models associated with the project (e.g., "Uh oh, Billy Bob's component is critical for this next version; if he's not ready, we can't release version 2.5 to the marketplace.") or the standard PERT/Gantt charts produced by project management packages like Microsoft Project (e.g., "Uh oh, Billy Bob is on the critical path of the activity network, and he's three days behind schedule, and he just went home with the flu.") The problem is that this information represents *power* in a highly political organization, and many project managers have adopted a working style of keeping the information to themselves. As a result, many projects are managed in such a way that none of the developers knows what their peers are doing, nor do they know the interdependencies involved in their work. Such a management style *can* work, but it means that the manager has to personally orchestrate and supervise any changes required to schedules, assignments, and behaviors.

ware projects:[4] "Never let a programmer disappear into a dark room." His point is that programmers sometimes have a tendency to go off on their own, programming all night long (and sleeping during the day), or working from a PC at home, without making it possible for the manager to see whether they're making progress or falling behind.

Of course, one way of preventing such a phenomenon is to make *all* of the work of *all* of the programmers publicly visible by putting it on a common network, where anyone can see its status and progress from a PC or Web browser. In the same context, the project management reports and defect-related information discussed later in this chapter can also be made publicly visible, so that *nobody* is in the dark.[5]

9.2 Managing the team's time

As mentioned earlier, the pressures of a high-intensity project are such that none of the developers can afford to waste any of their time. They have a natural instinct for avoiding what they perceive to be bureaucratic activities, but the very intensity of the project often makes it difficult for them to distinguish between what's *urgent* and what's really *important*. The distinction between the two categories creates four quadrants of time, as discussed in Stephen Covey's excellent book,[6] and as illustrated in Figure 9.1. Quadrant Q1 consists of the high-urgency, high-priority, "heart attack" activities, like dealing with a catastrophic system bug the night before a system is supposed to be released to the marketplace. Quadrant Q2 consists of the activities that are important, but not yet urgent, which tend to include most planning, organizing, and thinking activities. Quadrant Q3 is the disaster area for high-intensity projects: email, voice-mail, faxes, and uninvited intrusions into one's office or cubicle from someone whose request is urgent (indeed, the person is often extremely agitated and demands instant attention) but fundamentally *not* important. Finally, Q4 consists of the time-wast-

---

4. See *Dynamics of Software Development*, Jim McCarthy, Microsoft Press, 1995.
5. The logical progression of this idea is a concept called "visible processes," developed by Bangalore-based Mascot Systems, Inc. If the software development process illustrated briefly in Chapter 5 is developed in more detail, and formalized in an SEI Level-3 fashion (Mascot was actually awarded an SEI Level-4 status in June 2001), then the entire process can be put onto a project-wide Web site so that everyone (including the user!) can see the current process-related activities being carried out, as well as the overall status of the project.
6. See *First Things First*, Stephen R. Covey, *et al.*, Fireside, 1996. For an IT-related discussion of Covey's quadrants, see my Apr. 23, 2001, *Computerworld* article, "Finding Time to Think."

ers, like time spent on documentation that nobody is going to read, or time spent attending meetings to hear the latest announcements on the company's expense account policy, or a progress report on the Civic Committee's latest project to plant tulips in the town park.

From this perspective, it's safe to assume that the team members will generally find ways to avoid Q4 activities on their own; and while everyone will try to organize things so as to eliminate or minimize Q1 heart attacks, they can't be ignored if they do occur. One of the most helpful things the manager can do is help serve as a buffer to keep the Q3 interruptions from distracting the team members, and to remind them periodically that the Q2 planning activities *are* important, even if nobody is nagging them about such activities.

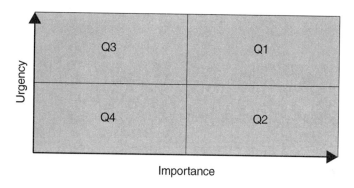

FIGURE 9.1 The four quadrants of time.

9.3 Project reviews, walkthroughs, and inspections

Another way to monitor the progress of a project is to conduct project reviews; these are primarily useful to the extent that a retrospective on past activities can help determine whether changes need to be made in the future.

In the traditional projects that took place in previous decades, there was typically only one postmortem review, at the end of the project. This often turned out to be a highly political event, in which the real problems and lessons were hidden to avoid political repercussions. Indeed, the very term "postmortem" is indicative of the status of the project at the time the review took place, that is, a review "after death."[7]

In today's high-intensity Internet-related project, it may or may not be useful to schedule project reviews at regular intervals of time, for example, once a week or once a month. More often, though, reviews take place at the end of significant events, such as the completion and demonstration/delivery of a new version of the system to the user community. These are usually relatively short meetings, lasting only an hour or two, during which the project team can review all of the successes and failures of the just-completed version to see whether things are still on track.[8]

A related concept is a walkthrough of any technical product. This is an approach that IT developers have used for decades, and it is well-documented in the literature.[9] We also know from past experience that developers often resist the notion of walkthroughs, not only because they object to having work products critiqued, but also because they feel it takes too much time. XP guru Kent Beck suggests that the first problem can be confronted by creating a project environment based on the "open source code" philosophy; that is, inform each developer that it's not "his" code or "her" code, but *our* code. Furthermore, create a set of processes and procedures that will allow anyone on the project team to modify any code (or design, or Web page, or requirement documents) created by any other member.[10] While this might seem like a radical approach employed solely to create controversy in the team, it often turns out to be an absolutely pragmatic, mandatory operational policy on high-intensity projects where programmers are working around-the-clock. If I discover a bug in your code at 3 a.m., I don't want to have to track you down, wake you up, and have an incoherent conversation about why your code isn't working the way it should; I want to be able to fix the bug *myself*, leave appropriate documentation about the nature of the fix, and then continue making progress on my own module before I collapse from exhaustion at dawn.

If the developers object because of the time, paperwork, and bureaucratic overhead associated with the walkthrough process, then you need to find a way to streamline it, so that the walkthroughs can take place as efficiently as

---

7. For a good discussion of how such reviews should take place, see Norm Kerth's discussion of project retrospectives in *Project Retrospectives: A Handbook for Team Reviews*, Dorset House, 2001.

8. See my Mar. 19, 2001, Computerworld article, "Mini-Postmortems," for additional discussion of this concept.

9. See my *Structured Walkthroughs*, Prentice-Hall, 1989, for guidelines on procedures and suggestions for conducting such reviews, and *Software Inspection*, Tom Gilb, Dorothy Graham, and Suzannah Finzi, Addison-Wesley, 1993, for a discussion of formal inspections.

10. Note that you *must* have a formal, disciplined, tool-supported configuration management environment to make this work. Part of that environment must be a mechanism that allows the originator of the work product to roll back to an earlier version, if necessary, so that well-intentioned but nevertheless erroneous "improvements" to an existing document or chunk of code can be undone.

possible. If the developers are geographically dispersed, then you may need to use various Internet-supported meeting and collaboration tools (e.g., Net meeting, or the new groove.net product). Also, consider videotaping project walkthroughs and meetings to reduce the amount of note-taking and paper-work.[11]

9.4 Defect tracking against quality targets

As we discussed in Chapter 8, testing can be a laborious, time-consuming activity in an IT development project; but from the perspective of this chapter, there is something even more important to say about testing: It's an area where things sometimes get badly out of control because an accumulation of open bugs can lead to unpredictable delays at the point where the project can least afford to cope with them, that is, near the deadline for delivery.

Thus, to keep things under control and to keep project costs and time delays from mushrooming, it's important to find and fix bugs as they occur. Ideally, the project team should have a goal for delivered defects per unit of work (e.g., per Web page, or thousand lines of Java code). Appropriate pro-cesses—walkthroughs, inspections, or just-in-time testing—should be implemented to identify the existence of defects as soon as possible after they are "injected" into the software, so that they can be fixed while they are still fresh in everyone's mind. Configuration management processes should be used to record the defects and trace them through to removal. And to ensure that all of the activity associated with this work remains *visible* to both the project manager and the members of the project team (to avoid unpleasant surprises), it's important to establish a culture in which *there is no such thing as a private defect*, meaning one that is detected and removed with-out being recorded.

One reason for establishing this culture is the strong suspicion—but a suspi-cion not yet substantiated by industry data—that Internet-related projects have at least one significant point in common with older, traditional projects: 80% of the bugs cluster in a mere 20% of the modules or compo-nents of the system. Bugs are like cockroaches: They don't live alone, and they tend to bring their brothers and sisters, cousins, and aunts and uncles with them when they infest a dwelling. Thus, if the team discovers a few bugs in a particular component of the Internet system, it's quite likely to be

---

11. For more details, see my article, "Internet Legacy Nightmares," Computerworld, July 31, 2000.

an infested component, which contains *more* bugs that simply haven't been found yet. To keep things from getting out of control, we need to spot these situations as early as possible.

You may recall that I suggested in Chapter 8 that the project manager should track the time required to close the bugs that have been identified, but not yet fixed. The reason for doing this is not only to improve the overall testing process, but also to get an early warning of whether the entire project schedule is at risk of being disrupted by the steady growth of difficult-to-fix bugs. At any given point, the project manager should know—as should the other members of the team—the average and maximum time to close a defect after it has been reported. Let's imagine, for the sake of argument, that the average time up through the release of version 2 of the system is one day and the maximum time is a week. Now we're working on version 3, and the project manager notices that the average time for defect closure has crept up to two days and the maximum time is two weeks. And, we've got one bug that's about to start its third week without having been fixed. There are various possible explanations for the phenomenon, and various strategies that the manager and team might choose to cope with the problem. The main point is that an alarm signal should be ringing at this point, and all team members should know that they're on the verge of losing control.

The casual reader might ask, "But wouldn't the situation be obvious at this point? How could anyone *not* know that the team was getting into trouble?" The point is that in a high-intensity project, everyone (including the manager) is so busy dealing with the day-to-day work assignments, pressures, and immediate problems that the emerging trends are *not* immediately obvious because nobody has any spare time to step back and *look* for the trends. But if metrics are being captured and reported on a regular basis, it's much harder to ignore an emerging trend.

By analogy: Some people involved in high-stress situations find themselves skipping their normal exercise regimen and increasing the amount of junk food they eat at the office, during rushed lunch-hours and late evenings. After a month or two of this kind of behavior, they may find that they've gained 10 pounds or more, by which time it might be fairly difficult to cope with the problem. But if their daily regimen also includes 10 seconds of standing on the scale in their bathroom while brushing their teeth in the morning, they can be reminded of their current weight without incurring any additional time or effort. And if their scale was sophisticated enough to display a graph of the last week's weight values, then an upward trend would be almost impossible to overlook. It's a lot easier to deal with a weight gain problem at the end of a week than it is at the end of a month.

As today's high-intensity Internet-related projects get larger, more complex, and more mission-critical in nature, it will become more and more important to measure and track not only the known defects, but also the *latent* defects, those that have not yet been discovered, but whose existence can be predicted on a statistical basis. For example, an IT organization may be building its first medium-sized Internet-related system today, and may not have much experience with the number of defects that are encountered *after* the official release and installation, when external customers begin using it. But 2–3 years from now, that same organization will have built 5, 10, or even a hundred such systems, and if it has monitored its defect removal activity carefully enough, it should be able to predict the *rate* at which serious defects are discovered and removed during the last few weeks or months of testing, and also the number of latent defects that somehow remained undiscovered until the first 30 days of use by external customers.

All of this data creates a knowledge base that may prove invaluable during the pressure-packed days before the official release of the company's first really, truly *big* Internet system, for which undiscovered defects could have devastating consequences. The Marketing Department is likely to be putting pressure on the project team with statements like, "We're about to launch a major TV advertising campaign, announcing that our new e-business system will be available on March 1. Are you techno-geeks going to be ready? Don't give us any sob stories about how hard you've been working—we've *all* been working hard! Just tell us whether or not your system will be ready, before we commit $25 million dollars in television commercials!"

The project team needs to be able to respond with a statement like this: "We told you that it was okay to promise the marketplace that we would deliver all the features in the high-priority category that we identified in our triage meeting last month, and we can assure you that we've finished developing *and* testing those features, with no known severity-one or severity-two defects."

"We also told you that we would try very hard to finish all of the medium-priority features, but that you shouldn't make any promises about them. As it turns out, there are three of those medium-priority features that we just won't be able to finish by the deadline. As for the rest of them, they're all coded and we've done a lot of testing, but there are still 7 severity-one defects and 13 severity-two defects that we haven't been able to track down and fix yet. Based on the data from our previous Internet-related projects, we have a 95% level of confidence that we can remove all of the severity-one defects and all but two of the severity-two defects before the official launch date."

One can imagine that the Marketing Department will grumble and complain about the three medium-priority features that the project team has confessed won't be finished in time, but overall, they should be relatively pleased with the news. But imagine that the official launch of the Internet-related system is expected to attract 10,000 visitors on the first day, 100,000 visitors *per day* by the end of the first week, and a million daily visitors once the massive advertising campaign has begun to seep into the consciousness of a nation of TV-addicted zombies. Given the stakes that are involved, it would be a good idea if the project team could also tell the marketing whiz-kids, "Oh, by the way, our experience with the last five Internet projects tells us that with the level of testing we've been able to do, we can expect one system crash per day during the first week of operation, followed by one crash per week during the next month of operation, followed by one crash per month for the remainder of the first year. "

"What?!?" the marketing people will yell, in stunned disbelief.

"Yeah, well, that's how it goes," the project team will respond. "If it's any consolation, the bugs that we experience during the first week will be fairly simple, and we should be able to get things fixed within 10 minutes. The next series of defects are likely to be somewhat more obscure, and they're likely to affect only about 10% of the people who are accessing the system when the problem occurs. After that, the problems are going to be much more infrequent, but they'll also be tougher to fix—most of those problems will take an hour or two to fix, and there will be a 10% chance that we'll be down for an entire day."

"What?!?" the marketing people will yell, far more loudly this time. "That's unacceptable! If you guys know all this stuff, why don't you do a better job of testing? Why are you *deliberately* leaving bugs in the system?"

If the same group of marketing people was involved in the planning and release of the last system, they should know the answer to this question; unfortunately, corporate politics are such that it may be an entirely new group of marketing people and business users who are forced to confront these real-world issues for the first time. The project manager may or may not find that it's politic to retrieve the memo that he or she wrote at the beginning of the project, warning that the schedule was too aggressive to do a sufficiently comprehensive job of testing; and he or she may or may not feel that it's politic to remind the users that he or she has been submitting weekly metrics data showing the discovery rate of new defects, as well as the closure rate of fixing those defects. Finally, he or she may or may not feel that it's politic to point out that one of the purposes of the three pre-release versions of the system, which were provided to the marketing people for internal testing and demonstration to key clients, was to provide a rough idea of the level of quality that could be expected from a project team working under the stress and constraints of a high-intensity schedule.

However unpleasant and ugly the dialogue between the marketing group and the project team might be at this point, it's better than the alternative: If there is no warning and no metrics data to quantify the expected number of post-release defects, there is a much more serious chance of severe frustration, embarrassment, and disappointment when the first 10,000 users hit the system, followed by the next 100,000, and culminating in that first million.

9.5 The "daily build" concept

In the discussion above, I assumed that the incremental deliverables produced by the project team would appear at intervals measured in months or weeks. That's what most of us are accustomed to from our past experience with normal projects, and it's consistent with the usual pace of business life (e.g., weekly staff meetings, monthly status reviews, quarterly presentations to senior management, etc.).

But high-intensity projects—whether Internet-related or not—typically need a different approach. When it comes to prototyping and incremental development, it often makes sense to organize the entire project around the concept of a "daily build." As mentioned briefly in an earlier chapter, this means compile, link, install, and test the entire collection of code produced by the team *every day*, as if this was the last day before the deadline and the team had to release whatever they had to the user tomorrow morning.

Realistically, the team can't start the daily build on the first day of the project. And while it might be possible to build the equivalent of a "Hello World" subroutine—which, for a typical Internet-related system, might be a single Web page that says "Under Construction"—on the second day of the project, it won't impress anyone unless *everything* about the project involves completely new technology. However, there's usually a point well before the first official demonstration or delivery of a prototype version of the system when the software developers have a reasonable collection of components, subroutines, or modules (e.g., a few Web pages, or a few hundred lines of code) that actually accepts real input, does real calculations or processing, and produces real output. That's the point when the daily build should begin, and a new (and hopefully better) version of the system should be built every day thereafter.

Why is this so important? As Jim McCarthy likes to say,[12] "The daily build is the heartbeat of the project. It's how you know you're alive." And there can hardly be a more important priority for the manager of a high-intensity Internet-related project. If a week goes by while everyone is spinning his or her wheels and nobody has quite had the nerve to tell the project manager that he or she just can't manage to get the new-fangled Web server to communicate properly with the Java servlet he or she is working on, the project may have fallen hopelessly behind schedule. As long as the project manager hears status reports delivered in a verbal fashion or documented in written memos (or UML models), it's all too easy to confuse motion with progress, and effort with achievement. But if the project manager insists on physically observing the behavior of each day's daily build, it's much more difficult to hide whatever problems are plaguing the project.

Some project managers will nod their heads and confirm that this is how they've *always* done it, but most will admit that they've settled for weekly builds, or monthly builds, or semi-annual releases of a system. While nobody can rightly claim to have invented the concept, many feel that Dave Cutler should be given the credit for popularizing it during the development of the original Windows NT operating system in the mid-1990s. The Windows 95 development project also used the daily build concept; the final beta version before the production system was released in August 1995 was known as "Build 951."

It's important to recognize that an approach like this effectively becomes part of the project team's *process* for developing the system: Imagine what it must be like to be part of a team that has to demonstrate a working version of its software on 951 consecutive days! To be effective, the daily build should be automated, and should run unattended in the middle of the night, when all of the programmers have gone home (or have climbed under their desks and into their sleeping bags!). Once again, this emphasizes the importance of having automated configuration management and source code control mechanisms, which we discussed in previous chapters. It also implies the existence of automated scripts of some kind to carry out the compiling and linking activities. But most important, it implies the existence of an automated testing process and regression testing tools of the sort discussed in Chapter 8, which can run all night long, pounding away on the new version of code to see if it still runs yesterday's test cases properly.

---

12. See *Dynamics of Software Development*, Jim McCarthy, Microsoft Press, 1995.

A few small tricks can add even more value to the daily build concept:

- The project manager should move his or her office to the test site or operation center once the daily build process begins. Dave Cutler did this at Microsoft, and there are apocryphal stories of the tantrums that he threw when he arrived at the office and found that the daily build had crashed in the middle of the night. Tantrums or not, the point is that the project manager wants to be *very* visible and *very* involved in the daily build process, rather than be the commanding general at the rear of the army, receiving daily reports on a battle taking place miles away. As mentioned earlier, one of the major objectives here is to ensure that the project manager has visible, tangible evidence of the project's status, and the best way to ensure that the evidence is indeed visible and tangible is to make sure that the project manager is there to see it, first-hand.

- Since it's likely that the daily build will require at least a small amount of manual supervision while it runs in the middle of the night, it may help to establish the following policy: Any programmer whose buggy code causes the daily build to crash gets the honor of supervising the operation of the (nightly) daily build until the next victim causes a crash. Obviously, there are advantages and disadvantages to such a policy, but at the very least, it makes the whole concept of the daily build much more real to the project team!

- Assign one of the programmers who normally comes into the office early in the morning the task of checking whether the daily build ran successfully, and then posting the results in a visible place. If nobody is willing or able to show up early, then hire a college student. One company instructed the student to plant a flag outside the building to warn everyone whether it was going to be a good day or bad day when they arrived: A green flag meant the daily build had succeeded, while a red flag meant that it had failed.

9.6 Conclusion

The discussion throughout this chapter assumed that the project manager actually wanted to *know* whether his or her project was under control or out of control. I also implied that marketing people, business users, and other stakeholders might want to know what's going on. It's the manager's job to assess progress on a day-to-day basis and take corrective action (or provide the information with which the developers themselves can take correction action) as needed. But one could certainly make a rational argument that the other stakeholders should be interested in assessing progress on, say, a weekly or monthly basis, and making that assessment as realistic as possible.

It's hard to imagine anyone disagreeing with such an assumption, but one can imagine the political culture of a high-intensity business environment in which a frazzled senior manager might say, "No, actually, I *don't* want to know the status of the project on a weekly or monthly basis. That's what I'm paying the project manager to do. I've got enough other problems to cope with. I just want the project to be finished, on time and within budget. Everything else is irrelevant."

Unfortunately, some IT projects are launched in an environment of unrealistic optimism about what's possible. And, sad to say, some projects are launched with schedules and budgets that are so aggressive that *nobody* on the project team believes they can be achieved; indeed, even the project manager knows that the assignment is impossible, but the political situation often precludes him or her from saying so out loud. Indeed, senior management sometimes makes it abundantly clear that they don't want to hear any expressions of doubt or pessimism; the schedule and budget are announced as edicts, and dissenters are told they can find employment elsewhere.

In cases like these, the question for the project manager and the rest of the team is whether they want to create unhappiness and frustration on the part of stakeholders and senior management in small doses at an early point in the project schedule, or in large doses at a later point in time, when it may be impossible to find an acceptable compromise or alternative. Interestingly, some developers will shrug and say, "Our senior management is so stubborn that they *never* want to hear bad news, and they'll deny reality even when it smacks them in the face. So there's no point going through all of this daily build and frequent release nonsense; they'll still go crazy when we miss the original deadline for delivering the final system. We might as well live a civilized life between now and then, and focus on learning some good technical Internet skills that we can put on our resume when the project is canceled and we have to go look for another job."

The interesting point to be emphasized here is that technical developers often have objectives and criteria for success that are not entirely aligned with project success or business success. If they've learned some technical skills, enjoyed their day-to-day programming activities, and earned a good salary, they may feel that *they* succeeded, even if their employer was unable to successfully deploy the Internet-related system they were building.

I won't attempt to judge the ethics or morality of such an outlook on life, but I will suggest that the project manager can rarely afford to be so cavalier about the outcome of a project. Aside from the question of ethics, the project manager is likely to be judged much more harshly than the technical developers when applying for his or her next job if the last project ended in failure. By contrast, the developers can merely shrug during their next interview and say, "I wrote some really *fantastic* Java code, but those idiot managers couldn't get their act together and plan things properly. So I decided to leave, a month after the deadline had passed, because I had finished all of the coding I was responsible for and I could see that the project would never be implemented successfully."

The project manager's track record is more likely to be tainted by a project failure or cancellation, regardless of whose fault it is. Therefore, it's not only arguably more ethical and moral, but also more pragmatic and beneficial to one's career to take whatever steps are necessary to: (a) keep the project under control; or failing that, (b) make it as unavoidably visible as possible when things start getting out of control. If the schedule and deadline are utterly unachievable, it's better to make that painfully obvious to stakeholders and senior management a week after the project has begun, rather than a week before the deadline … or even worse, a week *after* the deadline.

ᐭ ᐭ ᐭ ᐭ ᐭ

Managing Risk 10

To save all we must risk all. ■

Friedrich Von Schiller, *Fiesco, in Fiesco,* Act 4, Scene 6.

10.1 Introduction

Monitoring and controlling progress in a high-intensity Internet project, which we discussed in Chapter 9, could be regarded as one element of *risk management*. But if all the programmers quit in the middle of a project because they've been lured away by the promise of lucrative stock options in a startup company, then the project manager will have larger problems to worry about than a minor schedule delay. If the organization is sued because its intended use of the Internet provokes a competitor to claim that copyrights are being violated and intellectual property is being misused, then the project may be canceled, even if the programmers were ahead of schedule.

Of course, low-key, casually scheduled projects are susceptible to risk, too. *Everything* in our life involves some degree of risk, however minor and tolerable. But the very fact that we've used the term "high-intensity" to describe Internet projects in this book is an obvious warning that the risks are likely to be more immediate and severe than the usual, run-of-the-mill development projects that take place within an IT organization. And because of that, it may be appropriate to amend the statement we made in Chapter 9: Instead of just suggesting that a project manager's main day-to-day task in a high-intensity Internet project is to monitor and control progress, we should say that the task involves monitoring and controlling risk. Indeed, it's hard to imagine a manager of such projects who did *not* give some serious thought to the subject of risk on a day-to-day basis.

Unfortunately, even if the project manager performs a standard risk management review at the beginning of a project, things sometimes get out of hand as the project continues. In the best case, risks that were visible at the beginning of the project will be eliminated; in the normal case, however, they will continue to be worrisome risks throughout the project. But entirely new risks—things that nobody anticipated—can suddenly emerge, and because the team typically has very little slack, in terms of schedule, budget, and resources, these new risks can be killers.

As we discussed in Chapter 5, risk management and the monitoring of project progress are oversight processes that need to be applied throughout a project. To remind you of the pervasive nature of these two oversight processes, take a look once again at the software project life cycle in Figure 10.1. The reason for showing it again is to emphasize that risk management is not something to be done *once*, at the beginning or end of a project, but *throughout* the project, on a continuous basis.

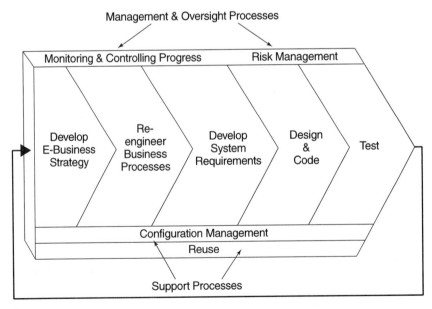

FIGURE 10.1 Risk management in the context of overall project management.

The most serious problem that I've encountered, having observed numerous Internet development projects in recent years, is that many project managers are content to use the intuitive, *ad hoc* risk management approach that served them well on projects that involved familiar technology, reasonable business users, and a civilized project schedule; unfortunately, this typically doesn't work in a high-intensity Internet project. Indeed, it's the existence of an effective, formal software risk management (SRM) *process* that makes some consulting/outsourcing organizations willing to go out on a limb and take on a high-risk project that would otherwise be certain suicide.

There is a substantial body of literature on risk management, and it's beyond the scope of this book to cover it all.[1] While it's important to be familiar with the standard, traditional SRM practices in the literature, it's also important to avoid having the "Risk Management Police" overwhelm a project with forms, reports, and other aspects of bureaucracy. Because of the limited amount of time for bureaucratic processes, project managers on some high-intensity Internet projects follow a very simple process of having the team identify and monitor the *top ten* risks in the project. These can be printed on a one-page form, and their status can be quickly reviewed on a weekly basis. A sample risk management form is shown in Table 10.1; it can be adjusted to suit the needs and preferences of a specific project.

Obviously, other approaches can work just as well, but the key is to ensure that you use an approach that will be understood, accepted, and followed by everyone on the project team (it's usually the peons at the bottom of the hierarchy—i.e., the developers—who are the first to see the emergence of new risks). In a high-intensity Internet project, we don't have time to let the information trickle up to the top of the management hierarchy by smoke signals or whatever antiquated communication mechanisms are used to convey political information; the risks have to be pounced on and attacked by the team as a whole to prevent them from getting out of control.

---

1. See, for example, *Managing Risk: Methods for Software Systems Development*, Elaine M. Hall, Addison-Wesley, 1998; *Assessment and Control of Software Risks*, Capers Jones, Prentice Hall, 1994; *To Engineer is Human: The Role of Failure in Successful Design*, H. Petroski, Vintage Books, 1992; *Computer-Related Risks*, Peter G. Neumann, Addison-Wesley, 1995; *Tutorial: Software Risk Management*, Barry Boehm, IEEE Computer Society Press, 1989; *Application Strategies for Risk Analysis*, Robert N. Charette, McGraw-Hill, 1990; and *Software Engineering Risk Analysis and Management*, Robert N. Charette, McGraw-Hill, 1989.

TABLE 10.1 A sample risk-management form.

ID	Person Responsible	Description	Last Week	This Week	Next Week (estimated)
6	Susan	System crashes with Netscape 4.75	♠	♦	♣
8	Rocco	Slow response to order inquiry	♦	♦	♣
11	Joshua	Vendor may be late on delivering unit X	♠	♦	♦
17	Mary Jane	MJ exhausted and burned out, wants to quit	♠	♦	♣
19	Billy Bob	BB wants starring role in *Tomb Raider* sequel	♦	♦	♦
23	Rocco	System won't work with new version of Oracle	♠	♠	♣
24	Josh	User *hates* Josh's new user interface	♠	♦	♣
25	Everyone	Competitor has pre-announced "killer" app	♠	♦	♣
33	Susan	HumDinger code crashes system	♠	♠	♦
47	Billy Bob	System violates new gov't privacy regs	♠	♦	♣
♠ = high risk ♦ = medium risk ♣ = low risk					

The word "control" is crucial here, for the project team has to distinguish among risk *assessment*, risk *control*, and risk *avoidance*. In the worst case, the project team must react to risks after they occur, for instance, by allocating additional resources for additional testing to alleviate the consequences of a newly discovered bug. This kind of "fix on failure" approach, where the risks are addressed *after* they have surfaced, often leads to a crisis mode form of fire-fighting that can lead to the utter collapse of a death march project team. Risk *prevention* is usually far better, but it means that the team must agree to follow a formal process of assessment and control to preclude potential risks from occurring.

An even more proactive form of risk management seeks to eliminate the root causes of failures and risk; this is often the focus of quality management initiatives within an organization. It tends to expand the scope of risk assessment to a broader horizon to allow the *anticipation* of risks, and it can lead to a very aggressive managing culture, which incorporates a risk-taking ethic by *engineering* the degree of risk that the organization can tolerate. I'm all in favor of such an approach, but it's a more strategic issue that ought to be discussed and implemented outside the context of a high-intensity Internet project. The project team has a very tactical perspective: It's not trying to change the culture of the organization, but merely attempting to survive and finish the project.

However, this may involve some cultural problems in the organization, especially if there is a perception that *other* projects have not been risky, and that this one is the first, last, and only risky project the organization will ever see—perhaps because of a naïve assumption that future Internet-related projects will be much calmer and more civilized. The problem is that the project team is not an island unto itself; if it were, then it could simply focus on the cultural problem of shooting the messenger who reports problems to higher level authorities.

But as risk management guru Rob Charette observes, the major causes of project failure often exist in the organizational environment or the business environment surrounding the project; this is illustrated in Figure 10.2. The organizational environment and business environment are almost always outside the project manager's jurisdiction and political control; but equally important, the project manager often doesn't know about those external risks until they come crashing into the project.

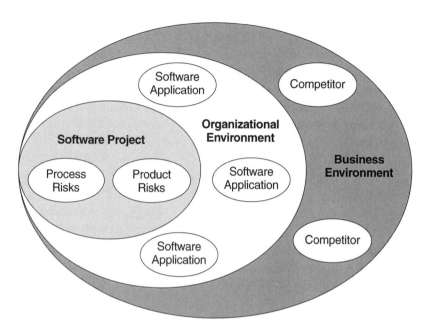

FIGURE 10.2 The scope of project risks.

Of course, the converse can also be true: The software project can create risks that affect the organization and external business environment. But everyone knows that! Indeed, the project manager can expect to be reminded *ad nauseam* that the entire organization—if not the universe, and all of civilization!—is imperiled by any delays or risks of failure associated with the high-intensity Internet project. But these same managers, who whine and complain about the fact that the project team is working only 167 hours per week to get the project finished, are often blissfully unaware of things going on in their sphere of control that could de-rail the project.

That's why it's important to have a risk management process that can assess project risks from several different organizational perspectives and balance them appropriately; after all, what the software developers see as a risk might be seen as an opportunity by the Marketing Department. This kind of global view of risk management is important, but I don't see it as often as I would like when I visit Internet development projects. And as noted above, the project team doesn't have the time, energy, or political clout to change the organizational culture by installing a global risk management process. Thus, the absence of such an organizational process becomes a risk of its own, which the team must assess.

Risk *assessment* is usually performed by evaluating the complexity of the system or product being developed, as well as evaluating the client environment and project team environment. Product complexity can be assessed in terms of size (e.g., number of function points), performance constraints, technical complexity, etc. Risks associated with the client environment are often a factor of the number of user constituencies involved, the level of user knowledge, the perceived importance of the system within the user's business area, the likelihood that when/if the new system is installed it will lead to a reorganization or downsizing activity, etc. And the risks associated with the team environment include the capabilities, experience, morale, and physical/emotional health of the project team.

Typically, there are a hundred or more risk factors that could be included in a comprehensive risk model; as noted earlier, some project teams will consciously narrow their focus to just the top ten risks. Some of the risks can be quantified in an objective fashion, for example, the response time performance requirements or the size of the system in function points. But other factors—for instance, the degree of user cooperation or hostility—may have to be assessed on a qualitative basis. As a practical management approach, it's usually appropriate to categorize such risks as "high," "low," or "medium" and to focus on getting a consensus on the state, or level, of the risk on the part of everyone involved.

A good summary of risks specifically related to e-business projects was provided in a recent article by Carole Edrich; those risks include the following:[2]

- *Most e-businesses are subject to immediate international access*—This point raises potential legal and regulatory risks. Indeed, the Internet project may be the first experience that an organization has had with online access to clients in other states, countries, and jurisdictional areas. There are certainly technical issues involved here (e.g., Do you have the necessary technology to ensure that an online customer cannot repudiate his or her purchase of a product you've already shipped?), but the largest risks are likely to be legal, and thus not something your developers can cope with. It's essential to get business managers and, if appropriate, the organization's internal and external legal counsel involved in this area as early as possible.

- *Internet supply chains behave very differently than those in a brick-and-mortar organization*—As a result, there is a risk of increased exposure to unstable suppliers. If you're building your first Internet-based supply

---

2. See "Risk Management for E-business," Carole Edrich, *Cutter Consortium Distributed Computing Architecture/E-Business Advisory Service* Executive Report, Vol. 3, No. 12, Dec. 2000.

chain system, you should remember that many of your erstwhile business partners may also be doing things for the first time, and while everyone has similar objectives of reducing inventories and the cycle time required to move things through the supply chain, it can lead to some ugly surprises (including bankruptcies) during the early stages of operation.

- *Pressure to be first to market in Internet space often leads to hasty decisions, creating technology risks as well as risks associated with sales and marketing*—With the recent collapse of the retail-oriented dot-com industry, this risk may have receded somewhat, but the first-to-market pressure existed before Web sites became popular in the late 1990s, and it will probably continue for at least the next several years. Thus, the project team may find that it is being rushed into premature technology decisions and commitments, or putting a great deal of faith in the promises of startup technology vendors ... along with a potentially unwarranted degree of faith in the new product announcements of established vendors.

- *Customer expectations are different (and often higher), while loyalty is typically much lower*—This is partly because of the ease with which a customer can click through to a long list of competitors' Web sites, which are bookmarked in his or her Web browser for easy access. Thus, while traditional systems could sometimes survive a shaky beginning because users were willing to overlook bugs and crashes, the new wave of Internet-based customers may not be as tolerant.

- *Intellectual capital is more difficult to protect when it can be accessed on your web site by competitors*—Whether you call it "competitive intelligence" or "industrial spying," there has always been some degree of risk associated with competitors who want to learn your product plans, marketing strategies, and technology secrets before you have released a new product. But if the entire product is an information-intensive product/service that's accessed via the Internet, then it's far easier than the old days of skulking through trash cans for discarded secrets. There are ways of coping with such risks, but you first have to identify and assess them before developing appropriate techniques for discouraging such competitive snooping.

Once the risks have been identified and assessed, the manager and team can sometimes identify appropriate strategies to minimize or eliminate as many as possible. This is common sense, of course, but it must be remembered that the very nature of a high-intensity Internet project is that there are commonly more than the usual risks, they're more severe, and they *cannot* be eliminated through simple actions. On the other hand, if the risks are extraordinary, sometimes the solutions are too. While the project team might never have dared to ask the CEO or senior vice president to eliminate a project risk on a normal project by spending an extraordinary sum of money or eliminating a severe bureaucratic constraint, it's not unreasonable to ask for such things in a high-intensity Internet project. And if you don't ask—which will often require going around the chain of command and circumventing several levels of brain-dead middle managers—then you'll never know whether you could have acquired the solution to your problem.

In any case, if there are high-risk factors that cannot be summarily eliminated, which is sometimes the situation in an Internet project, then they should be documented in a risk memorandum that identifies the risk impact, the possible higher-level actions, the contingency plans that need to be set in place, etc. This is not just a "cover your ass" political act, for if the risks do materialize and if they cause the project to fail, there will usually be dire consequences for everyone involved; after all, that's part of the reality of these projects. However, *denying* reality is also a common phenomenon on high-intensity projects. It's common for both members of the project team and for the various levels of users and managers surrounding the team to put on their blindfolds and steadfastly ignore the existence of serious project risks. It's not unreasonable to expect the project manager and team members to focus on internal risks with extreme diligence, but as noted earlier, the external risks often can't be controlled by the team members, because they're associated with organizational or business issues beyond their jurisdiction. Thus, a risk memorandum is an important *practical* activity to force the user and management communities to acknowledge what they would prefer to overlook and ignore.

10.3 Conclusion

It's easy to go overboard with the ideas I discussed in this chapter, and thus fall into the tar-pit of time-wasting bureaucracy. But it's far more common for the project team to exude a "Damn the torpedoes, full speed ahead!" air of bravado, act as if the best strategy is to ignore the risks, and then just overwhelm them by brute force if they should manifest themselves. There is also a tendency to assume that: (a) the Internet is new and wonderful; (b) all of the stakeholders and senior managers are extremely enthusiastic and excited about the prospects of the new system; and therefore, (c) those same stakeholders will rise to the challenge posed by any risks that appear on the horizon and do whatever it takes to support the project team. Alas, this is not always the case; indeed, the dot-com collapse has made some business executives quite skittish about everything associated with the Internet, and they may withdraw support if problems occur.

In any case, the very fact that such projects *are* highly intense, they involve a user community that is potentially global in scope, and they involve new Internet-related hardware technologies, new software technologies, and new (or re-engineered) business processes emphasizes that risk management is not something to be ignored. The project manager needs to begin identifying and assessing project risks on the first day of the project, and continue monitoring them until the very end.

🐾 🐾 🐾 🐾 🐾

Managing the Team
(adapted from Chapter 5 of *Death March*)

> "Surround yourself with the best people you can find, delegate authority, and don't interfere." ∎

Ronald Reagan, *Reagan's Reign of Error,* "Mission Impossible" (edited by Mark Green and Gail MacColl), 1987.

11.1 Introduction

If you're going to manage a high-intensity Internet project, chances are you're not going to develop all the software yourself, nor are you likely to be overseeing the efforts of a single super-programmer. More than life-cycle processes and development tools, the single greatest factor in the success or failure of your project is likely to be the *team* of people who actually do the work. So what advice can I offer when it comes to managing the team in such an environment?

Here's a summary: Insist on the right to choose your own team, or at least veto power to reject people who are completely unqualified.[1] Expect the team to work some overtime hours, but remember that they're on a marathon, and they should only be expected to sprint for the final 100 yards. Reward them handsomely if the project succeeds, but don't dangle extravagant rewards in front of them all through the project, for it will distract them. Focus on building a loyal, cohesive, cooperative team; it's important to have the necessary technical skills, but it's even more important to have complementary psychological constraints. That's all you need to remember.

Unfortunately, there's more to it for many project managers, for they work in organizations that have a miserable peopleware culture even for traditional projects. Though it might seem that such a culture would doom a high-intensity Internet project to certain failure, it sometimes turns out that just the opposite is true: Sometimes the project manager may have to accept an unreasonable schedule or budget, but can retaliate by being equally hard-nosed about various peopleware issues. Thus, the manager might insist on—and get away with—the right to hire the right people for the team, reward them properly, and provide them with adequate working conditions.

For precisely those reasons, the death march project will be perceived as a threat to those who want to maintain the bureaucratic status quo. The project manager may be able to circumvent the peopleware restrictions with an edict from senior management, but has to be aware that in doing so, he or she earns the permanent enmity of the "Office Furniture Police," the Human Resources Department, and various administrators. However, if the Internet project is a tremendous success, it may prove to be a catalyst to change the peopleware practices for subsequent normal projects.

In any case, my mission in this chapter is not to change the overall peopleware culture in an organization. Much has already been written about this, including chapters in my earlier books, *Rise and Resurrection of the American Programmer* and *Decline and Fall of the American Programmer*; you should also have a copy of DeMarco and Lister's *Peopleware* on your bookshelf, as well as Constantine's peopleware books[2] and the new edition of Weinberg's classic *Psychology of Computer Programming*.[3] The basic question addressed by this chapter is: If you're already familiar with the basics of peopleware, what's different about a high-intensity Internet project?

---

1. This doesn't happen much anymore, but it may have become part of the corporate culture in your IT organization—for example, you may hear a comment such as the following from a senior IT manager, or perhaps from one of the senior business users: "Hey, this Internet stuff isn't so hard to learn, is it? My kids tell me they write HTML in their high school classes. And Mr. BigWig, the senior executive in our End-user Department, has a nephew who really, *really* needs a summer job. How about taking him on as your network designer, or maybe your database wizard, or maybe he can do all the coding in...what was that language you guys were talking about? Java?"

2. *Constantine on Peopleware*, Larry L. Constantine, Prentice Hall/Yourdon Press, 1995, and *The Peopleware Papers: Notes on the Human Side of Software*, Larry L. Constantine, Prentice Hall/Yourdon Press, 2001.

3. *The Psychology of Computer Programming, Silver Anniversary Edition*, Gerald M. Weinberg, Dorset House, 1998.

11.2 Hiring and staffing issues

The first thing that's different about a high-intensity Internet project is the importance of forming an effective team, even though its individual members are likely to be drawn from a variety of heterogeneous backgrounds. Unless you've been living in a remote cave in the Himalayan mountains for the past couple of years, you should be aware of one significant change that has taken place in the aftermath of the collapse of the dot-com era, and the resulting layoff of a few hundred thousand "dot-com kids": You no longer have to offer a free car and signing bonus to attract people onto your team, and you no longer have to hire every idiot who stumbles in the door with a copy of *HTML for Dummies* under his or her arm. Now, once again, it's possible to hire experienced people to carry out the technical IT work, though the nature of many Internet projects is that your team may also have some *non-technical* people, particularly if your system is intended to have a multimedia Web-oriented user interface.

There are four common strategies for creating IT project teams:

- Hire superstars and turn them loose.
- Insist on a well-honed "mission-impossible" team that has worked together before.
- Choose mere mortals, but make sure they know what they're getting in to.
- Take whoever you're given and convert them into a mission-impossible team.

The first strategy is tempting, because the presumption is that the superstars are enormously productive and also clever enough to invent novel solutions to the ambiguous and demanding requirements they receive from the stakeholders and business users. However, it's also a risky strategy, because the superstars typically have super-large egos and may not work well together. And it's impractical in many organizations, because management isn't willing to pay the higher salaries demanded by the superstars—indeed, because of the dot-com collapse, there may be a corporate backlash against what was seen as the extravagant financial rewards that used to be necessary. And even if you *could* afford them, chances are they wouldn't be willing to work on an internal corporate Internet-related project—they're all working at Microsoft, or whatever high-tech startup company is still offering a combination of attractive salaries, lucrative stock options, good working conditions, and cool projects that offer the prospect of revolutionizing mankind and saving the world.[4]

The second strategy is almost certainly the ideal one for most organizations because it doesn't require superstars; it's also the kind of project team glorified by the *Mission Impossible* TV series. However, if your organization is embarking upon its first high-intensity Internet project, then such a team probably doesn't exist, even if the constituent members of the team are already employees. And if there were previous Internet projects that turned out to be suicide, kamikaze, or ugly-style projects,[5] then the teams are probably no longer together. Thus, a strategy of keeping a *successful* high-intensity Internet project intact usually has to be planned in advance, as a corporate strategy, on the assumption that such projects will occur again in the future.

The third strategy is the most common in the organizations I visit, for obvious reasons. Most organizations have no superstars, and they have no survivors from previous Internet projects.[6] Hence, each new high-intensity Internet project is staffed anew. The team members are competent, and perhaps better than the average developers in the organization, but they can't be expected to perform miracles. What's vital in this scenario is that the team members understand what they're signing up for; even though they're mere mortals, they will be called upon to perform extraordinary feats of software development.

The final strategy is one to be avoided at all costs. If the project turns out to be a dumping ground for personnel that no other project wants, then it's almost certainly a suicide project. Again, this has been glorified by Hollywood, especially in movies like *The Dirty Dozen*; the theme is that outcasts and misfits can be motivated by a tough, charismatic leader to perform miracles that nobody thought possible. Well, perhaps so, but Hollywood doesn't tell us about all of the misfit-staffed projects that failed. It seems to me that if you accept the assignment of managing (or participating in) a project of this kind, you've accepted the fate of suicide.

---

4. The details of such companies change from week to week, so I won't mention any specific names. However, at the time this book was being written in the spring and summer of 2001, the "hot" companies were typically involved in wireless technologies, peer-to-peer networking, and related technologies.
5. See Chapter 2 for a discussion of the categories of high-intensity projects.
6. In the best case (for them), they cashed in their stock options and retired. In the worst case, they burned out and collapsed, the project failed, and the entire dot-com division of the company was shut down in disgrace. An exception is the systems integrators and software consulting firms who survived the dot-com crash (e.g., companies *other* than MarchFirst, which declared Chapter 7 bankruptcy in the spring of 2001), and who often take on a succession of Internet-related projects for their clients.

This brings up the central issue of staffing the project team: To what extent should the project manager insist on the right to make the staffing decisions? As noted above, most project managers have to accept the fact that they won't be given *carte blanche* to hire the world's most talented superstars, and politics within the organization may make it impossible for the project manager to steal away the best people within the organization because they're already involved in other critical projects, or fiercely defended by other managers. Nevertheless, there is one aspect that I believe the manager should insist on as an absolute right: the right to *veto* an attempt by other managers to stick an unacceptable person onto the team. To do otherwise is to add an unacceptable level of risk to a project that's probably already over-burdened with other risks.

Obviously, this can lead to a variety of ugly political battles. The project manager is likely to hear soothing statements like, "Don't worry, Charlie has been having some problems on previous projects, but he'll be fine on your project," or ego-boosting statements like, "You're such a terrific manager that I'm sure you'll be able to turn Charlie around and get some real productivity out of him," or various appeals to loyalty, bravery, and other assorted Boy Scout virtues. My advice is to stand firm and insist on the right to reject anyone who you don't think will fit well into the team.

One of the criteria that should be used in such a decision is the likelihood of the proposed staff member leaving before the project finishes. Obviously, most software developers won't tell you if they're planning to quit midway through a project, but some of them *will* tell you about anticipated personal priorities—marriage, divorce, a prolonged mountain-climbing expedition to the Himalayas, etc.—that could rule them out of consideration. In general, it's crucial to avoid losing people in the midst of a short, high-intensity project of any kind, and Internet projects are no exception. It's also highly desirable to avoid having to add new people in the middle of a project.

11.3 Loyalty, commitment, motivation and rewards

Commitment is an essential element of the politics of such projects, but it's also a key element in the team dynamics that the project manager must try to maximize. Ideally (from the project manager's perspective), the team members will swear an oath of loyalty and dedication to the Internet project above all else. This was almost a trivial exercise a few years ago, when young dot-com kids assumed they would be getting stock options for participating in Internet-related projects, and that the options would make them richer than Bill Gates. In the aftermath of the dot-com collapse, you may find there is a certain degree of jaded cynicism that makes it difficult, if not impossible, to generate high levels of commitment and motivation.

Aside from the issue of cynicism about the dismal fate of high-tech stock options, the natural degree of motivation and commitment toward an IT development project will typically depend heavily on such things as the length of the project: Total devotion may be feasible for a 3–6 month project, but probably not for a 36-month project.

It will also depend heavily on the ability of the project manager to motivate the team members to *feel* loyal and committed. To some extent, this is a matter of charisma. Some managers generate such feelings of loyalty that their team members will follow them to the end of the earth, no matter how risky or unrealistic the project, and other managers are so uninspiring that their teams wouldn't exert any extra effort even if the project's objectives were to save mankind from an alien invasion.

Of course, one could argue that the project manager shouldn't allow anyone to join the team unless he or she *is* highly motivated. One could also argue that the issue is irrelevant because most software developers are already motivated. As DeMarco and Lister argue in *Peopleware*,[7]

> There is nothing more discouraging to any worker than the sense that his own motivation is inadequate and has to be 'supplemented' by that of the boss... You seldom need to take Draconian measures to keep your people working; most of them love their work.

There are levels, or degrees, of motivation. We might expect a software developer to exhibit a certain degree of motivation for a normal project, but high-intensity Internet projects demand a higher degree of motivation to sustain the team members through months of exhausting work, political pressure, and technical difficulties. And the project manager faces the practical difficulty of not knowing just how motivated the team members are when the project begins.

In many cases, the biggest factors in motivation/de-motivation will revolve around the dynamics of the overall team; I'll discuss that in more detail below. But there are two specific issues that also have a significant impact on motivation, and which are usually under the manager's direct control: rewards and overtime.

---

7. *Peopleware: Productive Projects and Teams*, Second Edition, Tom DeMarco and Tim Lister, Dorset House, 1999.

11.3.1 Rewarding project team members

Things would be easy if we could solve the motivation problem by dangling large sums of money in front of all of the project team members (and the manager, too!). But Frederick Herzberg suggests that money is not the answer:

> Money, benefits, comfort, and so on are "hygiene" factors—they create dissatisfaction if they're absent, but they don't make people feel good about their jobs and give them the needed internal generator. What does produce the generator are recognition of achievement, pride in doing a good job, more responsibility, advancement, and personal growth. The secret is job enrichment.[8]

Interestingly, Herzberg made his comments in a 1987 publication, and they probably made sense at the time. But one can imagine him being hooted off the stage if he had made a similar comment at an Internet conference during the late 1990s, a time when the prevailing attitude of many IT workers was best articulated by actor Cuba Gooding in the popular movie *Jerry Maguire*: "Show me the money!" Money may not have been the only motivation during those heady years, but one could certainly argue that it dominated most other factors.

In today's chastened post-dot-com world, Herzberg's statement may be an accurate assessment for normal projects in IT organizations, and it's likely to still be a potential factor for the typical high-intensity Internet project. Indeed, it may be an over-riding objective for the project as a whole: There are still Silicon Valley startup companies embarking upon frantic projects in such emerging areas as wireless technology and peer-to-peer networks, hoping that they will be able to develop a "killer app" and sell millions of copies to an eager marketplace.

If the project team members have stock options and profit-sharing plans, then financial rewards are obviously a very large part of the motivational structure of the project. Indeed, many Silicon Valley companies have traditionally pegged their salaries at 20–30% below the prevailing market rates, but provide ample stock options and/or profit-sharing plans to motivate the members of their technical staff. It's not quite as easy to persuade young college graduates that this is an attractive prospect, especially when these IT professionals see their peers on the unemployment line, holding worthless

---

8. "One More Time: How Do You Motivate Employees?", Frederick Herzberg, *Harvard Business Review,* Sep.-Oct. 1987.

stock options. But hope springs eternal, and if you can't offer substantial financial rewards to someone who's expected to invest extraordinary amounts of time and energy on a high-intensity Internet project, you'd better have *something* that will provide motivation.

Of course, there *are* legitimate, exciting Internet projects for which money is irrelevant. A software developer who is offered the once-in-a-lifetime chance to work on the equivalent of the Apollo 11 lunar landing doesn't need money; he or she will cheerfully agree with Steve Jobs' comment about the Macintosh project: "The journey is the reward."

At the other extreme, we're now beginning to find Internet-related projects starting up in moribund government agencies, where the project is intrinsically boring and there is no hope of increased financial reward for *anyone* in the organization. Salaries are determined by one's civil service grade level, and the salary structure is fixed by law; there are no bonuses, profit-sharing rewards, or stock options. In cases like this, it's obviously silly to even discuss financial rewards as a motivator: All it will do is frustrate the team.

But what about the organizations that have some degree of flexibility? If the Internet project is important enough to the organization to justify a high-intensity work effort on the part of the project team, then it's not beyond the realm of possibility to set aside a significant bonus pool to reward the team if it succeeds in delivering the project on time. The possibility of bonuses comes up in normal projects, too, but the monies involved are usually much more modest. It's nice to get a bonus check of $1,000 at the end of a normal project, but the tax authorities usually take a third for themselves, and the remainder is not enough to have a noticeable impact on the lifestyle of a typical middle-income software professional. But things *can* be different if the stakes are high enough for the organization: A $10,000 bonus check might be enough to buy a new car (albeit a pretty modest one these days!) or finance a vacation to Bali; a $100,000 bonus check is enough to finance a child's Ivy League college education or to buy a house (or at least the down payment on a house); and a $1,000,000 bonus check is enough to make retirement a serious possibility.[9]

Assuming that such a bonus is possible, here are a few observations:

---

9. As this book is being written in the spring of 2001, I'm not aware of any IT organizations offering bonus checks of a million dollars in cold, hard cash; indeed, even a $100,000 bonus check would be pretty extraordinary. But for the entrepreneurial software ventures, it's still possible to find IT project managers who are negotiating three-year employment contracts with a stock-option package that *could* be worth a million dollars if the market recovers and the company's fortunes take off. And it's still possible to find senior IT professionals who are negotiating similar contracts that have a potential value in the low six-figure range.

- Remember that a 20% salary increase means much more to a junior programmer earning $25,000 per year than it does to a senior programmer making $75,000 per year. At the higher salary, the marginal tax rate is usually much higher, often as high as 50%; thus, the programmer doesn't take home much more, and the salary increase is more likely to be regarded as a hygiene factor. For the junior programmer, though, the tax rate is still reasonably low, and the extra 20% might be sufficient to cover the monthly payments on the programmer's first car, or justify moving out of his/her parents' home to a first real apartment.

- Remember that the possibility of large sums of money can motivate people in a variety of ways. Management may assume that it will simply make everyone work harder, but it can also make other team members excessively critical and suspicious. For instance, a team member may complain bitterly, "George had the audacity to take Christmas Eve off just to be with his stupid family, right when we were at a critical stage of testing. He's gonna screw us out of our bonus!"

- Remember that the size of the bonus doesn't have a direct, linear correlation with the productivity of or number of hours worked by the project team. I've watched senior management in some organizations attempt to bribe project teams by offering to double the size of the bonus, usually because the project is behind schedule and management apparently believes that doubling the bonus will double the number of work hours by the project team. But if the team members are already working 18 hours per day, the laws of physics prevent even the most dedicated effort to double the work hours.

- For a bonus to work as a motivator, the project team has to believe that it really exists and that senior management won't find a devious excuse to withhold it. Obviously, if the rewards are associated with success in the marketplace—for example, if the project succeeds, then the company can go public—then everyone understands that the final value of the reward will depend on the fickle nature of the stock market. But if the reward is entirely at the discretion of senior management, and if the team believes that previous high-intensity project teams have been unjustly cheated out of their rewards, then the promise of a bonus will probably be a *negative* motivator. Similarly, if the project team concludes that they have little control over the successful outcome of the project—for example, because, in addition to their software, the project depends on new hardware being developed by an outside vendor—then they may view the bonus being promised by management as a random lottery rather than as a motivating device.

- The team must also believe that the bonus will be distributed in an equitable fashion. That doesn't necessarily mean that every team member will get exactly the same share, but if the team believes that the project manager will get the overwhelming lion's share of the reward, and that they'll end up with the crumbs, then the results are predictable. This needs to be discussed at the beginning of the project. It's unlikely that the team members will be pacified by statements from the manager like, "Trust me, don't worry—I'll make sure everyone is taken care of in a fair manner."

For projects that cannot or will not consider extravagant bonuses, it's important for the project manager to remember that there are a wide variety of non-financial rewards that can have an enormous impact on the motivation of the project staff. Again, this is an issue that we frequently see on normal projects, but it's more important here because everyone is being stretched to his or her limits. It's also important to remember that the pressure of the death march project team is felt by the spouse and/or family members of the death march staffers.

It can be *extremely* meaningful, for example, to provide practical rewards to family members, especially the spouse who is left juggling all of the household and child-care responsibilities while his/her significant other is working 'round the clock on the death march project. A thoughtful project manager might check to see whether the spouse needs a taxi service to pick up or drop off a child from school, or whether someone from the office could pick up some groceries on the way home to help the spouse who is stuck at home with sick children. And if the children are *really* sick and need medical attention, the project manager will move heaven and earth—and utterly destroy any bureaucratic obstacles—to ensure that the appropriate services are provided, to minimize anxiety on the part of the project member.

Of course, the examples mentioned above *do* require money, but it's usually a very small amount of money, and it can usually be covered in the miscellaneous part of the project's budget. There's a good chance that the Accounting Department will whine and complain if they find out about it, for such expenditures usually don't conform to officially sanctioned procedures. The project manager who caves in to this kind of pressure is, in my humble opinion, a spineless wimp; if necessary, the manager should pay for such expenses out of his or her own pocket, since he or she is usually making a much higher salary than the technical staff members. In any case, it's the manager's job to deal with the corporate bureaucracy here; the last thing you want is to have the technical staffers wasting their time and emotional energy fighting with the Accounting Department about whether it was reasonable to order a pizza with two extra toppings rather than the economy pizza for a midnight dinner when the team was working late.

Modest rewards of this kind throughout the project will certainly help, but what about non-financial rewards of a more lasting nature when the project finishes? I'm not thinking of promotions or new career opportunities here, for those fall into the same category as overt financial rewards. Here are some examples of rewards that might not be quite as motivating as a million-dollar bonus check, but would nevertheless help ease the pain of a death march project:

- *An extended vacation*—If the project succeeds, give the team members a vacation of the same duration as the project. Most of us aren't quite sure what to do with a two-week vacation, but if we had a six-month *paid* vacation, it might motivate us to take that 'round-the-world sailing trip we've always dreamed of. An interesting test: Try this idea out on your manager and watch the reaction. If it's something like, "What?!? Are you nuts? Six months' vacation for a six-month Internet project?!? We'll give you a couple days off, but don't push your luck!" It will give you a strong indication of management's implicit belief that software developers are nothing more than indentured servants. Such an attitude speaks volumes about the organization's concept of a social contract.

- *A paid sabbatical*—When the death march project is done, assign the team members to a six-month stint on "Project X." Question: What's X? Answer: Anything they want it to be. Rather than immediately being assigned to another high-intensity Internet project (or equally bad, an utterly boring non-Internet project), the team members can look forward to six months of learning about new versions of Java, or researching the latest object-oriented methodologies, or even returning to college to get their Master's degrees. You'll have to be a little creative about the official name for X to confuse the bureaucrats; something like "the advanced nimbo-heuristic strategic forecasting client/server system" might do the trick.

- *A fully-equipped computing environment at home*—Even though PC hardware has gotten much cheaper and we all have something set up in our home offices, it's usually not the most up-to-date equipment; many of us have a sluggish 486-, or even an ancient 386-based machine, while the rest of the world races ahead to gigahertz Pentium machines. The interesting thing about high-intensity IT development projects is that they often accumulate extra computer equipment because management is often prepared to throw extravagant sums of money into the budget on the theory that advanced technology will save the project. If there is leftover equipment at the end of the project, give it to the team members as a bonus; if an outright gift breaks too many bureaucratic rules, then loan it to them.

11.3.2 The issue of overtime

If bonuses and extended vacations are motivators, then overtime during a project would normally be considered a de-motivator. But, it's almost inevitable on high-intensity Internet projects; indeed, it's usually the *only* way that the project manager has any hope of achieving the tight deadline for the project. And, as noted earlier, it often occurs without any explicit requests from the manager: Young, fanatical, unmarried team members who are excited by the challenge and advanced technology associated with the project will happily work 60, 80, or 100 hours per week.

Nevertheless, overtime has to be managed properly to avoid de-motivating the team and endangering the success of the project. One way to manage overtime is to ensure that senior management knows how much it costs. Regardless of whether or not the team members are being compensated for their overtime work, the worst mistake is not recording the overtime on the theory that since the developers aren't being paid for it, it's "free." While this may be an accurate perception on the part of the Accounting Department, overtime is *not* free from the project manager's perspective. Even if we assumed that all team members could work 18-hour days forever, without ever becoming tired, it's crucial for the manager to keep track of how many "invisible" overtime hours are being contributed throughout the project; this is the only way the manager can accurately gauge the productivity of the team and the likelihood of reaching each mini-deadline throughout the project.

And as everyone knows, people *can't* work 18-hour days forever; and even if they try, they get tired. When they get tired, they get cranky and short-tempered; they also work less productively, and they make many more mistakes. All of this has a dramatic impact on the progress of the overall project, and the manager has to know when to relax the pressure and when to ask for more overtime. This may not seem so important for a 3–6 month project, when a young, energetic project team can work flat-out from beginning to end. But on longer projects, which we're beginning to see more and more often now, careful management of overtime effort is crucial; the effects of long periods of heavy overtime are insidious, but nevertheless quite real.

One of the dangers that the project manager must watch for is excessive *voluntary* overtime on the part of enthusiastic, young software engineers who don't know their own limits, and who don't appreciate the potential side-effects of working when they're exhausted. As suggested by Figure 11.1, net productivity might actually *increase* during the first 20 hours of overtime work, based on adrenaline, concentration, etc. But sooner or later, everyone reaches a point of diminishing returns, and at some point, productivity begins to diminish because of increased errors and lack of focus and concentration. Indeed, there comes a point when a team member becomes a "net negative producer" because the rework effort caused by mistakes and defects exceeds the positive contribution of new software developed. Thus, assuming that the scale in Figure 11.1 is accurate (which it may or may not be for any individual software developer), the manager will probably want to encourage the developer to work as much as 60 hours per week; the period between 60 and 80 hours per week is where the manager should begin letting the developer set his or her own limits; and beyond 80–90 hours per week, the manager should insist that the developer go home and rest.

11.4 Team-building issues

As mentioned earlier, it's crucial that the project manager have the freedom to choose his or her team members. It can be helpful to use techniques such as the Briggs-Meyers personality assessment tests to help anticipate how team members will interact with one another.

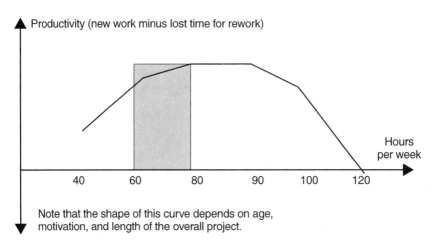

Note that the shape of this curve depends on age, motivation, and length of the overall project.

FIGURE 11.1 Net productivity vs. hours worked.

Yet another ingredient involves the concept of team *roles*. Many project managers focus on technical roles such as database designer, network specialist, user-interface expert, and so forth. While these are all important, it's also important to think about the psychological roles that will be played by one or more team members. These roles are visible in normal software projects, too, but they are more crucial in death march projects. Rob Thomsett has described the eight key project roles as follows:[10]

- *Chairperson*—Controls the way in which a team moves forward toward the group objectives by making the best use of team resources, recognizes where the team's strengths and weaknesses lie, and ensures that the best use is made of each team member's potential. As might be imagined, this person is often the official project leader; in self-managing teams, it could be any individual.

- *Visionary*—Shapes the way in which team effort is applied, directs attention, and seeks to impose some shape or pattern on group discussion and on the outcome of group activities. This individual may have the official title of "architect" or "lead designer," but the key point is that it's a visionary role. Especially in a high-intensity project, where everyone is highly focused on his or her individual assignment, it's crucial to have a single, clear focus on what the problem is and what the solution (design) should be.

10. "Effective Project Teams: a Dilemma, a Model, a Solution," Rob Thomsett, *American Programmer*, July–Aug. 1990.

- *Provocateur*—Advances new ideas and strategies with special attention to major issues and looks for possible new approaches to the problems with which the group is confronted, to help find innovative solutions to help solve the technical problems confronting the team.

- *Critic*—Analyzes problems in a practical manner, and evaluates ideas and suggestions so that the team is better poised to make balanced decisions. In many cases, this person balances the optimistic proposals of the shaper and the plant. The critic is aware that new technologies don't always work, vendor promises about the features of new tools and languages are sometimes broken, and things in general don't always go as planned.

- *Company worker*—Turns concepts and plans into practical working procedures; carries out agreed-upon plans systematically and efficiently. In other words, while the visionary is spouting grand technological visions, the provocateur is proposing radical new solutions, and the critic is looking for the flaws and shortcomings in those proposals, the company worker is the person who hunkers down in a corner and churns out tons of code. Clearly, a high-intensity Internet project needs to have at least a couple of these folks; but on their own, they may not bring the project to success because they don't have any grand visions of their own.

- *Team worker*—Supports members in their strengths (e.g., building on suggestions), underpins members in their shortcomings, improves communications between members, and generally fosters a team spirit. In other words, this person is the diplomat of the team. It may be the project manager, but it could also be any individual on the team who happens to be a little more sensitive than the others about bruised egos and sensitive personalities. Again, this is often a crucial role in a high-intensity project because the team is often under a great deal of stress, and at least one or two of the team members is likely to begin behaving in an insensitive, "macho" fashion.

- *Scavenger*—Explores and reports on ideas, developments, and resources outside the group, creates external contacts that may be useful to the team, and conducts any subsequent negotiations. This is the person who knows where to find a spare PC, an available conference room, an extra desk, or almost any other resource the team needs. Such resources might or might not be available through official channels, but even if they can be procured in the normal fashion, it often requires filling out 17 forms in triplicate and then waiting six months for the bureaucracy to process everything. A high-intensity project operating on an aggressive schedule can't wait that long, and can't afford to have all its progress brought to a halt because the vice president's administrative assistant jealously guards access to the organization's only available conference room. The team scavenger often has a network of friends and contacts throughout the organization from whom the critical resources can be begged, borrowed, or stolen; and the most important thing is that the scavenger *enjoys* this activity.

- *Completer*—Ensures that the team is protected as far as possible from mistakes of both commission and omission; actively searches for aspects of work that need a more than usual degree of attention; and maintains a sense of urgency within the team. It's common to see this person taking on the dominant role during the testing activities at the end of the project life cycle, but it's just as important in the earlier stages, too. The team sometimes needs to be reminded—daily!—that it's not involved in a lifetime career, but rather a project with a hard deadline, with intermediate inch-pebbles that need to be accomplished in a timely fashion to avoid falling behind.

Unfortunately, even with all this effort, there's no guarantee that the project team will come together, or "jell," in a cohesive fashion. As DeMarco and Lister put it in *Peopleware*:

> You can't make teams jell. You can hope they will jell; you can cross your fingers; you can act to improve the odds of jelling; but you can't make it happen. The process is much too fragile to be controlled.

If the jelling process is successful, there will usually be some visible signs. As DeMarco and Lister observe, successful teams typically have a strong sense of identity, a sense of eliteness, a feeling of joint ownership, and (at least on the mission-impossible-style projects) a feeling that they can do good work *and* have fun. On the other hand, while the organization may not be able to guarantee a successfully jelled team, it *can* cause what DeMarco and Lister refer to as "teamicide," that is, a conscious or unconscious decision to give up and abandon all efforts to maintain a focused, cohesive team structure. The practices that typically lead to teamicide are these:

- *Defensive management*—Here, the management does not trust the team. Note that this is an area where the notion of a team champion, discussed in Chapter 2, becomes essential.
- *Bureaucracy*—Here, there is too much paperwork. If the team has any sense, it will simply refuse to do the paperwork, or will make vague promises to catch up with all of it after the project has finished.

- *Physical separation of team members (e.g., in different buildings, different cities, different countries)*—Electronic mail and groupware tools can obviously reduce this problem, but physical proximity is necessary to maintaining the team spirit so essential to the success of a high-intensity project.[11]

- *Fragmentation of people's time*—This is especially applicable in situations where the team members devote part of their time to the official death march project, but another part of their time to maintaining an old legacy system, or serving on the committee for the company Christmas party.

- *Quality reduction of the product*—While the team may be prepared to accept a certain level of quality reduction to deliver "good-enough" software on time, there is usually a threshold below which they will refuse to go. The quality issue may involve defects (bugs), missing functionality, a primitive user interface, or shoddy documentation.

- *Phony deadlines*—These are deadlines so aggressive that the team has absolutely no faith in its ability to meet them. This form of teamicide usually transforms a mission-impossible team into a suicide team.

- *Clique control*—Here, the team is split up when the project finishes. As noted earlier in this book, some teams find that the project they're working on is intrinsically boring, and the users to whom they will deliver the software are ungrateful louts, so the satisfaction to be derived from the project comes from the pleasure of working with a certain group of people. Indeed, the satisfaction may be so great that the team members look forward to the prospect of continuing to work together on future projects. But ironically, the team spirit that made the team succeed is often regarded as a political threat to management; hence, they employ the common practice of breaking the team apart upon the completion of the project. This in turn is such a demoralizing prospect that the team disintegrates even before the project deadline.

---

11. For obvious reasons, some Internet-related project teams feel that the very technology they are developing for their business users can be employed to re-engineer their own work processes, stay in close contact with distant users throughout the project, and make themselves more productive. This may well turn out to be the case, but the tools have to be *very* good, the supporting infrastructure has to be in place, and the overall corporate culture has to be supportive of the concept. In my experience, the technical developers may be in a position to "eat their own dog food" and use their own Internet-based tools, but the users with whom they must interact are not always equipped with sufficient tools and/or comfortable with the use of those tools.

A final point about team jelling: Even when it happens, it doesn't happen on the first day of the project. A typical team goes through a four-stage evolutionary process before it can be considered fully jelled:

- *Forming:* Team members define goals, roles, and the direction of the team.
- *Storming:* The team sets rules and decision-making processes, often renegotiating (arguing over) team roles and responsibilities.
- *Norming:* Procedures, standards, and criteria are agreed upon.
- *Performing:* The team begins to function as a system.

In the ideal case, a project team may have gone through most of the forming and storming stages before the project even begins, because the team members have worked together on previous projects. However, every project is different, and every project team usually includes one or two new people, which is bound to cause a certain amount of forming and storming. But whether the overall process takes a day, a week, or a month, it has to occur; if at all possible, the project manager will try to get to the team members assigned to the project well before the official kick-off date of the project, to be at the performing stage when the project officially begins.

It's also important to remember that even when a team has jelled, it can fall apart because of the pressure of the project. In the worst case, though, the team might never get past the first two stages; or to put it another way, the team may commit teamicide because of the various problems listed earlier. And by the time the project manager (or some level of management above the project manager) notices that teamicide has occurred, it's probably too late to form a new team. *C'est la vie.*

11.5 Workplace conditions for high-intensity Internet projects

The issue of decent offices—versus Dilbert-style cubicles—has been debated for so many years in the software development field that it seems pointless to bring it up again. Tom DeMarco and Tim Lister, whose work has already been cited numerous times in this chapter, have discussed the benefits of decent office working conditions at length in their *Peopleware* opus. Software developers who say their workplace is acceptably quiet, for example, are one-third more likely to deliver zero-defect work than those who work in noisy office environments with uncontrollable interruptions. And in a survey of some 600 software developers, DeMarco and Lister were able to make a persuasive argument that those working in reasonable office conditions—with the ability to divert phone calls, silence the phone, close the door, and prevent needless interruptions—were approximately 2.6 times more productive than those working in the usual office environment.

Though DeMarco and Lister published their work in 1987, it doesn't seem to have done much to the workplace conditions for more software developers throughout the 1990s and even in the current decade, *except in software product companies*. The working conditions at Microsoft, and in many software companies throughout Silicon Valley, are civilized indeed: private offices with doors that close; access to kitchens stocked with soda, juice, and other beverages; and a "permanent" phone number that follows the programmer in the event he or she is reassigned to a different office.[12]

As for the software developers who work in banks, insurance companies, government agencies, manufacturing organizations, and the hundreds of other companies for which software is still generally regarded as an overhead expense, offices tend to be replaced with cubicles, and the ability to concentrate on one's intellectual efforts ranges from poor to non-existent. Stale Muzak wafts through the air, phones ring incessantly, dogs bark, people yell, and there is no way to prevent anyone from the mailroom messenger to the CEO from sticking his or her head into your office to interrupt you. As DeMarco and Lister put it,

> Police-mentality planners design workplaces the way they would design prisons: optimized for containment at minimal cost. We have unthinkingly yielded to them on the subject of workplace design, yet for most organizations with productivity problems, there is no more fruitful area for improvement than the workplace.

> As long as workers are crowded into noisy, sterile, disruptive space, it's not worth improving anything *but* the workplace.

Unfortunately, my complaining about the situation has not had any more of an effect on the industry than DeMarco and Lister's far more detailed and eloquent discussion. But remember that we're talking about *high-intensity* projects here: different rules apply, and I believe that the project manager should adopt the philosophical position that *no* rules apply.

---

12. Here, too, things went overboard during the heady days of the dot-com era, with Internet startup companies using their newly acquired venture capital funding to equip their offices with everything from exercise equipment to video-arcade machines, from ping-pong tables to fully-equipped kitchens and cappuccino machines. I'm not suggesting that programmers need opulent surroundings or frivolous toys, just a comfortable environment where they can concentrate on the intellectual tasks they are performing.

If you're the manager of a high-intensity Internet project with a nearly impossible deadline, then the message that decent office conditions can lead to a 2.6-fold improvement in productivity should be enough to motivate you to break *lots* of rules. Whatever you accomplish probably won't be permanent: As soon as the project is over, the "Furniture Police" will swoop in and reassign everyone to the same miserable cubicles occupied by the rest of the staff. But if the Internet project lasts only three months, and if you're clever, you might be able to provide decent working conditions without the "Furniture Police" even figuring out what's going on.

Here are some possibilities:

- *Frontal attack*—If you have a project champion and/or project owner desperate to get the project finished, explain to him or her just how important it is to put your project team into an effective environment. If the project champion is a high-level manager, it should be relatively easy to arrange a temporary transfer of the project team.

- *The "skunk-works" mystique*—Most senior managers have heard of the notion of a "skunk-works"; thus, rather than asking to locate your project team in the executive suite, where each office has its own private bathroom, ask for permission to relocate the team to an abandoned warehouse.

- *Squatter's rights*—Commandeer empty office space that has been sitting unoccupied while the "Furniture Police" try to figure out how many hundreds of people they can cram into it. Possession is 90% of the battle; while the bureaucracy complains, debates, and sends angry email messages back and forth, you might even be able to finish your project and disappear back into the anonymous cubicles again.

- *Telecommute*—Tell everyone to work at home, and arrange to have your weekly status meetings at the local MacDonald's (at 9 a.m., the place is likely to be empty). It may take weeks for anyone to notice that the project team has disappeared. As an additional diversion, you can put scarecrow-style dummies at the desks normally occupied by the project team; management will have a hard time distinguishing them from the other zombies in the office.

- *Switch to the graveyard shift*—This is more extreme, but can be effective if much of the project work can be carried out without interacting with the user community. It's unpleasant asking everyone to change his or her work schedule to the midnight-to-eight shift, but it's virtually guaranteed to eliminate the normal interruptions. A strategy like this is sure to evoke the wrath of bureaucrats throughout the organization, but the wonderful thing is that the bureaucrats aren't in the office in the middle of the night! They'll send angry memos and email messages. The best strategy is to ignore them and pretend that you never received them. If that doesn't work, then simply refuse to change your schedule; unless they turn off the lights or change the locks on the office door, there's not much they can do within the duration of a typical Internet project.

- *Barricades and buffers*—If your team is in a typical open office environment and the strategies discussed above aren't feasible, then do whatever you can to ensure that the project team members are located in contiguous cubicles. Next, take whatever further steps are necessary to barricade that set of cubicles from access by the rest of the office herd. Disable the intercom and loudspeaker that blare noise from the ceiling (and be prepared to do so weekly, as the janitorial service will probably do their best to repair it). If you can take over an entire floor, or a whole building, so much the better. Erect a pirate flag atop the building, as Steve Jobs did with the Macintosh project team at Apple, and install a guard to shoo away unwanted visitors.

Some of these actions will provoke a more violent response from the corporate bureaucracy than others. The team and its manager will have to decide which strategy is most effective. But I want to emphasize that I'm serious about *all* of these strategies, despite the obvious fact that they violate the rules that one finds in almost every large company. Confronting the bureaucracy in this fashion is not for the timid; but by the same token, high-intensity Internet projects are not for the timid. If the project manager isn't willing to stand up and fight for decent working conditions, then why should the project team be willing to make extraordinary sacrifices on behalf of the organization and project manager?

11.6 Conclusion

Talented people, cohesive teams, and decent working conditions are not enough to guarantee success in a high-intensity Internet project, but the absence of these elements is almost enough to guarantee a project's failure. And since the collapse of the dot-com era, managers have no longer had the easy (indeed, *too* easy) strategy of offering obscene amounts of money to programmers to lure them into high-intensity Internet projects; instead, they must pay more careful attention to the long-established peopleware principles discussed in this chapter.

Indeed, there was a perception for a few years that the *only* thing necessary to make a high-intensity Internet project succeed was a group of super-geeks with extraordinary physical stamina who would literally code until they dropped from exhaustion. Methodologies and software processes weren't important, the theory went; indeed, given the chaos surrounding everything else associated with the project, any attempt to impose rigorous processes was likely to be a disaster. All one needed was good, energetic, well-motivated people; and with good people, *anything* was possible. From that perspective, one could make the argument that I should have placed this chapter near the beginning of the book, *before* the detailed discussions about managing the analysis, design, coding, and testing processes.

Well, good people *are* important, and motivation, teamwork, and decent working conditions are important, too. The next time we see the IT industry inundated with radically new technology, chaotic business conditions, and irrational investments of money, perhaps we'll return to an environment where the *only* thing that matters is people. But the crazy days of the Internet are now behind us, and even though organizations will probably continue to launch thousands of high-intensity Internet projects for the rest of this decade, we're now beginning to return to the days where software processes are relevant, risk management is taken seriously, and fundamental principles of project management are being rediscovered.

So yes, *do* pay attention to the people on your project team, but don't forget about everything else!

ટ. ટ. ટ. ટ. ટ.

Managing Tools and Technology 12

(adapted from Chapter 6 of *Death March*)

A long time ago, in a galaxy far, far away, I had dinner with an amiable group of mid-level Microsoft managers. During the course of the discussion, I asked if it was common for Microsoft project teams to use such methodologies and development processes as object-oriented design or structured analysis. The answers ranged from "Sometimes" to "Ummm, I guess so" to "Not consistently" to "What's that?" And when I asked about the use of CASE tools (which were still fairly popular throughout the rest of the industry at that point in time), I was told that the common opinion of Microsofties was that such tools were for "people off the street." This was a term I hadn't heard before, but the rough translation is: "ignorant savages who have just come out of the primeval forest and who are just learning to program, unlike *real* programmers, who don't need no such artsy-fartsy tools."

Somewhat depressed, I asked whether the project teams used *any* tools, and was told that, in fact, each Microsoft team could choose whatever tools it felt were appropriate for the project it was working on. Seizing on that, I asked: What does a typical project team consider its most *important* tool for a software project?

"I asked one of the project teams the same question the other day," replied one of the managers. "And you know what their answer was?"

"A high-speed C++ compiler?" I asked. "An assembler? A powerful debugging tool for all those bugs in their code, heh heh heh?"

"None of the above," the manager responded. "The answer was: *electronic mail*. The average Microsoft programmer gets a hundred email messages a day; he *lives* on email. Take away email and the project stops dead in its tracks."

The interesting thing is that this anecdote took place in 1992, that is, *before* the explosive growth of the Internet had begun, before the World Wide Web was available, and before anyone at Microsoft had even begun thinking about the .Net development environment that was emerging while this book was being written. I was staggered at the thought of anyone getting a hundred email messages a day; in 1992, I was deliriously happy if I got two or three email messages a day. But as you can imagine, if the same question about the most important tool was raised today, the answer might well be "World Wide Web" rather than email; by contrast, the answer might have been "Fax machine" in 1987, "PC workstation" in 1983, "Online terminal" in 1976, and "My own telephone on my desk" in 1965.

Obviously, we don't expect a high-intensity Internet project team to survive with only one tool, or with something as rudimentary as email. Most teams, even for normal projects, have a wide variety of tools, and quite an assortment of technology to accomplish their day-to-day work. But sometimes they have too much, and sometimes they have technology that's too new, and sometimes they have tools they don't want foisted upon them by Dilbertesque managers. And, in some cases, they're prevented—for financial, political, or cultural reasons—from getting the one tool they believe critical for accomplishing their objectives.

In case you were worried, let me assure you that I'm not going to advocate esoteric, advanced software tools that somehow communicate telepathically with the programmer to generate bug-free Java code from disorganized thoughts. But I do want to discuss the notion of a "minimal toolset" for Internet projects. I also want to emphasize the critical relationship between tools and processes, especially since the processes in a high-intensity Internet project are likely to be different from those used in the rest of the organization. And finally, I want to issue a warning against introducing completely *new* tools of any kind into an Internet project team environment that could end up discovering that a new tool is the straw that breaks the camel's back.

12.1 The minimal toolset

In Chapter 6, I strongly recommended the notion of *triage* as a prioritization strategy for dealing with user requirements. The same concept applies to tools and technology for the project team: There are some tools the team "must have," and some that they "should have," and a bewildering variety of tools they "could have." And, there are some obvious reasons for applying the triage prioritization in a conscious, cold-blooded fashion at the beginning of a project.

The most obvious reason is economics. Even if the tools worked and everyone was familiar with them, it would cost too much to acquire them, and it would take too long to order them—by the time the procurement process in a normal corporate bureaucracy was finished, the project would be finished. In many death march projects, it's important to focus on a few critical tools and then try to persuade senior management (or the "Tools Police") to acquire them.

But suppose the team is operating in a large environment that already has hundreds of different tools that have been acquired over the years. Should they all be used? Obviously not! Even if they all worked, the mental effort required to remember *how* they worked, and the additional effort to make them all work together, would usually exceed the incremental benefit obtained. Consider the analogy of a team of mountain-climbers, trying to decide what equipment to take with them as they prepare for an assault on a peak. There are some essentials (tents, drinking water, etc.) they'd better have; and if it's an easy climb, they might want to take along some new-fangled gadgets they read about in their favorite mountain-climbing magazine. But if they're planning to climb Mt. Everest without the assistance of burros or Sherpas to carry everything, then they can't afford the burden of carrying 300 pounds of gear per person on their backs.

Exactly what tools *are* critical and what should be left behind is a decision the project team should be allowed to make on its own, regardless of whether it conforms to organizational standards. I'm staggered by the number of organizations I visit where the project manager tells me sadly that there's an organizational mandate that *all* projects must be done in Java because it has been decided that it's what God intended—even though it's abundantly clear that Java is utterly inappropriate for *this* project. Baloney! Throw it out! Use the tools and technology that make sense! To do otherwise is roughly analogous to someone telling the leader of the Mt. Everest mountain-climbing team, "Our committee has decided that your project team should take along a detailed map of the New York City subway system because most projects have found it very helpful."[1]

I think it's essential that the team members agree on common tools *within* the project; otherwise, chaos will ensue. Obviously, this has to be interpreted with a certain degree of common sense. It probably doesn't matter which word processor the team members use to write their documentation, but it probably *is* important that they all use the same compiler for their C++ code. One of the problems with a high-intensity Internet project is that the software developers believe it creates a license for complete anarchy at the individual level: If they want to use an obscure C++ compiler they downloaded from a university Web site, they believe it's their inalienable right. Not so: It's the *team* that has the inalienable right, and the project manager must enforce this strictly in any area where incompatible tools could make a significant difference.

This means that unless the team members have worked together on several previous projects, they will have to come up with a minimal toolset that everyone agrees to use. Thus, triage emerges again: The "must have" toolset is also the "must *use*" toolset. Once a consensus has emerged on that set of tools, then the team can discuss the "should have" tools, where the problems are likely to be a combination of consensus-building within the team and management approval for the purchase of new tools. Beyond that, there may or may not be sufficient time and energy to discuss the merits of the nearly infinite number of "could have" tools that various team members might be interested in.

I suggested above that the project manager should be prepared to enforce a consensus; indeed, this could be one of the criteria used by the manager to select potential members of the team. Note that the same could be said about the software processes that we discussed in Chapter 6. And as we'll see below, it's even more important than that because tools and processes are intimately related to one another.

With all of these caveats in mind, it's impossible for an outsider like me to casually enumerate the recommended tools for any specific Internet development project. When asked the question, my answer—"It depends..."—is usually confused with the consultant's weasel-worded tendency to avoid

---

1. Imagine, for example, an Internet project team at Sun Microsystems announcing that it wants to use Visual Basic as its programming language, or a project team at Microsoft announcing that it wants to build its new Internet system to run on Linux rather than whatever version of Microsoft Windows has been anointed as the "Greatest Operating System Ever Developed."

giving a straight answer to any question. So, as long as you keep my earlier advice firmly in mind, here is the list of tools I would normally look for:

- *Email, groupware, Internet/Web-based collaboration tools*—Like the Microsoft example above, this is at the top of my list. Today's Web-based collaboration tools are not only more efficient than old-fashioned email, they facilitate coordination and collaboration. Basic email and access to the Internet should be considered resources on essentially the same level as oxygen and electricity, though I would be happy to negotiate as to *which* vendors and products should be used. It matters far less to me whether you use Microsoft Outlook or Eudora, WebEx or Lotus Notes, as long the whole team is on the network and keeps all of its project memory on the network.

- *Prototyping/RAD development tools*—As we've discussed in earlier chapters, virtually all Internet projects use some form of prototyping or incremental development approach; consequently, they need tools to support this effort. It's hard to find a popular development environment today that describes itself as anything else *but* a RAD environment, and almost all such tools have a visual, drag-and-drop user interface to help the programmer get more code developed more quickly. Whether the tool should be based on Microsoft's Visual Studio or IBM's VisualAge (or a dozen other possible choices) is something I can't recommend on any kind of global basis. But remember the comment above: It's not sufficient to have a consensus that we're all going to use a language like Java or Python; we have to agree on a common toolset from a common vendor. To have part of the team using Microsoft's development environment while the others use tools from Sun or an IBM product may be technologically feasible, but it's still downright stupid.

- *Configuration management (CM)/version control*—Several of my colleagues feel that this should be at the top of the list. There is an obvious benefit to having the CM tools well-integrated with the other primary development tools. Thus, Microsoft's SourceSafe may or may not be the best version control software, but the fact that it's well-integrated with Visual Basic is a big argument in its favor. Similarly, many other development tools are integrated with Merant's PVCS or other comparable CM tools.

- *Testing, debugging tools*—Many of us would automatically include these with the basic development tools that allow us to create code, compile it, and run it. But as we moved from mainframe online applications to GUI-oriented client/server systems to Web-based systems, we gradually realized that an entirely new set of testing tools was not only appropriate, but often essential, and tools from vendors like Rational, AutoTester, and Mercury Interactive still aren't widely enough distributed in the organizations I visit.

- *Project management (estimating, scheduling, PERT/Gantt, etc.)*—There's a tendency to think of these as the "manager's toolkit," and that may be the case; perhaps it's only the project manager who needs to recompute the project's critical path on a daily basis. But in this same category, I would include estimating tools like ESTIMACS (developed by Howard Rubin, and available from Computer Associates), CHECK-POINT (from Software Productivity Research), and SLIM (from Quantitative Software Management); these are essential tools, in my opinion, because they support the dynamic re-evaluation of schedules and deadlines throughout the project.

- *Toolkit of reusable components*—If the project team is familiar with the concept of software reuse, and if they regard it as a strategic weapon with which to accomplish high levels of productivity, then a toolkit of reusable components needs to be on the list of "must have" tools. This might be a collection of VBX components for Visual Basic, or the Java components associated with IBM's San Francisco project, or Microsoft's MFC class library for C++; obviously, it could also include some in-house components developed by other project teams within the organization. The choice is usually language-dependent, and it's another one of those areas that needs to be used consistently by everyone within the project team.

- *CASE tools for analysis/design*—Some project teams regard CASE tools as a crutch for novice developers, but others consider them as essential as word processors. My preference is for the CASE tool that's simple, inexpensive, and flexible; aside from that, I won't recommend any particular vendor because the real answer to the question of which CASE tool to use is, "It depends..."[2] As I'll discuss below, the biggest problem with CASE tools is that they encourage (and sometimes enforce) a methodology that the project team doesn't understand and doesn't particularly want to use.

---

2. Among the popular choices today are Rational ROSE, the tool suite that helps to automate and enforce the use of UML for object-oriented projects, and Togethersoft's "Together" tool suite that guarantees to keep visual UML models fully and interactively synchronized with either Java or C++ code.

12.2 Tools and process

The issue of CASE tools, mentioned above, is probably the most obvious example of a truism: Tools and processes are inextricably linked together. There's no point using a formal, heavyweight, object-oriented design tool if you've never heard of the UML (Unified Modeling Language). Such a CASE tool is not only useless, but an incredible burden if the project team sincerely believes that UML use case diagrams and object interaction diagrams are meaningless forms of bureaucratic documentation produced solely to get the "Methodology Police" off their back.

The situation is not so black-and-white in many cases: The project team might feel that UML diagrams are useful, but only as an informal modeling tool. Thus, a flexible CASE tool might be considered a benefit, while a hard-line CASE tool would be rejected. Consider the obvious analogy with a word processor: We all appreciate the benefits of the spell-checker, but we don't want to be forced to use it, and it's quite likely that we will *never* use the grammar-checker because it's too slow and clumsy (at least that's *my* excuse for not using it on Microsoft Word!). We would be even more annoyed if the word processor steadfastly refused to allow the word "ain't" within a document, or required that any phrases it considered racist or sexist to be approved in advance by the Political Correctness Committee. A few more "features" like that would be enough to make us all go back to paper and pencil.

What this means, of course, is that the project team must *first* agree on the processes and methodologies it intends to follow, and it must decide which of those processes are going to be followed in a heavy fashion (and which ones will be honored in spirit, but perhaps not to the letter of the law). Once this has been decided, the tools and technology can be chosen—or rejected!—accordingly. In this same fashion, the project manager may decide to adopt a particular tool to enforce a process that everyone agrees on intellectually, but is likely to practice in a sloppy fashion; a good example is version control and configuration management.

One of the biggest myths about software tools in *any* software project—and a particular danger in a high-intensity Internet project—is that a certain tool will be a "silver bullet" that will somehow accomplish miracles. Miracles, of course, are what senior management is looking for, and even the project manager may be tempted by a vendor's advertising claims that programming, testing, or various other activities will be improved by a factor of 10 through the genius of its tools.

Aside from the problem that such tools are usually brand-new and nobody knows how to use them (which I'll discuss below), there's a more fundamental point to consider: The only way such a tool *could* be a silver bullet is if it allows or forces the developers to change their process. For example, if I write a program and then compile it, I do so according to a particular process; perhaps I conduct a peer-level walkthrough before the compilation, or perhaps I precede the programming activity with a formal, detailed design process. Now, if you give me a compiler that's 10% faster than the one I was using before, I'll be happier and somewhat more efficient—maybe the productivity of the overall project will increase by some incremental amount— *but I won't change my process.*

On the other hand, if you give me a compiler that's 10 times faster, then it *will* change my process. That's what happened when we went from batch-mode, overnight compiles to online compilation in the 1970s, and then to compilation on one's own PC/workstation in the 1980s, and then to various combinations of incremental compiling (*a la* Borland's Delphi) and interpretive execution (*a la* Visual Basic). Because of this, many developers have eliminated detailed design prior to coding on the theory that they can compose programs extemporaneously. The practice of walkthroughs has also been eliminated in many projects on the assumption that the programmer can find and change his or her own defects efficiently.

Hardly anyone objects to the prospect of using improved technology that permits the *elimination* of processes that were considered boring and tedious. But it's more difficult to introduce new technology that requires us to *add* processes, or *modify* processes we were comfortable with. A good example is the process of reuse and the associated technology of reuse libraries, browsers, and related tools. The project teams that use this technology effectively can raise their level of reuse from approximately 20% (a level that I call "accidental" or "ad hoc" reuse) to 60% or more; indeed, if the technology is matched with a corporate-wide reuse process, then the level of reuse can reach 80–90% or more.

The difference between a 20% level of reuse and an 80% level of reuse is equivalent to a four-fold improvement in productivity. And as Paul Bassett points out,[3] the subsequent incremental increases in reuse have more profound benefits than you might think. If the level of reuse rises from 80% to 90%, it means that instead of having to develop 20% of the code from scratch, the project team only has to develop 10%. Thus, their workload has effectively been cut in half.

---

3. *Framing Software Reuse: Lessons from the Real World*, Paul G. Bassett, Prentice Hall, 1996.

This is all very exciting—indeed, it's worthy of being called a silver bullet—but it's utterly irrelevant if the project team (and ultimately the entire organization) is unable or unwilling to change its software processes with regard to reuse. The irony is that most organizations will blame their failures on the technology itself: They'll buy an expensive library of Java components, or they'll replace their old software development methodology with object-oriented techniques on the theory that objects are synonymous with reuse, and when they eventually find they've achieved no measurable increase in reuse, they'll blame the problem on objects, or on the vendor of the class library, or on whatever other technology they've depended on. Meanwhile, the process is exactly the same as it was before. The culture of such an organization is expressed with the phrase: "Only wimps reuse other people's code; *real* programmers write their own damn code!"

From the perspective of a high-intensity Internet project, there's a very simple moral here: If the introduction of new tools *requires* the team's standard process to be changed dramatically, then it will add significantly to the project risk and probably contribute to the failure of the project. This sometimes gets muddled with the issues of training and of learning the mechanics of how to operate the tools; I'll discuss these issues below. But the more fundamental problem is usually that of changing behavior, which is what software processes are all about. It's hard enough to do under normal circumstances, where we feel that we have lots of time and a supportive environment to slowly become comfortable with the new process. And for obvious reasons it's usually a disaster in a death march project, when we don't have enough time, and we don't have a supportive environment.

12.3 Risks of choosing new tools

As noted above, some high-intensity projects grab onto new tools and technology as a silver bullet to achieve far higher levels of productivity than would otherwise be possible. Let's assume, for the moment, that we've found some way to solve the cultural and political problems of process change that were discussed above. What else do we have to worry about?

The two most likely risks are technical issues and training. In many cases, the silver bullet tool is so new that it's not even available in a commercial form—someone on the project team downloaded a preview version from the Internet. Or, the tool can't be integrated with any of the other tools used by the project team; the vendor has made vague promises, but in the meantime, their import/export capability is riddled with bugs. Or, the tool isn't supported; it was developed by a graduate student in Uzbekistan, or (even worse!) it was developed in-house by one of the software developers who sees nothing strange about the idea of a bank developing its own visual development tool or an insurance company developing its own network design tool.

Let's assume for the moment that the tool is solid, reliable, and available from a reputable vendor that provides top-notch support. In that case, the problem is likely to be one of training, for if the tool was already being widely used throughout the organization, nobody would have characterized it as the "silver bullet" that would miraculously save the project team from certain disaster. Occasionally, you'll find a project team that begs for permission to use a powerful tool that they've all used in a previous job, but this is rare indeed. In most cases, neither the project team members nor anyone else in the organization has ever seen or used the tool before.

As mentioned before, any non-trivial tool usually has strong implications about the corresponding software process; thus, a new tool often implies a new process. Though such a correspondence should be obvious, it's remarkable how often the vendor's training representative gets halfway through a five-day workshop on how to operate the tool before finding that the students (whose managers are already panicked about falling five days behind schedule as a consequence of attending the workshop!) have absolutely no understanding of the process supported by the tool. It's awfully demoralizing, for example, to spend two days showing a reluctant student how to draw a class-hierarchy and then have him or her ask, "By the way, what *is* an object? And since I'm gonna program everything in Visual Basic, why should I care about all of this stuff?"

But let's assume that the project team members understand the process supported (and automated) by the tool, and that they have enthusiastically agreed that they will carry out the practice in their project (from 10 years of experience with object-oriented methods, I know that this is a naive assumption, but there's no point going further unless we do). So, *if* we assume that there are no technical problems with the tool, and *if* we assume that the corresponding software processes won't cause a problem, *then* all that is left is the training and practice associated with the tool itself.

How long does this take? Obviously, it depends on the nature and complexity of the tool, as well as its user interface, its online help features, and assorted other issues. In the best case, the developers will be able to figure out how to use the tool without any formal training at all; that's what the project manager and various other managers outside the project desperately want to be true, for they regard *any* training as a waste of time and a distraction from the real work of the project. But the more realistic estimate is that it will take an hour, a day, or a week to learn how to use the tool. Whether that takes the form of a classroom session, or reading a book, or just playing with the tool, it still takes time.

Keep in mind that the training activity does *not* provide a thoroughly trained, infinitely experienced user of that tool. Training is not a binary phenomenon: The project team members don't go from a state of utter ignorance to a state of sublime mastery of the tool at the end of a one-week training class. This should be obvious, but it somehow baffles senior management, which tends to grumble and complain, "Okay, we spent all that money for those high-priced trainers, and we wasted all that time in the classroom while those lazy, good-for-nothin' programmers could have been programming. Now I want to see some *real* productivity with that silver bullet tool you talked us into getting for them!" Perhaps it's not so surprising that senior management would be so naive, since they wouldn't know a software tool if they fell over one, but sadly, I've seen the same reaction from many technically oriented death march project managers.

My colleague, Meilir Page-Jones, argues that there are seven stages of mastery in software engineering; in a wonderful article on the subject,[4] he focuses on *methodologies*, but I believe that his ideas apply equally well to tools and technology. In the list below, I've added my own estimates for how long it would take the average software developer to reach various stages, assuming that the tool or technology was of average sophistication and complexity:

1. *Innocent* (has never heard of technology X)—This obviously requires no time at all.

2. *Aware* (has read an article about X)—Roughly an hour, in most cases, is enough for a software developer to be in a position where he or she can voice strong opinions about the advantages and disadvantages of the tool, even though he or she has never seen or used it.

3. *Apprentice* (has attended a five-day workshop)—For the period of a week, which has perhaps been compressed into two days because of the pressure of the high-intensity Internet project, the developer has probably done nothing more than play with canned tutorials provided by the vendor, or dabbled with a small exercise to illustrate the features of the tool. He hasn't encountered the glitches, shortcomings, and "got-

---

4. "The Seven Stages in Software Engineering," Meilir Page-Jones, *American Programmer*, July-Aug. 1990.

chas" of the tool; he or she hasn't seen how (or if) it will scale up for large, complex projects; he or she hasn't tried to integrate it with most of the other tools in the environment.

4. *Practitioner* (ready to use X on a real project)—A month is probably required to explore the nuances of a tool and become sufficiently comfortable to use the tool on a real project.

5. *Journeyman* (uses X naturally in his or her job; complains bitterly if it is taken away)—This usually takes 6-12 months, and if the tool really is a silver bullet, then the developer becomes an evangelist, doing his or her best to persuade everyone that it's the most wonderful tool on earth.

6. *Master* (has internalized the details of X; knows when he or she can break the rules)—This usually takes 2–3 years, which also means that the developer has survived two or three new product releases, has found all of the support groups and discussion groups on the Internet, and knows all of the unlisted phone numbers for the technical support gurus at the vendor's organization.

7. *Expert* (writes books, gives lectures at conferences, looks for ways to extend technology X into new galaxies)—Page-Jones was focusing on methodologies in his paper, and it's not clear that this applies to tools and technology.

12.4 Conclusion

Does the gloomy discussion in this chapter mean that we should use no tools at all? Are we supposed to abandon all technology and resort to old-fashioned dumb terminals? Should we assume that technology can *never* save us?

The rhetorical nature of these questions is intended to remind you that common sense should prevail in all such discussions. When the stars and planets align themselves just *so*, maybe technology *will* save us, at least on one or two Internet projects. And we should certainly take advantage of as much advanced technology as we can, because it can leverage our intellectual efforts and relieve us of time-consuming, error-prone, tedious tasks associated with software development. In the best of all worlds, the software developers will have had a chance to learn, experiment, and practice with high-powered tools in a less risky environment; indeed, in the best case, advanced tools have already been deployed throughout the organization and are part of the culture and infrastructure of the organization.

In this case, we wouldn't need to have any discussion about tools and technology at all; we would simply pick up our tools and go to work on the project. The reason for the discussion in this chapter—and the reason all of this *is* relevant in most death march projects—is that the organization is using mediocre tools, *or* someone believes that a completely new form of technology, just announced breathlessly by a startup vendor last week, will somehow save the day. The former scenario is depressing, but all too common, and the latter scenario is also common for the simple reason that technology advances quickly and relentlessly in our field.

If new technology could be introduced without any impact on our software processes, and if it didn't require training and practice on the part of the developers, then we would be faced with a simple cost/benefit decision. And since the natural instinct of many higher level managers is to assume that a problem can be eliminated by simply throwing money at it, I find that there tends to be far more brand-new technology used on high-intensity Internet projects than on normal projects. The irony, as I've tried to explain in this chapter, is that the new tool can be the straw that breaks the camel's back, and the project's failure is then blamed on the tool.

So, use whatever tools make sense for your death march project, regardless of whether the rest of the world thinks they are advanced or old-fashioned. And remember that if you *do* use new tools, it's going to have an impact on the people and processes within the death march project. As Thoreau put it so eloquently 150 years ago:

But lo! men have become the tools of their tools.   ∎

Henry David Thoreau, *Walden*, "Economy," 1854.

ᖾ ᖾ ᖾ ᖾ ᖾ

Final Thoughts 13

I began programming in the early 1960s, a couple of years before IBM's
introduction of the 360 family of computers ushered in the mainframe era.
My first job was at Digital Equipment Corp., where we were convinced that
we were creating a revolution as significant as the invention of fire, by introducing a so-called "mini" computer called the PDP-5. It was about the size
of a household refrigerator, cost a mere $30,000, and had the computing
capacity of today's digital wristwatch. A couple of years later, I started
working for General Electric on an ill-fated project that attempted to introduce "on-line" systems into hospitals. The concepts of online and real-time
systems were considered so revolutionary that when I presented a seminar
on the topic for a bank in Stockholm in the early 1970s, the CEO stood up at
a formal dinner banquet and quoted from Chairman Mao's "little red book"
to impress upon us how radical he thought the IT department's plans were.

Since then, of course, we've experienced such revolutions as the personal
computer,[1] client/server systems, relational databases, the Internet and the
Web. As I've lectured and consulted to managers on these topics over the
years, I've found that in the early stages of a new technological innovation,

managers typically want to know about *the technology itself*. Indeed, the quirks and nuances of the technology tend to fascinate us all, and the early adopters often concentrate enormous energy on figuring out how to work around the glitches and idiosyncrasies so that the technology can be used to achieve a significant advantage.

In the early days of online systems, the hardware vendors typically didn't provide an operating system that would support remote terminal users, so anyone who wanted to build such a system often found that he or she had the additional challenge of developing an operating system along with the applications. Having supervised the team building an operating system for our ill-fated GE project, which took place concurrently with the equally ill-fated GE Multics project, I was deeply immersed in the technology, and I recall giving dozens of seminars to glassy-eyed IT managers around the world, attempting to explain the intricacies of preemptive scheduling algorithms and dynamic memory allocation strategies.

"What's this got to do with developing high-intensity Internet projects?" the patient reader might be muttering at this point. Well, if you had been appointed to lead an Internet development project in the mid-1990s, chances are you would have been subjected to technical lectures on the inner workings of the TCP/IP protocol, and perhaps even the syntax of HTML. That's now considered technology suitable for teaching at the high-school level; as this book was being written, managers were probably sitting through lectures on Microsoft's incipient Hailstorm technology and .Net development tools. They may have been learning about security protocols available for peer-to-peer networks, or the best programming language for developing applications on wireless, handheld computing platforms. By the time this book reaches the end of its useful life, managers will be learning about things that aren't even available as commercial products today.

But why do we do this? Why is it necessary for managers of high-tech projects to be immersed in books, lectures, and seminars about the technology itself? As we've noted in earlier chapters, there are certainly some instances where the manager is a player-coach who participates in the technical development work; but in most cases, he or she is supervising the

---

1. To illustrate that I was not at all prescient about some of these revolutions, I should point out that when I began writing my *Techniques of Program Structure and Design* book in the early 1970s, the introductory chapter admonished the reader that "unless you're very rich or very eccentric, you'll never have your own computer." By the time the book was published in 1975, it should have been obvious that such a prediction was short-sighted … but I didn't think to change it, and it has reminded me ever since that we all have our own personal blind spots.

work of other people who actually know what all of the latest technobabble really means. So, why bother giving managers the illusion that they actually understand the technology?

Perhaps the most obvious reason is that the manager is involved in the technical decisions that have to be made throughout the course of the project. He or she may have to confirm a technical choice recommended by the development team—"We're gonna use Python for this project, boss! It's really great stuff! I know you've never heard of it, and we know that it violates the company mandate that everything should be written in Visual Basic, but trust us, boss, it will be really, *really* cool!" And of course, the manager is even more likely to be involved if the technical decisions involve expenditures of large sums of money. Thus, it's understandable that the manager wants to know enough about the technology to offer good advice to the developers, to spend the organization's money wisely for technology investments, and to help make wise choices if the project requires choosing, say, between two competing vendors.

These are all relevant explanations for learning about new technology. What they mean is that, as a manager of a high-intensity Internet project, chances are that you'll be expected to sit through an intense seminar on whatever leading-edge technology your project is using. But I believe there is a far more important reason for managers to acquaint themselves with technology, and it has to do with the discussion in Chapter 10: *risk management*. If the company you work for is a laggard when it comes to adopting technology,[2] then technical risk is not likely to be a major element. As this book was being written, for example, it was safe to say that client/server technology was sufficiently mature that hardly any new technological risks could be expected. As for the Internet, some aspects of it (like TCP/IP) are even *more* mature than client/server technology; and while Web browsers and HTML may still be evolving, they are not sufficiently risky that a manager has to worry about them very much.

But there are other Internet-related technologies that *are* risky, and the manager needs to learn enough about them so that he or she can participate in the decision-making process from a risk management perspective. As this book was being written in the spring of 2001, for example, it wasn't clear whether Microsoft's ambitious new .Net strategy would be available and technically adequate for the needs of a specific project, *in the short term*. It's fine to say that Microsoft is rich enough and stubborn enough to make a

---

2. Refer back to Chapter 1 for a discussion of Geoffrey Moore's characterization of innovators, early adopters, and laggards in the marketplace.

strategic technology investment like .Net pay off eventually … but will it pay off this year or next year? In other words, would it be better to avoid taking that risk and depend instead on more traditional Internet languages, tools, development environments, and related third-party products?

In situations like this, the end-users, senior managers, and other stakeholders are not likely to contribute much to the decision-making process. They may have some opinions on the matter, and they may articulate some financial or political constraints; but if the project manager feels out of his or her depth when dealing with leading-edge technologies, chances are that the stakeholders will, too. Meanwhile, the technical members of the project team may or may not be in a position to provide a good technical assessment. If they are savvy, experienced veterans, then they will be able to assimilate the technical details and figure out how to use the technology, but if they are junior developers with very little previous background in the IT field, they may be as overwhelmed as the manager.

The main thing to remember, though, is that the psychology of the development team is probably biased *in favor* of taking on the risks of new technology. From the developers' perspective, it will be fun and exciting; it will give them bragging rights when they meet their fellow developers at the nearby pub to swap gossip, lies, and war stories. It will look good on their resumes and prove valuable when seeking their next jobs, regardless of whether *this* project succeeds, and regardless of whether the new technology contributed to its success or failure. Beyond that, many developers are suckers for any vendor's marketing hype: They actually do believe that the new Internet-based development tools will make then 10 times more productive than they were on the previous project, and that it will help the business user achieve staggering levels of success. Perhaps on some subconscious level they've begun growing a little skeptical about the constant exaggerations and glib promises from the vendor whose new product they're about to recommend … but *this time*, maybe it will work.

And indeed, maybe it will. Maybe it will be wonderful, and maybe it really will contribute to both the success of the project and the success of the business user who asked for the new system. But the project manager has to evaluate all of this as realistically as possible, and that often means balancing the excessive optimism of the developers with some skepticism about the associated risks. There are risk management questions that need to be asked, and the developers may not be willing or able to ask those questions. There are also risk management assessments that need to be made, along with risk management contingency plans that need to be established; and it's likely to be the project manager who plays the leading role in those activities.

So, the bottom line is this: In a high-intensity Internet project, the manager *will* have to learn something about the specific technologies being used, indeed perhaps more than he or she really wanted to learn. But the reason for doing it is to acquire the necessary information with which to make realistic risk management decisions. Keep that point in mind and don't be seduced by the glamour of the technology itself.

While technical risks may be a significant factor on these projects, my experience over the past 3+ decades is that it was rarely the technology that caused a project to fail. Sometimes it was the unwillingness, or inability, of responsible managers to adequately assess the technical risks, but the project failures were more likely to be associated with failures in basic areas of management: planning, organization, scheduling, etc. This was a major factor with the early online systems, with client/server systems, and it continues to be a factor in today's Internet projects. But as we discussed in Chapter 1, there is (at least) one major difference between the projects of yesteryear and the projects of today: the "intensity" of the schedule. This involves some political issues, which we discussed in Chapter 2. It's quite likely that plans, schedules, deadlines, and commitments will be made at the beginning of the project, and the consequences are far more profound than the technical issue of whether Microsoft's latest development environment actually does all the things they've promised.

Thus, it may turn out that the single biggest factor in determining the success or failure of a high-intensity Internet project is the manager's willingness to say "No!" to a set of constraints (schedule, budget, and/or resources) that are clearly impossible. But if it's inappropriate or impolitic to say "No," then the next best thing is to adopt an agile, lightweight, iterative development process that delivers interim results as frequently as possible. As we discussed in Chapter 5, the notion of an iterative development life cycle is certainly well-understood at this point (even the laggard organizations are beginning to adopt it!), but the light nature of the development process is still being debated, discussed, and refined by the industry's best thinkers. Thus, if the project manager is going to devote any time and resources to seminars, conferences, and other forms of education, I would recommend that it be focused primarily on learning the latest ideas about XP, agile methods, and other related concepts rather than learning the technical nuances of an arcane programming language.

In the areas of scheduling, planning, and organizing the project, if I had to reduce my advice to a single statement, it would be this: *Base your plans on the assumption that it's <u>impossible</u> to get everything done by the deadline.* The very nature of a high-intensity project almost guarantees this to be the case: Why would we describe such a project as "high-intensity" if senior management gave us enough time, enough money, and enough people to do it in an orderly, civilized, 9-to-5 fashion? That much is obvious, but there are still lots of well-intentioned managers who continue to believe that if they work hard enough, fast enough, and long enough (i.e., enough hours of overtime, weekends, and holidays), and if they bully their developers into doing the same thing, it will somehow be possible to get *all* of the work done.

But such a strategy is doomed to failure in today's business environment. After all, if it was possible, then the last manager in the IT department would have done so on the last project. And once it became evident that it *was* possible, then the business managers would up the ante: They would demand that the next project (i.e., *your* project) be done faster, and/or with fewer people, and/or with less money. Perhaps this relentless business pressure for "Faster! Cheaper! Better!" will eventually moderate, but it probably won't happen this year, and it probably won't happen on your project. In the best of all cases, your stakeholders will acknowledge that they're asking for more functionality, more quickly, and more cheaply than they have a right to deserve, and they'll work with you to help identify which parts of their expectations are most important, and which parts are merely somewhat important.

That's what triage is all about, as we discussed in Chapter 6. Though it's possible that you'll have some rational discussions about all of this in the early planning sessions for the project, it's far more likely that it will become a relevant topic when the system requirements are being articulated and documented. Whatever else you do as a manager, don't fall prey to the siren song from your developers: "We don't need no steenking requirements, boss, we're gonna prototype everything! We can save lots of time that way, boss, and we'll be able to let the users change their minds as often as they want to!" I won't repeat the detailed arguments that I made in Chapter 6, but I want you to remember that even a one-sentence articulation of a requirement is better than nothing because it provides the basis for rational triage decisions to be made at an early stage in the project. If you do actually manage to implement 100% of the requirements articulated by the stakeholders, it will be a miracle; you (and they) should be very proud of yourselves if you get 80–90% of the requirements finished when the deadline arrives. If the project is really ambitious and truly "high-intensity" in nature, you may only get 50–60% of the requirements finished, in which case, it's obviously crucial to get the *right* 50–60% done.

In the final analysis, though, the *business* success or failure associated with your high-intensity Internet project is unlikely to depend on technical risks, or even project planning risks; instead, it will depend on the re-engineering and strategy issues that we discussed in Chapters 3 and 4. Again, that's not a new experience: It was true when companies first began building online systems in the 1970s, when they introduced PCs in the 1980s, and when they developed client/server systems in the 1990s. The sad reality is that many cannot or will not recognize this point, and they will continue to use new technology to provide faster, cheaper implementations of a business process that became obsolete 20 years ago.

As noted earlier, the technical developers may or may not care about this. If you ask them what they do for a living, they're not likely to say, "I work for a bank, so I must be a banker," or "I work for an airplane manufacturing company, so I must be an airplane person." Instead, they're more likely to say, "I'm a Java programmer," or "I'm a database designer," which are special case versions of the general statement: "I am a software engineer," or "I am an IT professional." If the current project fails, or if the entire organization comes to a screeching halt, they're likely to shrug, update their resume, and move on to the next place where they can practice their profession. Obviously, they *do* care, to some extent, about the success of their project and the success of the organization that provides their paycheck. But caring is a relative matter, and the *focus* of one's caring can be substantially different for a developer, a project manager, and a business stakeholder.

For obvious reasons, this book has taken the position that the business success of a high-intensity Internet project is likely to be far more important to the project manager than it is to the technical developers on the team. Consequently, the issues of BPR, and overall business/IT strategy development are of crucial concern to the project manager. What's the point of using the latest technology and developing a staggeringly complex system on time and within budget if it doesn't help the business users achieve their goals of increased revenues, increased market share, and/or increased productivity and quality?

All of this suggests that managing a high-intensity Internet project is a thankless, high-stress job. And perhaps it is, at least for some projects and some managers. But if you anticipate the problems in advance, you can avoid most of them and cope with the rest. If all the planning and hard work enables you to succeed—not only on a technical basis, but on a more fundamental basis, with a system that actually helps your business stakeholders achieve dramatic improvements in their business—then the effort will hopefully be worthwhile. Indeed, the project may then fall into the category of a "mission-impossible" project, as I described it in Chapter 2.

If high-intensity Internet projects are not only successful, but fulfilling and fun as well, what more could you ask? As E.B. White put it, perhaps in the midst of one of his own high-intensity projects:

> I wake up each morning determined to change the World ... and also to have one hell of a good time.
>
> Sometimes that makes planning the day a little difficult.

Amen to that! And best of luck on your next high-intensity Internet project. May you change the World, and have a hell of a good time while you're at it!

🙚 🙚 🙚 🙚 🙚

Index

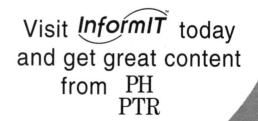